This is the first book to examine the world of the playwright in nineteenth-century Britain. In a fascinating account of the frustrations and the rewards of dramatic authorship, Stephens offers a new perspective on the playwright's growing professional status, and uncovers fresh information on earnings, relationships with actors, managers, and publishers, and the struggle for copyright reform. Among the authors discussed are Planché, Fitzball, Boucicault, Pinero, Grundy, Gilbert, Tennyson, Jones and Shaw.

THE PROFESSION OF THE PLAYWRIGHT

THE PROFESSION OF THE PLAYWRIGHT

British theatre 1800–1900

JOHN RUSSELL STEPHENS

Lecturer in English, University College of Swansea

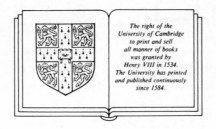

The right of the
University of Cambridge
to print and sell
all manner of books
was granted by
Henry VIII in 1534.
The University has printed
and published continuously
since 1584.

CAMBRIDGE UNIVERSITY PRESS

Cambridge
New York   Port Chester
Melbourne   Sydney

Published by the Press Syndicate of the University of Cambridge
The Pitt Building, Trumpington Street, Cambridge CB2 1RP
40 West 20th Street, New York, NY 10011-4211, USA
10 Stamford Road, Oakleigh, Victoria 3166, Australia

First published 1992

Printed in Great Britain at the University Press, Cambridge

A catalogue record for this book is available from the British Library

Library of Congress cataloguing in publication data

Stephens, John Russell.
The profession of the playwright, British theatre 1800–1900 / John Russell
Stephens.
p.   cm.
Includes bibliographical references and indexes.
ISBN 0 521 25913 4
1. Theater – Great Britain – History – 19th century.   2. Theater and
society – Great Britain.   3. English drama – 19th century – History and
criticism.   4. Drama – Publishing – Great Britain – History – 19th
century.   1. Title.
PN2594.S75   1991
792'.092'241 – dc20   90-25605   CIP

ISBN 0521 25913 4 hardback

SE

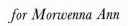

for Morwenna Ann

Contents

Preface

Dr Johnson's characteristically blunt assertion that 'No man but a blockhead ever wrote, except for money' is a convenient departure-point for a book on the profession of the playwright, since a large part of it is about money. Money is at the root of the idea of professionalism. The dramatist's sense of himself as a professional and of his chosen career as a profession is largely dependent upon the respect which he feels for his work and the respect which his work inspires in others, especially the actor and the manager. None of that makes any realistic sense if he is not paid the rate for the job.

It will be apparent that the earnings' levels of dramatic authors are very closely linked to the economic health of the theatre, and I have tried throughout to give due weight to the varying economic condition of the theatre; but that is a topic in its own right and the present work does not pretend to be a detailed economic history of that kind. On the whole, authors' salaries run in parallel with, but at a lower level than, actors', though the top end of the latter's was distorted by competition amongst managements who were forced into offering absurdly high fees. This was not a feature of the remuneration of authors. At 50 guineas a performance during his first season at Drury Lane in 1804–5 a runaway (though short-lived) sensation like the 'Young Roscius', Master William Betty, was making as much in ten days as a dramatist like Frederick Reynolds made in total (including copyright) from a reasonably successful comedy. A somewhat less exceptional comparison might be made with John Philip Kemble's combined salary of £56 14s a week as actor and manager at Drury Lane in 1801–2, where the earnings for most of the actors at the same time fell into the range of between £10 and £20 a week. Near the bottom of the scale the gap between actor and author was much greater. Hack writers who grubbed away for 30 shillings a time (such as George Dibdin Pitt in the 1840s) made no more than the equivalent of one week's wages for a minor player. The most depressed period of authorial remuneration coincides with the low point of the theatre in the 1840s and early 1850s, when actors' salaries were also much reduced.

The low level of dramatic earnings in general until the last few decades of the century is one of the main reasons for the furious productivity of so many nineteenth-century dramatists, especially the hacks who wrote for the minor theatres or for East End venues. The dramatic market was insatiable; and, in the attempt to achieve a decent income from their playwriting, authors were at the same time satisfying the constant demand from managers for new pieces at very short notice, perhaps as little as twenty-four hours. Although the long run later in the century reduced the demand for plays, its secondary consequence was that dramatists had more leisure to write their plays. And the money was so much better because not only was the theatre economically more healthy, but entrepreneurial dramatists like Boucicault and his successors exploited their ability to produce highly successful plays by insisting on sharing in the profits, thus opening the way for the playwright to compete on the same level as the novelist.

Important though money was to the professional playwright, the working conditions of the nineteenth-century theatre involved several other considerations. Many of them are hinted at in Frederick Reynolds's mild caricature of the frustrations and hardships of the dramatic profession in the person of Vivid the playwright (quoted in the epigraph to the present work). To the list must be added the issues of copyright and publishing. Dramatic property had little formal protection from piracy and its relative security in terms of proper copyright protection was achieved only slowly, through a series of copyright law reforms over a period of more than fifty years. Just as vital to the profession was the incentive to publish, which was itself closely dependent on adequate copyright protection, and furthermore to publish in durable as opposed to ephemeral form. Most of the dramatic texts of the century are available only in the flimsiest of acting editions and only towards the end of our period does dramatic publishing gain a degree of respectability through the interest of major publishing houses. Such improvements in the working life of the professional dramatist were essential for the respect for the playwright as an artist and as a professional in the theatre. The emergence of the author-director by the end of the century is the climax of a long struggle for recognition, a search for his own identity which is not imposed from above by the manager or imprinted upon him by the actor. It is when the playwright ceases to be a servant and becomes master of his own play that his true professionalism emerges.

Professional dramatists have inhabited the theatre since Shakespeare's time. What is different about the nineteenth-century stage is that more than any other it has come to be known as the actors' theatre – in the sense that audiences tended to be attracted to the theatre by a particular actor's name on the playbill rather than that of the playwright. In some ways it is the strength of the Victorian theatre. Some dramatists found that they liked the security attached to writing for a particular player whose talents and characteristics were well known and whose acceptance of his play was one of the surest guarantees of success. Indeed many wrote only to order, and were at a loss to do anything different. Equally, others considered the practice to be a humiliation of the artist and an unacceptable restriction on his freedom as a writer.

Compared with the actor's, whose profession a star performer like Macready continued to regard as a poor and degrading art, the dramatist's status was, until late in the century, still lower. Analogies with the trade of the carpenter or shoemaker were common. Even W. S. Gilbert, who was partly responsible for its improved reputation in the second half of the century, denigrated playwriting as an intellectual activity, regarding it as requiring merely 'shrewdness of observation, a nimble brain, a faculty for expressing oneself concisely, [and] a sense of balance both in the construction of plots and sentences'. Nonetheless, in a theatre which embraces so much diversity of talent in so many genres – from Reynolds and Tom Dibdin, through Fitzball, Moncrieff and Stirling to Boucicault, Robertson, Burnand and Albery, and eventually to Pinero, Jones, Wilde, and Shaw – it is proper to recognise the ever-growing professionalism with which many dramatists approached the writing of a play and sometimes also its staging. A hack writer (the vast majority of nineteenth-century dramatists) would always be a hack writer, but that didn't necessarily prevent him from having a sense of belonging to a writing community. At the top of the profession, especially at the end of the century, the playwright tended to be highly conscious of his role as an artist. External pressures on dramatists of all classes were enormous, by virtue of the often conflicting demands of managers, actors, actor-managers, stage-crew, box-office, audience, critics, and the sometimes suffocating limitations imposed by official censorship. Yet for the professional playwright it was expedient as well as pragmatic to acquire a respected, independent, functional identity, or as much of one as was possible in whatever theatrical niche he found himself placed. This book is an outline of that process.

Acknowledgements

I am indebted to the following institutions for permission to use extracts from copyright material: the Trustees of the British Museum (archives of Covent Garden Theatre, Sydney Grundy–William Archer correspondence, and letters of Henry Arthur Jones to Messrs Macmillan Ltd); the Theatre Museum, Covent Garden (archives of the Lyceum Theatre); and the Tennyson Research Centre, Lincoln (letters of Henry Irving and Frederick Macmillan to Hallam Tennyson), courtesy of Lincolnshire Library Service. Material quoted from the Lord Chamberlain's papers in the Public Record Office is in Crown copyright.

It is a great pleasure to thank those individuals and institutions who have helped me in the writing of this book. This task is tinged with sadness, however, because Emeritus Professor Cecil Price, who shared with me information on his extensive collection of late eighteenth- and early nineteenth-century dramatic texts, died while this book was at the copy-editing stage. It is many years now since he first introduced me to Victorian theatre research, but he continued to take a keen interest in my work and for that, as well as for his model scholarship, and his friendship, I shall always be grateful.

I am indebted to the following for advice, suggestions, and other practical assistance: Dr Russell Jackson of the Shakespeare Institute, Birmingham; Professor Peter Wearing of the Dept of English, University of Arizona; Dr J. D. Dawick, Palmerston North, New Zealand; my colleagues Dr James A. Davies and Mr Andrew Varney; the Curator and staff, Theatre Museum, Covent Garden (especially Anna Jackson and Andrew Kirk);

Susan Gates, Tennyson Research Centre, Lincoln; the staffs of the Library, University College of Swansea, Westminster Central Reference Library, and the Reading Room and MSS Students' Room of the British Library, in particular Mrs Sally Brown (Curator of Modern Literary MSS), who made arrangements for me to consult long runs of the Lord Chamberlain's plays; and the editorial staff at Cambridge University Press (Sarah Stanton and Victoria Cooper), and my copy-editor Chris Lyall Grant, for making this book freer of errors than it might have been. I record also my appreciation to the Senate and Council, University College of Swansea, for the grant of two terms' sabbatical leave during the early stages of my research.

My small daughter Sarah deserves a special word of thanks for her continual reminders that there is life beyond the word-processor; but most of all I want to thank Ann, my wife, to whom this book is dedicated, for her generous support and encouragement.

Abbreviations

In addition to standard forms for periodical literature and *DNB* (for *Dictionary of National Biography*), the following abbreviations have been employed throughout. Full details may be found in the bibliography.

Burnand   Francis C. Burnand, *Records and Reminiscences.* 4th edn. 1905.

Dibdin   *Reminiscences of Thomas Dibdin.* 2 vols. 1827.

Fitzball   Edward Fitzball, *Thirty-Five Years of a Dramatic Author's Life.* 2 vols. 1859.

Genest   [John Genest], *Some Account of the English Stage from the Restoration in 1660 to 1830.* 10 vols. 1832.

Jones   *The Life and Letters of Henry Arthur Jones*, ed. Doris A. Jones. 1930.

Macready   *The Diaries of William Charles Macready, 1833–1851*, ed. William Toynbee. 2 vols. 1912.

Nicoll   Allardyce Nicoll, *A History of English Drama, 1660–1900.* 6 vols. 1965–7.

Pinero   *The Collected Letters of Sir Arthur Pinero*, ed. J. P. Wearing. 1974.

Planché   *Recollections and Reflections by James Robinson Planché.* [19]01.

Reynolds   *The Life and Times of Frederick Reynolds.* 2 vols. 1827.

Shaw, I   *Bernard Shaw. Collected Letters 1874–1897*, ed. Dan H. Laurence. 1965.

Shaw, II   *Bernard Shaw. Collected Letters 1898–1910*, ed. Dan H. Laurence. 1972.

1832 *Report*	*Report from the Select Committee on Dramatic Literature*
1866 *Report*	*Report from the Select Committee on Theatrical Licenses and Regulations*
1878 *Report*	*Report of Commission on Home and Colonial Copyright*

In the text, references to plays are normally accompanied by a note of theatre and year of first performance. Names of theatres have been abbreviated as follows:

Adel	Adelphi
Ave	Avenue
Brit	Britannia
CG	Theatre Royal, Covent Garden
Cob	Coburg (= Victoria)
Com	Comedy
Crit	Criterion
Crt	Court
Dal	Daly's
DL	Theatre Royal, Drury Lane
EOH	English Opera House (= Lyceum)
Gai	Gaiety
Gar	Garrick
Glo	Globe
Grec	Grecian
Hay	Theatre Royal, Haymarket
Lyc	Lyceum (= English Opera House)
Lyr	Lyric
Olym	Olympic
OC	Opera Comique
Pav	Pavilion
PoW	Prince of Wales (Tottenham St)
P'cess	Princess's
Roy	Royalty
SW	Sadler's Wells
St J	St James's
Sav	Savoy
Shaft	Shaftesbury

Stan	Standard
Str	Strand
Sur	Surrey
Ter	Terry's
Vaud	Vaudeville
Vic	Royal Victoria (= Coburg) (Old Vic)
Wynd	Wyndham's

All references to money are to the pre-decimal system of pounds, shillings, and pence (£ s d), in which 12 (old) pence made one shilling (modern equivalent five pence), and twenty shillings one pound. A guinea was twenty-one shillings (or £1 1s) (modern equivalent £1·05).

... his *first* difficulty consist[s] in pleasing *Himself* – his *second* difficulty in pleasing the *Manager* – his *third*, in pleasing the *Actors* – his *fourth*, in pleasing the Licenser – his *fifth*, in pleasing the *Audience* – his *sixth*, in pleasing the *Newspapers*; and, in addition to all these, the actors must *please* not to be taken ill, the weather must *please* not to be unfavourable, the opposing theatre must *please* not to put up strong bills; and then! – what then? – why then – '*Please* to pay the bearer the small sum of * * *;' and, N. B. which sum is sometimes, *par accident*, not paid at all.

Frederick Reynolds, *A Playwright's Adventures*,
London [1831]

CHAPTER I

The smell of lamps and orange peel

Our image of the early nineteenth-century playwright is coloured by Dickens's 'Mr Johnson' (alias Nicholas Nickleby), who in the space of twenty-four hours is expected to write a play designed 'to bring out the whole strength of the company', while contriving simultaneously 'to introduce a real pump and two washing-tubs' which the manager happens to have bought cheap at a sale the other day. Just the same as they do in London, says Mr Crummles, where '[t]hey look up some dresses and have a piece written to fit 'em'.

While it is by no means the whole truth about a profession as diverse as that of the nineteenth-century dramatist, Dickens's fictional account had a secure basis in reality at the middle and lower reaches of the market in mid-century. Sam Wild, proprietor of one of the best-known portable theatres in the north of England, reckoned that 'there were always to be found authors prepared at short notice to write a new piece, or to adapt an old one to meet the capabilities of an establishment'. No more was necessary than 'to state what talent you had, your scenic resources, and the extent of your wardrobe, and they would get you a new piece out in a couple of days'.[1] Few performers perhaps could have been quite as difficult to fit up with a part as Mr Crummles's daughter, 'the infant phenomenon'; but Nicholas Nickleby's task was rivalled if not exceeded in absurdity by Tom Dibdin's commission from David Morris of the Haymarket Theatre in the early 1820s to write a piece to suit a herd of reindeer and a diminutive family trio of singers, dancers, and fiddlers – the man shaped 'like an oil barrel', his wife with the dimensions of 'a half anker', and a son 'about the height of a Dutch cheese'.[2]

Dramatic authorship was never an easy profession and for much of the century provided neither security nor status. Yet one of the extraordinary features of the theatre is that, at the same time that it was execrated by those who thought it either sinful or had simply disgraced its heritage through being swamped by foreign adaptations and adulterated by performing animals, so many wanted desperately to write plays: 'to persevere' (as a contemporary says of Frederick Reynolds, one of the first professionals of the period) 'through all obstruction and discouragement, and be a dramatic author, or NOTHING'.[3]

Epitomised for James Planché by 'the smell of the lamps and the orange peel',[4] the living theatre had a special magnetism. For all sorts of reasons it attracted a vast range of writers: most of the century's best-known poets from Coleridge, Byron, Shelley, Browning, and Tennyson down through lesser-known ones such as Felicia Hemans; major and minor novelists like Charlotte Smith, Bulwer Lytton, Charles Dickens, Wilkie Collins, Charles Reade, Robert Buchanan, Henry James, R. L. Stevenson, and Hall Caine; essayists like Charles Lamb and Mary Russell Mitford; periodical writers, journalists, dramatic critics, lawyers, surgeons, military men, clergymen, teachers, clerks, shopkeepers, printers, actors, stage managers and scene painters – and in unprecedented numbers. Nicoll's *Handlist* records more than 700 dramatists for the period from 1800 to 1850 and that is by no means exhaustive. On that basis alone the drama was not dead, not even dying, but actually full of vibrant (if not literary) life even at its darkest period towards the middle of the century, when in response to the debilitated economic state of the theatre authors' fees fell to their lowest point. In the increasingly more optimistic climate of the second half of the century the number of dramatists more than quadrupled to around 3,200, though a high proportion, larger than in the earlier period, comprised single-play authors and the number was also inflated by an expanding body of writers active only in the provincial theatres, which had taken on new life. A more realistic picture of general dramatic activity would suggest that overall through the century the number of authors who wrote fairly regularly for the metropolitan and provincial theatres was not much above 10 per cent of the total, while those with outputs of more than fifteen to twenty plays apiece is much smaller again at somewhere between 3 and 4 per cent.

The social origins of nineteenth-century playwrights tend to be reflected in the status of the theatres for which they wrote. On balance most East End dramatists came from lower down the social scale than did patent theatre writers or, later in the century, those who wrote for the major theatres within, say, a half-mile radius or so of Charing Cross. Yet the profession was a broad church, which afforded opportunities for writers from many walks of life. Some wrote merely for amusement or for publication rather than stage performance – the number of closet tragedies is remarkable, especially before 1850 – but there was room for the leisured gentleman-amateur, the poet or novelist testing his way, the strolling player turned hack writer, as much as for the dedicated professional playwright. The widest band was occupied by a great multitude of writers for whom dramatic authorship, dependent on individuals' circumstances, provided a greater or lesser proportion of their income, and who also followed other paid employment, often within the theatre itself or perhaps in one of the professions.

In the first half of the century it is probably true to say that the number of female dramatists about matches their proportional involvement in the literary profession as a whole. The tradition established in the Restoration period by Aphra Behn – the first professional woman dramatist – and taken up by Susanna Centlivre and Hannah Cowley continues into the early nineteenth century with Elizabeth Inchbald and Joanna Baillie, though the latter's reputation was mainly literary rather than theatrical. While Mrs Inchbald is the only one at this period who could properly be considered a full-time professional writer for the stage, there were a number of other women playwrights who, having gained some reputation in literature, also wrote for the theatre and were granted honorary membership of the Dramatic Authors' Society.[5] After 1850 there was no shortage of female dramatic authors, but the majority were amateurs and few achieved any special distinction. Many wrote only one play, or were known only in the provinces, and those who made it to

London usually advanced no further than the afternoon matinée, which by the 1880s became established as one of the routes
whereby a new dramatic author might have a trial before being
accepted for the evening bills. Among the exceptions was Sarah
Lane (widow of the former manager Samuel Lane), who
energetically ran the Britannia and wrote a cluster of melodramas for her theatre in the 1870s and early 1880s. Invariably,
those who made any sort of name for themselves (like Frances
Hodgson Burnett, Mary Elizabeth Braddon, and the Anglo-
American Pearl Craigie) were predominantly novelists; and
except for the last-named's *The Ambassador* (St J 1898), which
ran for a whole season, their occasional excursions into the
drama were little regarded in comparison to the dramatised
versions of their novels. These were usually independently
worked up for the stage by other hands, such as Colin Hazlewood, who produced one of the many versions of Miss Braddon's
enormously successful *Lady Audley's Secret* (Brit 1862).

One feature of the world of the playwright stands out above all
else: that the broadest avenue into dramatic authorship was
through the theatre itself – as actor or stage manager, separately
or in combination. It was the great leveller. The eponymous
hero of Dickens's *Nicholas Nickleby* effects a rather swifter
translation from raw, untried actor to house dramatist and
leading player in Vincent Crummles's travelling company than
would have been typical, but nevertheless the principle holds
true. A lowly strolling player might indeed one day find himself
writing plays not just for booths and fairs or minor provincial
venues but for the London theatres. Acting or stage management were useful preparatory work as well as stimuli for writing,
and it is no coincidence that many of the best-known and most
successful dramatic authors served their apprenticeship in either
or both of those arts. To know the theatre has always been the
dramatist's first responsibility, and the majority of nineteenth-
century playwrights acquired their intimate knowledge of it
from the inside.

For many dramatists the theatre was a kind of self-perpetuat-
ing institution.[6] George Colman junior emulated his father in

combining the art of playwriting with management of the Haymarket. Brothers Charles (junior) and Thomas Dibdin came from a theatrical family and the latter's son George Dibdin Pitt became a prolific writer, mainly for the East End theatres. Both Thomas Morton's sons (Thomas junior and John Maddison) elected to follow their father into the dramatic profession, as did Douglas Jerrold, whose own son William Blanchard continued the connexion. Joseph Ebsworth's wife Mary was also a playwright and his father-in-law was the pantomimist Robert Fairbrother. Likewise Fanny Kemble helped to sustain her family's strong theatrical tradition as actress (albeit reluctantly) and subsequently as playwright. In Tom Robertson's case, both parents were busy professional actors and provincial managers, while Edward Leman Blanchard, though he never acted himself, was the son of William Blanchard the comedian. Actor-dramatist-managers such as Charles James Mathews (who married Madame Vestris), and Edmund Yates were also sons of actors. In the East End, where the Conquest family had strong theatrical ties as actors and managers during the second half of the century, George Conquest wrote for the Grecian under the management of his father Benjamin and later on for the same theatre and the Surrey under his own.

Throughout the century many of the best-known dramatists as well as the humblest followed the traditional route from acting into authorship. A number started out as actors with amateur companies. Although James Kenney began his working life in a London bank his real interest was acting with local amateurs, for whom he wrote his first piece, the farce *Raising the Wind*, the success of which led to its adoption by Covent Garden for performance in 1803. Thereafter Kenney wrote regularly for the two main patent theatres. James Robinson Planché had a similar kind of initiation. At first articled to a bookseller, he began his long theatrical career as an amateur, acting in private theatres. Like Kenney he wrote his own play, the burlesque *Amoroso, King of Little Britain* (1818), which, unexpectedly announced for the professional stage at Drury Lane without his prior knowledge, 'at once determined [his] future'.[7] It proved to be his entry point into regular writing, first for the Adelphi, then for Covent Garden, Drury Lane, the Olympic, and the Haymarket, in a varied and distinguished career embracing the theatre, antiquarianism, and heraldic office that lasted for more than fifty years. Such direct movement into the glories of writing for the patent theatres was not usually quite so easy, and a provincial starting-point was more common. Edward Stirling actually paid to act his first parts with an amateur group in London before becoming a strolling player and then, at the age of twenty-two tested out his abilities as a dramatic author on an 'easily pleased' audience of sailors and their girl-friends at Gravesend with an 'artfully rechristened' melodrama *Tilbury Fort* (1829), founded on Scott's *Kenilworth*.[8]

Dion Boucicault's long theatrical career began simultaneously and pseudonymously as actor and playwright in 1838. But it was his writing that first brought him to prominence with *London Assurance* (CG 1841) and *Old Heads and Young Hearts* (Hay 1844). He continued to act, often in his own plays, though it was eight years before he had another successful piece on his hands with *The Corsican Brothers* (P'cess 1852) and a further eight before he became properly established in Britain. His younger contemporary Tom Robertson was steeped in the theatre from the beginning, having started as a child actor, stage-hand and prompter in his parents' provincial companies. For more than a decade until 1860, when he retired as an actor, Robertson's writing for the stage ran in parallel with his acting, prompting, and stage-managing career in London and the provinces. In contrast, Arthur Wing Pinero was expected to join his father in the legal profession, but threw it up to become a provincial player, while his contemporary R. C. Carton trained as an architect before succumbing to the same temptation. Both were sometime members of Irving's company during the mid- to late 1870s, but Pinero was the first to abandon acting once he became established as a professional playwright in the mid-1880s; Carton (who was a better actor) continued performing until he began writing in earnest for George Alexander at the St James's in the early 1890s.

Against the usual trend, Henry J. Byron established himself

first as a dramatist and then as a manager (at the Prince of Wales with Marie Wilton) before trying a successful experiment as actor. He already had more than ten years' experience of writing burlesques and extravaganzas before making an unscheduled debut as Sir Simon Simple – Edward Sothern had refused the part – in his own drama *Not Such a Fool as He Looks* (Glo 1869). Thereafter Byron, like so many of his colleagues, combined the two professions by continuing to act in his own pieces.

Acting at whatever level, from 'walking gentleman' upwards, was a natural and useful accompaniment to or catalyst for dramatic writing. A large number remained in the acting profession, even very prolific authors like John Beer Johnstone, who is said to have written upwards of 200 dramas for the minor theatres. He was in middle-age before he wrote his first play and went on writing until he was nearly eighty, but spent his whole working life as a small-time actor. William Travers, who wrote for the East End theatres and was resident dramatist at the City of London in the 1860s, was also that theatre's leading player. Those like Edward Stirling, who continued to act even in a small way at the same time as being writers for the stage, found the continuing practice of actors' benefits useful supplements to their dramatic income.[9] More unusually, Brandon Thomas came to dramatic authorship by way of journalism and part-time composition and performance of music-hall songs before joining the acting company of John Hare and the Kendals at the St James's in 1879. While continuing to perform – Pinero considered him for casting in *The Second Mrs Tanqueray* – he wrote more than a dozen plays, including *Charley's Aunt* (Roy 1892), the farce which made him famous and brought him a considerable fortune.

Yet although most actors-turned-dramatists were competent players, few of them could be said to have truly excelled in the acting profession. Sheridan Knowles, Robertson, and Pinero were useful, but never in any way outstanding, as actors. Indeed, it was suggested that Knowles's surprising popularity with audiences as an actor actually rested on the strength of his reputation as a dramatist.[10] Ben Webster and John Baldwin Buckstone were admittedly held in some regard in comic and character parts, but the playwright who came closest to excellence in acting was undoubtedly Dion Boucicault, whom Joseph Knight, writing of his performance as Conn in *The Shaughraun* (DL 1875), described as 'probably the best stage Irishman that has been seen'.[11] As a general rule no great actor made even a mediocre playwright; but mediocre and middle-ranking actors sometimes made highly successful careers in dramatic authorship.

The acting label was difficult to shed for those of humbler status who had come up through the ranks, such as Andrew Cherry. Having made his acting debut at the age of fourteen, he became a strolling player and eventually rose to provincial theatre management in charge of companies on the South Wales and western circuits. By degrees he achieved reasonable success as a patent theatre playwright, but Genest insisted on his origins by describing his best-known play *The Soldier's Daughter* (DL 1804) as 'written by Cherry the actor'.[12] Nevertheless the metamorphosis of actors into prompters, stage managers or theatre managers and then into authors was common. Among them were John Fawcett, James Cross, Joseph Ebsworth, William Emden, William Oxberry, Thomas Longdon Greenwood, John Brougham, Thomas Hailes Lacy (who gave up writing when he went into business as theatrical publisher), and Robert Soutar, the comedian and sometime stage manager at the Gaiety under John Hollingshead. George Dibdin Pitt made his acting debut at the Surrey in 1827 and went on to stage management at other minor theatres, including the Coburg and Pavilion. His extraordinarily fecund career as dramatic author – he is said to have written more than 700 pieces, coupled with duties as acting manager – was spent almost exclusively at the Britannia Theatre in Hoxton writing melodramas for the Lane family. His successor was Colin Henry Hazlewood, formerly (in the theatrical jargon of the period) a 'low comedian' on the provincial circuits, who came to London in 1850 and joined the Surrey and City of London companies, all the while producing dramas, farces, and burlesques in rapid succession.

That the appetite for dramatic writing amongst actors and managers was sometimes better resisted than indulged is illustrated in the case of Wilson Barrett. Although as an actor he never rose to the first rank, he stands as an example of a dramatist who was actually better as an actor and certainly as a theatre manager and adviser to dramatists (notably Henry Arthur Jones) than he was at authorship. While he achieved some success in collaboration with Hall Caine, whose novels he dramatised, his own greatest triumphs at the box-office were cheap and sentimental religious melodramas like *The Sign of the Cross* (Leeds 1895, Lyr 1896) and *The Daughters of Babylon* (Lyr 1896), in which he also acted the lead roles.

Despite Sir Fretful Plagiary's horror (in Sheridan's burlesque *The Critic*) of the breed of manager who '[*w*]*rites himself*', some theatres, like the Haymarket, Adelphi, Grecian, and Surrey, all with longish periods of management continuity, benefited from managers who did exactly that and acted into the bargain. Ben Webster, who ran away from school to try his fortune on the stage as a dancer like his father, eventually rose to management of the Haymarket and Adelphi theatres, where most of his own plays were produced and in which he continued to act the character parts. In like fashion, his successor at the Haymarket, John Baldwin Buckstone, started out with a travelling company, graduated to low comedian in the minor theatre, and then went on to appear in his own and others' plays for the next fifty years. He began by appearing in his domestic melodrama *Luke the Labourer* (1826), the acceptance of which on terms of a guinea a night for thirty nights at the Adelphi Theatre (which Ben Webster eventually went on to own) occasioned his transfer from the Coburg acting company, where he had played comic parts for 30 shillings a week. Lower down the dramatic scale was George Conquest, who became perhaps the most stunning actor-acrobat of his time. With the help of collaborators – mainly Henry Pettitt, Paul Merritt, and Henry Spry – while manager of the Grecian (1872–8) and Surrey (1881–1901), he kept his theatres supplied with a constant stream of pantomimes and nerve-tingling melodramas, many of which were graced with suitably athletic roles for their author.

The theatre, Henry James observed in 1879, was 'just now the fashion' and 'perpetually talked about' in fashionable circles, where 'members of the dramatic profession are "received" without restriction'.[13] But things had not always been so. Playwrights sometimes suffered almost as much as actors from the rather snobbish, evangelically inspired, prejudice which tended to colour attitudes to theatre-going amongst sections of so-called respectable society. When Douglas Jerrold was not invited to the first performance of his penultimate play, the comedy *St Cupid; or, Dorothy's Fortune*, before the Queen at Windsor Castle in 1853, he commented that 'English authors have not yet, it would appear, proved themselves worthy of an obscure corner, on any occasion, in any ante-room, of Buckingham Palace or Windsor'.[14] In fact, however, the reason was probably more political than social and it was his punishment for satirising the monarch and other sacred institutions of the period in the columns of *Punch*. The Queen herself, especially in her early years, was a lover of the theatre – indeed, did much actively to support it – and she was sufficiently appreciative, for example, of Bulwer Lytton's *Lady of Lyons* (CG 1838) to send backstage a message of congratulations ('full of courteous expressions') to author and leading actor. Yet, in general, contemporary dramatists seem to have been held in low esteem by the Queen's early advisers at Court. Lord Melbourne said of Thomas Noon Talfourd (unaware of, or choosing to ignore, his profession as a lawyer): 'He writes plays and I don't think a man who writes plays is ever good for much else.'[15]

Dramatic authorship had more than a touch of bohemianism about it. It was an engaging world, a strange mixture of tawdriness and grandeur, raffishness and respectability. Most of the more prominent dramatic authors tended to be members, not just of the Garrick, which was formed under aristocratic patronage specifically for the theatrical fraternity and their supporters, but of a whole range of smaller, less formal clubs. The Savage, the Re-Union, the Cosmopolitan, and the Arundel all had a strongly non-conventional flavour, and were complemented by a profusion of lesser-known groups and coteries of theatrical and literary men who would meet for a smoke, a drink, and a meal at regular intervals, much along the lines of the group known as the 'Owl's Roost', affectionately portrayed in T. W. Robertson's play *Society* (PoW 1865).

Since the emergence of coffee-house societies in the eighteenth century, dramatists, like their fellows in other branches of literature, had long been attuned to club life, often in association with others outside the theatrical profession. All the Covent Garden authors and the principal actors connected with the theatre at the turn of the century were members of the Covent Garden Theatrical Beef Steak Club, described by Tom Dibdin as 'a most agreeable society' and numbering amongst its extra-theatrical members 'several eminent commercial and legal characters'.[16] From the early 1820s onwards, the grandest club in London for men of literature and the fine arts was the Athenaeum, but for dramatic authors it was rapidly overtaken in popularity and importance by the Garrick, whose secretary at its foundation in 1831 was James Winston, the former acting manager of Drury Lane. To Alfred Bunn (prior to his election as a member) it was merely 'a theatrical gossiping society'. On the other hand, as Planché records, not only did it bring together 'the majority of the principal dramatists and actors then living', but membership was not limited to theatrical folk, and its most engaging feature was 'the social intercourse between men of all ranks'.[17] As it attracted mainly established dramatists, novelists (including Dickens and Thackeray), and actors, the Garrick went on to develop a rather staid, establishment atmosphere – 'old-fogey-ridden' Francis Burnand called it when he became a member in 1865[18] – and by and large the smaller, more raffish clubs proved more useful as nurseries for aspiring authors. George R. Sims describes the Unity Club in Holywell Street, whose members included dramatic critics, publishers, editors, and journalists, as 'my jumping-off place for the world of authorship'.[19] And at the Savage Club, where the Brough brothers were founder-members and Tom Robertson an early recruit, the qualification for membership (originally limited to 100) was to be '[a] working man in Literature and Art'.[20]

Later, in the 1860s and 1870s, even the Dramatic Authors' Society endeavoured to conceal its essentially commercial nature by adopting the pretensions, as John Hollingshead put it, of 'a somewhat exclusive club – in which no man could be admitted who was not fit for the Carlton or the Garrick'. This led him to doubt wryly whether Shakespeare or David Garrick would have qualified under character or occupation for admission. A predominantly minor theatre hack like Edward Fitzball, formerly a country printer, was allowed membership, he alleged, only because of 'his great personal respectability'.[21] Candidates were permitted to offer themselves for election only after having had a play staged 'in a theatre of consequence'. Outside London this was defined as including major Theatres Royal (like Edinburgh, Glasgow, or Liverpool) but such lower-grade institutions as the theatres at Grimsby or Blackburn apparently did not qualify.[22]

For all its apparent size the world of the dramatic author was a relatively close one. Outside the clubs, many of the better-known playwrights were also members of social and literary circles, where, especially in the second half of the century, they mixed as a matter of course with prominent men in Victorian letters. At the upper end of the social scale was James Planché, whose scholarly and antiquarian pursuits in addition to his theatrical interests qualified him as a regular attender at conversaziones, breakfasts, and soirées, where, as he records in his memoirs, 'I met and was introduced to most of the notabilities then living in London.'[23] John Westland Marston's house in Regent's Park Road was the venue for regular Sunday evening and Monday levees, where favoured fellow dramatists, like W. G. Wills and Herman Vezin, might mix with such notables as Dante Gabriel Rossetti, William Morris, Ford Madox Brown, and A. C. Swinburne. As newcomers to wealth and influence, the Boucicaults, for a couple of years until the profits of *The Colleen Bawn* ran out, also wined and dined literary and dramatic society on a grand scale at their spacious mansion in the Brompton Road in the early 1860s.

The majority of the best-known nineteenth-century dramatists were connected to the mainstream of literary life; but the proliferation of Bohemian clubs, coteries, and societies, especially in the middle and later Victorian period, helped to promote more ready contact with men of all professions and callings. The Arundel, which occupied upstairs rooms off the Strand, was a favoured gathering-place for dramatic critics after first nights. It cultivated a distinctly relaxed and informal air: cards, billiards, and late hours were numbered amongst its attractions, while in hot weather members were permitted to wear shirt-sleeves rather than frock-coats. Burnand's impression of the place, to which he was introduced by Edward Leman Blanchard in the 1860s, was of 'a very meagerly furnished room' inhabited by 'some queer-looking men, shabbiness being their chief characteristic, smoking and drinking'. Most striking amongst them was the young burlesque writer Francis Talfourd, described as '[t]he most irregular of irregular livers, and the most careless'. Clement Scott, commenting on its membership diversity at about the same time, asserts that '[w]e had as many barristers, solicitors, artists, men of science, and musicians as actors and dramatists'.²⁴ Indeed the social mix to be found at the Arundel and similar institutions was a fair reflection of the variety of professions from which many new authors were drawn into playwriting.

After the theatre itself, journalism and the law were the most popular modes of entry into dramatic authorship. Yet, with the exception of Douglas Jerrold (who had early distinction as a playwright and later as a writer for *Punch*), and perhaps E. L. Blanchard, no journalist attained any very high standing in the profession. Possibly this was because journalism afforded such a wealth of opportunity for the writer, from the penny weeklies to the magisterial monthly journals. Instead, it was the law, heavily oversubscribed and packed with students who had no particular vocation for it, that tended to provide the theatre with playwrights of more dedication. As Burnand put it, the law was 'neither very attractive nor primarily productive; the drama, on the other hand, was both. The law meant possibilities *in futuro*, considerably *in futuro*; the drama was "cash down".' On the other hand, he warned those possessed of what he called 'the dangerous facility' for lightweight writing to avoid mixing journalism and the drama. Yet, as Burnand himself confessed to devoting 'at least a couple of days a week' to regular work for *Punch*,²⁵ it was hardly surprising that most of his playwriting friends in the 1860s, like Shirley Brooks and Tom Taylor (subsequently editor of the same journal in 1874) paid no attention to his advice.

Among the journalists-turned-playwrights were Albert R. Smith (originally a surgeon), who diversified into novels, drama, and periodical publication; Andrew Halliday, one of the founders of the Savage Club and collaborator with William Brough in the 1860s at the Adelphi and elsewhere; Henry Farnie, author or adapter of more than seventy pieces, including a number of successful comic French operas; and John McArdle, who wrote mainly for provincial theatres, and Joseph Stirling Coyne, a proprietor of *Punch* and sometime Secretary to the Dramatic Authors' Society. For some dramatists the additional income derived from journalism was not just useful but essential to their economic well-being. Colin Hazlewood (resident dramatist at the Britannia in the 1860s and 1870s), despite the very large quantity of plays he wrote, survived only by his extra work for the penny weeklies. And Edward Blanchard made journalism the financial mainstay of his life, even though his first love was writing for the theatre. Forced to make his own way in the world after the death of his father, he wrote dramatic pieces from his late teens onwards. By 1841 (at the age of 21) he was also editor of Chambers's weekly *London Journal of History* and, at the same time, appointed stock dramatist at the Olympic. In addition, he was a writer and reviser of guide books, among them *Bradshaw's Descriptive Railway Guides*, and a regular contributor to various newspapers, including the *Era*. While employed as dramatic critic for the *Daily Telegraph* for twenty-six years between 1863 and 1889, he continued to supply the annual pantomimes for Drury Lane and other theatres.

In addition to Blanchard there was a sizeable group of dramatists who were also dramatic critics. In the late 1850s and 1860s this group included John Oxenford and Tom Taylor (*The Times*), Edmund Yates and John Hollingshead (*Daily News*), Leicester Buckingham (*Morning Star*), William Bayle Bernard (*Weekly Dispatch*), Frederick Guest Tomlins (*Morning Advertiser*), John Heraud (*Illustrated London News*), and John Westland Marston (*Athenaeum*). Later, George R. Sims and H. Chance Newton (under their respective pseudonyms of 'Dagonet' and

'Carados') wrote on the theatre for the *Referee*. None of them seems to have recognised any particular conflict of interest between the two activities. But Sydney Grundy, who served his apprenticeship to literature by ten years of journalism, including dramatic criticism, on various Manchester newspapers, warned his fellow critic William Archer (who, as translator of Ibsen, was liable to fall into the same trap) that 'my excessive honesty in those days has been a terrible stumbling block in my path as a writer for the stage'.[26] Indeed, a contributor to *The Theatre* in 1895 (possibly with Bernard Shaw in mind) went so far as to assert that 'to be a writer of plays and to sit in judgment upon the plays of others – is to be placed in a position of dangerous embarrassment . . . The two avocations are obviously incongruous.'[27]

At the end of the century both Shaw – the most prominent critic-dramatist of the century – and J. M. Barrie entered dramatic writing by the common way of journalism and the lesser-travelled route of the novel. After a stint as dramatic critic in the provinces and then as leader writer for London newspapers, Barrie made a modest name for himself in fiction before his first successful plays were produced in 1891–2. Though, like Barrie, Shaw was a novelist before he was a playwright, he eased himself into paid journalism in 1885 and made his first reputation in the early 1890s as music critic of the *World* and later as dramatic critic of the *Saturday Review*. Ever conscious of the professional overlap between dramatic critic and dramatist, Shaw strove very hard to keep them distinct. As with his fellow countryman Oscar Wilde, who never seriously contemplated any career but a literary one, Shaw waited patiently for the inevitable to come about in the sure belief that fame was the natural consequence of the possession of genius. Perversely, he was gratified that his first play *Widowers' Houses* (Roy 1892), though it wasn't an artistic or financial success, at least made him 'infamous as a playwright'.[28]

The various niches of the law harboured a number of writers anxious to make their mark in the theatre. Near the bottom was William Thomas Moncrieff, reputedly the original of 'the literary gentleman' who attends Vincent Crummles's farewell supper in *Nicholas Nickleby*. One of the period's most prolific hack playwrights, he began his working life as a humble clerk in a London solicitor's office, later returning briefly to work as a law stationer after a period in theatre management. Other dramatists were originally solicitors or articled clerks, such as John Westland Marston, John Oxenford, Frederick Broughton, John Kingdom, and Shirley Brooks. William Dimond, Richard Lalor Sheil, and F. C. Burnand were all law students when their earliest plays were produced in the London theatres, though the last-named as a student at Trinity had some pieces staged previously by Cambridge ADC, which (with J. W. Clark) he founded in 1855. All three later obtained legal qualifications, but other authors such as Frederick Reynolds, Thomas Morton and Henry J. Byron promptly abandoned their legal training in the first flush of success as dramatists.

Among those qualified barristers who turned to the theatre were Thomas Noon Talfourd MP (who became a serjeant-at-law in 1835, the year before his first tragedy *Ion* was staged at Covent Garden), Tom Taylor, Wilkie Collins, Charles Kenney, Montagu Williams (Burnand's contemporary and collaborator), Sydney Grundy, and W. S. Gilbert. To begin with, Gilbert was a clerk with the Education Department of the Privy Council, 'in which ill-organised and ill-governed office', he stated later, 'I spent four uncomfortable years'.[29] After 1863, when he began to write plays, he practised law for a time on the northern circuit until the late 1860s. Like Burnand, he experienced the penury of a lawyer's life and claimed to have pocketed only £75 out of law work in two years. But at the same time he was making a reasonably satisfactory income through contributions to *Punch*, heavyweight periodicals like the *Cornhill* and *Temple Bar*, and as dramatic critic to the *Illustrated Times*. Until 1871, when seven of his plays appeared on the London stage, Gilbert's income from playwriting was negligible and journalism his only means of support.

A number of other professions were represented in the ranks of dramatic authors. Sheridan Knowles, who was both a teacher and an actor before he became a dramatist, originally studied medicine at Aberdeen University; Michael R. Lacy was a musician; Samuel Beazley an architect, responsible for the 1822 remodelling of the interior of Drury Lane; John Millingen a physician; Henry Robert Addison an officer in the Dragoons; Edward Mayhew a veterinary surgeon; George Croly and Henry Hart Milman were Church of England clerics; and Joseph Ebsworth (formerly secretary to David Morris at the Haymarket and actor-prompter at the Theatre Royal Edinburgh) combined playwriting with a parallel career as bookseller and teacher of music and singing. A few dramatists were also painters: the patent theatre dramatist Isaac Pocock, Samuel Lover (one of Madame Vestris's authors at the Olympic), W. G. Wills (who wrote novels as well as plays, but made his best income executing commissioned portraits), and Joseph Mackay (sometime collaborator with Sydney Grundy in the late 1870s and early 1880s). Most colourful of all, perhaps, was Henry Archibald Major, writer of melodramas for East End theatres such as the Soho, Grecian, and Britannia. Combining the activities of artist, actor, postman, and hack dramatist for nearly thirty years, he is said to have gone under the sobriquet of 'The Postman artist of Lincoln's Inn Fields'.

New dramatists came into the profession from various other areas of employment such as mercantilism, banking, insurance, and the Civil Service. James Cobb was an Assistant Secretary in the East India Company and George Lovell, Secretary to Phoenix Insurance. The Civil Service provided Charles Dance, who rose to chief clerk in the Court for Relief of Insolvent Debtors, while Gilbert Arthur à Beckett (having been trained in the law) was a clerk in the office of Examiners of Criminal Law Accounts. In the upper echelons of government service were Henry Reeve at the Privy Council and Sir Henry Taylor at the Colonial Office. As Clement Scott put it, 'Her Majesty's Service has from time to time given many hostages to literary fortune.'[30] But dramatic authorship also served as a more exciting alternative to the mundane life of the clerk for writers such as William Bayle Bernard (Army Accounts Office), Frank Marshall (Audit Office, Somerset House), who, like the former, wrote theatrical criticism for the newspapers, and F. G. Tomlins (another part-time critic and journalist), whom John

Hollingshead describes as having 'cultivated literature on a City clerkship'.[31]

The most conspicuous recruits from the world of Victorian business were James Albery and Henry Arthur Jones. The former, having given up his early training as an architect, became a partner in the family rope-making business in Black-friars Road, close to the Surrey Theatre; and the latter worked as an assistant in his uncle's drapery shop in Ramsgate from the age of 12 at a salary of £20 a year, then as a warehouseman in Bradford. In his early twenties Jones became a commercial traveller in the west of England on a salary of £150 plus commission on orders over £8,000 per annum. After his first great success *Two Roses* (Vaud 1870) Albery distanced himself from the business, but remained a partner until 1878. Jones made a bolder and more risky break in 1879, following the acceptance of three of his comedies at provincial theatres and, with the practical encouragement of Wilson Barrett, his London debut with the comedietta *A Clerical Error* (Crt 1879). At the time Jones confessed to a friend that the question of whether 'to give up bagmanship' in favour of a professional career as a dramatist (which Barrett strenuously urged upon him) had reduced him to 'a wretched state of ferment'.[32]

The dilemma for the would-be dramatic author was always between the relative security of employment outside the theatre and the uncertainties within. For Andrew Cherry, Planché, Douglas Jerrold (also for a short time a midshipman in the Navy), and the Brough brothers (who all had early connexions with the printing and bookselling business), the pull of the theatre was too strong; but Edward Fitzball used his trade as an insurance against failure during his formative years as a play-wright. His rise from printer's apprentice and the obscurity of a Norwich printing business, first into provincial theatre, then to minor theatre in London and finally into patent theatre writing concluding his long career as reader for Drury Lane but still turning out plays – there are over 150 of them as well as four novels and six volumes of verse – is the classic illustration of the determination and sheer energy of the middle-ranking, popular Victorian playwright. But, then, as he claims in his autobiography, his success as a dramatist was directly attributable to his possession of 'the felicitous art of suiting myself to my audience'.[33]

Looking back on his most prolific period of writing (which would have been the 1830s), Fitzball maintained that '[a] man with a tolerable share of genius and *industry* could turn himself respectably about and gain a genteel living'.[34] Certainly this marks an important watershed between an era when it was possible to sustain a career wholly dedicated to dramatic authorship and a period around mid-century when it clearly wasn't.

In economically more healthy times at the beginning of the century dramatists like Elizabeth Inchbald, George Colman junior, Thomas Morton, Frederick Reynolds, and Tom Dibdin stand out as professionals, each drawing their primary income from the theatre and dramatic composition. Inchbald represents the rather more cautious author, who carefully prepared the ground of her dramatic career. Not until June 1789, by which time she had had nine plays staged in five years and was about to produce another, could she judge it safe to relinquish her small but regular income as an actress and become a full-time dramatist (with occasional excursions into the novel). But the professional dramatist was in keen demand at the turn of the century for all kinds of related functions. Mrs Inchbald and Tom Dibdin both had relatively lucrative editing assignments for series of dramatic texts published by Longmans and Charles Whittingham respectively;[35] and Dibdin went on to stage and theatre management, at first for the patent theatres and then on his own account. Reynolds was perhaps the more typical playwright of the period because, having lost his patrimony, he was for long periods totally dependent upon his income from dramatic authorship and was forced into producing plays at regular intervals in order to satisfy immediate financial demands, whereas Morton (who seems to have had some private income) was able to 'wait better than his friend the temptings of a good dramatic subject, and write at leisure'. It is true that, as Boaden says, both dramatists, for most of their respective

careers, 'avoided the engagement of a regular profession' outside
playwriting,[36] but (as in the case of Tom Dibdin) they were both
eventually tempted into quasi-managerial functions in the
theatre. Morton held out longest before accepting positions as
reader of plays for Covent Garden and Drury Lane in the late
1820s and 1830s; but Reynolds's involvement, like Dibdin's, was
more comprehensive. Fifteen years or so into his dramatic career
he took on advisory duties at Covent Garden under Henry
Harris. Though untitled, the position was wide-ranging and
time-consuming: '[s]ome called me "*whipper* in to the
tragedians"; many, "*ferret* to the painters and composers"; and
others, "*maid of all work*" to the manager, who, himself, called me
"*thinker*"; at the same time, kindly allowing me, without injury
to my morals, to be a *free* thinker'.[37] Not surprisingly Reynolds
had begun to devote less and less time to dramatic composition
and by the time he went to Drury Lane between 1823 and 1824
(as replacement to Tom Dibdin) to become part of the management cabinet, acting as 'private advisor and reader of plays at
home' for Robert Elliston at a salary of £200 a year,[38] writing
plays had become very much a secondary activity.

The same drift away from dramatic writing is even more
obvious in George Colman junior, who, from about 1808, found
his managerial duties at the Haymarket and precarious finances
precluded anything more than the occasional addition to his
dramatic canon. According to James Winston, in 1821 he was
offered tempting employment by Elliston at Drury Lane as
'supervisor of plays, etc.' at the exorbitant salary of £1,000.[39]
But instead, to the wonderment of his friends, colleagues and
enemies in the theatrical profession, in February 1824 he
accepted the quasi-sinecurial post of dramatic censor (officially
Examiner of Plays to the Lord Chamberlain) at £400 per
annum plus fees for every play licensed. Colman turned his
attention to his new duties with startling zeal and transformed
himself from self-confessed 'careless immoral author'[40] into a
kind of dramatic policeman. He wrote no more plays.

Unpropitious as the 1830s were for new entrants into the
dramatic profession, those like James Planché, already well
established and with a reasonably high reputation, were finan-

cially secure within the professional theatre only because writing plays was but one element in a career which embraced a variety of other professional duties. For Planché this included at various times not only employment as reader of plays for the Olympic and Covent Garden theatres, but stage management and costume design. However, times were hard and even Sheridan Knowles, the best-paid playwright of the period, found his way back into acting before mid-decade simply to make ends meet. 'To my brief success as an actor', he wrote, 'I owe what I should in vain have looked for as an author – emancipation from debt, a decently furnished house, the means of giving my children ample education, relief from the doubt whether to-morrow might not bring short commons, or none at all.'[41] Knowles's profits from acting, alleged by his son to have been 'very considerable', suggest that he must have done quite well out of end-of-season benefit nights, since his regular salary, even if it was a bit above average, wouldn't have amounted to more than about £15 to £20 a week. Certainly it could have been nothing like the £30 per performance which a star performer like Macready extracted from Alfred Bunn in the mid-1830s.

Dramatists who came into the profession in the 1840s and later were nearly all men of the theatre in the wider sense. The range of opportunities afforded by the theatre as a whole, in addition to authorship, provided them with necessary life-lines, because writing plays was in itself such a financially unreliable occupation. Outlining his career to date to the members of the 1866 Committee, Dion Boucicault proclaimed a single-minded commitment to the profession in which he alone enjoyed truly commercial success: 'I commenced as a dramatic author at 18', he explained, 'and I have never quitted it up to my present age, which is 43. I have never done or attempted anything else.'[42] Yet in truth, despite a couple of isolated successes, Boucicault's early career was nearly as much of a struggle as was Tom Robertson's or any of the other aspiring authors who managed to claw their way into the theatre by means which did not rely exclusively on their productivity as playwrights. Robertson was forced into selling some of his copyrights for the miserable price of £3 and earning a few extra pennies by revamping, at the request of the bookseller and publisher T. H. Lacy, successful West End adaptations of French plays for 'East End and transpontine theatres'.[43] Boucicault too was a survivor; he was nothing if not uncompromisingly realistic. The drama was for him essentially a means for making money, and John Hollingshead described him in 1866, three years after his second bankruptcy, as a 'patient and constant worker – a temperate man, simple in his habits, who treated dramatic authorship as a trade. He worked harder than a banker's clerk.'[44]

The dramatic profession was always a trial, but especially so in the 1840s and 1850s when fees for writing plays were so depressed. Yet whereas Boucicault and Robertson, whatever the difficulties, remained committed to the theatre as full-time professionals, their contemporary Tom Taylor followed a quite different course. Though a loyal member of the Dramatic Authors' Society, he had simultaneous career interests completely independent of the theatre. Hollingshead's description of him as 'otherwise occupied; he is an eminent civil servant'[45] is a crashing understatement for a playwright, of all Victorian dramatists the most highly educated, who managed an extraordinarily diverse extra-theatrical career. Despite writing more than eighty plays spread over more than thirty years – during which he was house writer for the Olympic (1853–60) and for the Haymarket (1857–70) – he was never wholly dependent upon the drama for his income. He was variously a Cambridge Fellow and tutor, Professor of English in the University of London, barrister for three years on the northern circuit, art critic on *The Times* and *Graphic*, leader writer for the *Morning Chronicle* and *Daily News*, and a highly placed civil servant for twenty years with the Board of Health. After retirement from the Civil Service he took on the editorship of *Punch* and continued to write plays to within a year or so of his death in 1880.

Burnand asserts that when he began to write for the commercial theatre in the early 1860s no one could seriously contemplate making a proper living out of the dramatic profession. As in so many aspects of theatrical life the exception was of course Boucicault – he could earn 'more in two weeks than any one of the old stagers had been accustomed to make in two years' – but for the rest the playwright 'could just manage to exist by his trade; that was all'. Planché, the Brough brothers, Tom Taylor, Charles Dance, Stirling Coyne, 'and all of the dramatists of that day had a hand-to-mouth existence as far as the stage brought any contribution to their incomes. Except Tom Taylor and Planché [who had earnings from other sources], they were none of them in what is known as "society", and therefore the calls on their pocket were not extravagant.' In Burnand's view little had changed by 1880 when, in a symposium conducted in *The Theatre* on the state of authorship, he maintained that 'there is no dearth of dramatic authors, but there are very few who live entirely by their work for the stage'.[46] James Albery tried it and was comfortably successful for a time during the 1870s; but by the mid-1880s his popularity was on the wane and his income (put at a total of about £650 for 1883 and 1884) was just not enough to support a wife and three children.[47]

Albery was representative of an earlier generation in which only Boucicault and W. S. Gilbert, by dint of their impressive negotiating powers, enjoyed really substantial financial success. For the newer generation, however, the future held promise of better things. The quality of life of the professional dramatist was necessarily dependent upon the health or otherwise of the theatre, and dramatists who came into the profession during the last quarter of the century benefited from the increasing confidence in its economic state. The long run, now well established, helped to spread production costs and, given the right play, box-office receipts were more stable and predictable. Dramatic authorship in consequence became less of a foolhardy enterprise. At the beginning of the 1880s George Sims, though he owed money at 60 per cent interest to a loan-shark, still happily gave up his secure job with his father's wholesale and export business in the City to concentrate exclusively on playwriting and journalism.[48] Well before the end of the century theatrical management and proprietorship again became a highly lucrative business: as Arthur à Beckett put it in 1896, '[i]t is a modern fashion to consider (and find) theatrical property a paying investment'.[49] And dramatists did not fail to recognise it as such. While to begin with the number who devoted themselves to

writing plays and nothing else was small, they formed a significant and growing minority, including Sydney Grundy, Henry
Arthur Jones, and, by the mid-1880s, Arthur Wing Pinero. At
the same time Gilbert (with his partners) was making so much
money out of the Savoy operas that in 1889 he was able to
finance the erection of a new four-tiered, 1,500-seater theatre for
the actor-manager John Hare, the Garrick in Charing Cross
Road, thus giving himself the distinction of being the first
Victorian dramatist to build a theatre wholly out of the fruits of
his own labour. As a profession the drama had come a long way
by the end of the century, when Francis Burnand's considered
advice to the aspiring writer was to ignore journalism 'light or
heavy', ignore the novel (unless intent on producing dramatisations of one's own work) and simply '*stick to the drama*'.[50]

CHAPTER 2

'A devil of a trade'

Of all the uncertainties in the life of a dramatic author in the nineteenth century none was more prominent or vexatious as money. 'What profession', enquired Frederick Reynolds at the end of a forty-year career, 'can be considered so laborious, and at the same time so *precarious*, as an author's?' But, though he pointed out in 1827 that a sum of just over £19,000 was not really a great deal to show for a life of 'incessant labour, struggle, and uncertainty', it was nonetheless, as he admits, 'a sum, hitherto unequalled in the history of dramatic writing'.[1]

In a sense Reynolds was actually very fortunate. Although 'woeful experience' taught him that '[a]n author's is a sort of *hand to mouth* profession', it was still possible, at the turn of the century, to make a living solely or principally out of the drama and, as Reynolds did, to support a wife and family out of it. Such relatively favourable conditions did not, however, persist long into the nineteenth century as the minor theatres' war of attrition against the patent houses bit ever deeper. The economic record until about 1860, when Boucicault helped to wrest the contractual initiative out of the hands of the manager and put it into the author's, is of the gradual descent of the playwright into a financial trough. As George Colman junior, who knew the heights and the depths, put it, the playwright's was 'a devil of a trade'.[2]

In 1800 the economic state of the theatre showed few signs of its subsequent swift decline. For authors especially, the omens were good. Within the previous decade the old benefit system based on authors receiving a share of takings at the box-office, after deduction of house expenses, on the three traditional authors' nights – the third, sixth, and ninth – had given place at least at the patent theatres to a less risky and more professional arrangement whereby authors contracted with theatre managers for a fixed sum. It was evidently a matter worth commenting on when in February 1793 John Philip Kemble noted in his private memorandum that there 'was no Benefit for the Prize, the proprietors giving Mr Storace and Mr Hoare 150 Pounds in lieu of it'.[3] This suggests the beginning of the transition between traditional authors' benefits (which had subsisted since at least the beginning of the eighteenth century and probably earlier) and fixed payments on contracts which guaranteed certain sums as long as the play stood its expected course. In this respect the patent theatres seemed to work more or less in concert. During the next season at Covent Garden Frederick Reynolds, who until then had been paid in the traditional way, received the fixed sum of £33 6s 8d every night for the first nine nights of the run of *The Rage* (1794), followed by a lump sum of £100 on the twentieth night, which, together with an additional £100 on the fortieth night, brought him in total £500 for the play. Reynolds describes his contract on this occasion as 'the foundation of that bargain between manager, and author' which was still current in the late 1820s. He also laid claim to the alternative arrangement, beginning with *Laugh When You Can* (CG 1798), whereby the first £300 was paid to him in three equal instalments on the third, sixth, and ninth nights of representation, followed by £50 on both the fifteenth and twentieth nights.[4] This scheme, it was maintained, superseded the former and constituted a precedent for later arrangements entered into by Morton and Inchbald, though in fact the two types of contract (which in any case produced the same income up to twenty nights) ran in parallel and, with minor variations and adjustment, supplied the theoretical framework for paying authors of legitimate dramas at the patent theatres at least into the 1830s. With both forms the skeleton of the old benefit system was retained but, instead of dependence on the level of patronage at the box-office, authors were guaranteed their fees on a fixed scale, subject only to the length of the run.

The benefit system for dramatists did not disappear overnight. Authors' nights survived into the early years of the nineteenth century at the Haymarket (where writers of farces were reminded of the inferior nature of their chosen genre by the delay of their initial benefit until the sixth night of representation). Outside the patent theatres, older practices continued for decades longer in the provinces and in some minor theatres where regular writers supplemented their income with occasional authors' nights.[5] Even at the main patent houses there are a few stray examples of authors who were obliged to submit to the indignities of the old system, certainly up to about 1800, with results that confirmed the superiority of the newer alternative. Charlotte Smith's success as a novelist wasn't repeated in the theatre. Her comedy *What is She?* (CG 1799) attracted such a poor audience to her first (and only) benefit night that receipts barely covered house expenses, resulting in an income for the author which couldn't have exceeded £30.[6] Yet at the other end of the spectrum a dramatist like Elizabeth Inchbald (whom her first biographer describes as 'better skilled in the art of dealing with theatres than most of her cotemporaries [*sic*]') was confident enough to suggest her own terms to Covent Garden. Though not successful on every occasion, she did persuade Thomas Harris to remunerate adaptations on a scale commensurate with the often considerable work involved. For *The Wise Man of the East* (CG 1799) (adapted from Kotzebue) Harris rejected her request for £300 for nine nights and £20 a night thereafter up to and including the thirtieth night, making a projected total of £720; but his counterproposal of £500 in full settlement was a fair one and Mrs Inchbald 'was too wise to refuse'.[7]

Patent theatre authors tended to be better off under the fixed payment scheme than under the old benefit system. There was naturally still a substantial element of risk involved but it was on the whole a much more equitable arrangement. Thomas Morton declared that it was his purpose in negotiating with the patent theatres 'to share in their prosperity, or to take my share in their adversity, as well as I could; my bargains were made on that principle'.[8] Of the more prominent patent theatre authors at the turn of the century, it was probably Mrs Inchbald who asserted most strongly the right of the author to fair and adequate remuneration for the labour involved in every species of dramatic composition. She had tasted poverty in early life as an actress and was determined not to do so again. All her income was carefully controlled and properly invested. As Boaden says, 'the love of money was always strong in her'.[9]

Many late eighteenth- and early nineteenth-century drama-tists, fortunate enough to be carried along on a rising tide of theatrical fortunes, found that the fixed payment system, depen-dent on length of run, modulated into a guaranteed lump sum which absolved the dramatist from all risk. In some special cases payment was even made on acceptance of the MS rather than in the course of performance. These exceptions tended to attract high fees. Reynolds noted that Elizabeth Inchbald's superior bargaining-power secured her £800 for *Wives As They Were, and Maids As They Are* (CG 1797) before representation. And it was with more than a hint of jealousy that he noted that his friend Thomas Morton had managed to negotiate no less than £1,000 for *Town and Country* (CG 1807) also before it was acted.[10] But the highest fee of all at this period seems to have been reserved for George Colman junior's *John Bull* (CG 1803), which enjoyed an unusually long run of forty-seven nights. Its success considerably exceeding his expectations, Thomas Harris improved upon what was at the time his already unprecedented purchase price of £1,000 by making two *ex gratia* payments to Colman of £100 each to give the author an aggregated income from the play of £1,200.[11] Such fees were well beyond the usual levels of remun-eration, but at Covent Garden occasional supplements to agreed fees were not uncommon. Most of Colman's plays were said to have attracted extra payments of between £100 and £200 and, on a lower level, Frederick Reynolds records that for *Delays and Blunders* (CG 1802), Harris, 'liberally giving me a share in the profits', added another £50 on top of the negotiated fees.[12] The practice earned Thomas Harris a reputation, for the most part, of fair dealing in a world where such a virtue was untypical.

As middle-of-the-road professionals Frederick Reynolds and Tom Dibdin were able to command sufficiently good terms to enable them to sustain wholly adequate and even well-to-do livings out of their careers as professional playwrights. In both cases however (as with contemporaries such as Colman, Inchbald, and eventually even Morton, whose early career was assisted by a private income) this was supplemented by earnings in one or more of the usual occupations for a playwright of the period – stage management, theatre management, editing collections of plays, or a position as reader of plays – all of which were useful and sometimes very necessary second strings. Of the two Reynolds was the more financially secure. Indeed he had something of a reputation (undeserved, as he continued to point out) of being a rich man. But, unlike Dibdin, he never went bankrupt and he retained, more or less, his pre-1800 income level into the new century. In general Reynolds cleared between £300–500 a play. This meant that in a fairly average year like 1805, between productions at the Surrey and Covent Garden, he could make a very respectable middle-class income of £800; but in an exceptionally good year like 1808, with the revenue from the successful comedy *Begone Dull Care* added to the £600 made by the opera *The Exile; or, the Deserts of Siberia* over a 22-night run with receipts averaging over £400 a night, he realised as much as £1,100.[13] Dibdin's income per play was lower but he made up for it in quantity. At Covent Garden during the first decade of the century he could normally count on about £300, including sale of copyright, though occasionally the fee was closer to £400. Under a 'hit or miss' contract with the normally less generous Haymarket in the sum of £200 for *Five Miles Off; or, the Finger Post* (1805), Dibdin was delighted to receive from Colman – 'who most liberally and laughingly said he did not scruple breaking an agreement made in his own favour to serve a friend' – an extra £75 on top of the original contract price, which, together with the sale of the copyright at £100, netted him a total of £375.[14]

To the casual observer in 1800 the theatre seemed robust and financially secure. Everyone who could do so wanted to write for it and share in the reputedly substantial incomes to be made. The recognition of just how profitable dramatic authorship could be attracted to the theatre some whose instincts were not primarily theatrical. Charles Lamb, eagerly awaiting a response from John Philip Kemble, to whom he had sent a MS, wrote at the end of 1797 that 'the profits of acting plays are now so large, that a very shadow of a hope ought to make me glad.'[15] Essentially, the same awareness underscored the attempts of the Romantic poets at dramatic authorship. Of the first generation, Wordsworth and Coleridge wrote plays, but only the latter's came to the stage and he was fully briefed in the financial advantages involved in acted, as opposed to closet, drama. His revised tragedy *Remorse* (DL 1813) – Sheridan had rejected the original version at the same theatre in 1797 – secured Coleridge an income which far outstripped anything he had made previously. 'It has been a good thing for the Theatre', he wrote to Thomas Poole, since they would make between £8,000 and £10,000, '& I shall get more than all my literary labours put together, nay thrice as much', amounting to £400 inclusive of copyright.[16]

But the enormous success of a few productions in the early years of the century masked a serious underlying decline in theatrical finances, the danger signals of which were largely ignored or misinterpreted. Actors' salaries for top performers went to ruinously high levels – for instance, Edmund Kean, after a brilliant debut at Drury Lane in 1814, eventually commanded £50 a night. In the costs behind the very success of certain productions there were worrying long-term consequences, not least for dramatic authorship. Sheridan's *Pizarro* (DL 1799), though it brought in 'the enormous sum' of £30,000 in the first sixty nights, also bled an almost equal amount of money out of the theatre. As Reynolds pointed out, there was, 'a vast difference between the expenses attached to the production of what is technically termed a "blue coat, and white waistcoat play," and those of a "spangled and processional play"'. Similarly, the first forty-one nights of the revival of Colman's *Blue Beard* (DL 1798) in 1811 brought Covent Garden 'above *twenty-one thousand pounds*'.[17] Yet while on paper the play evidently contributed a large proportion of the total receipts of the 1810–11 season – inflating them to an artifically high level at £98,110 4s 8d – the expense of hiring live horses from Astley's for the production must have made deep inroads into the profits.

Reynolds insisted on praising the adventurousness, liberality and managerial expertise of Henry Harris, who had taken over Covent Garden Theatre from his ailing father Thomas in September 1809. But the picture in terms of hard cash was far less encouraging. On the surface the theatre, with average receipts between 1809 and 1820 at just under £78,000, appeared to be prosperous.[18] It seems however that for the whole of the second decade of the century the theatre was entirely dependent for its profit on the annual pantomime, most of which were written by Harris himself. For the benefit of the 1832 Committee Francis Place calculated that for the seasons 1810–1 to 1820–1 no regular drama made any profit at all and that the average annual surplus on the pantomime – effectively the basis of the profit for the season – amounted to £3,267, from which a further sum for production expenses would need to be deducted.[19]

The factors said to be responsible for the general decline in the theatres, which was widely recognised by the early 1830s, were lengthily debated at the proceedings of the Select Committee set up to enquire into the drama in 1832. Incompetent management, the level of actors' salaries, excessive production expenses unmatched by receipts, unwelcome competition provided by the attack on the patent monopoly from the proliferating minor theatres, religious scruples, even late dinner-hours, were all adduced as evidence for the deterioration. At Covent Garden after 1820–1 even the old standy-by the pantomime failed to make money. Competition from the minors was reckoned to cost Covent Garden as much as £20,000 in fall-off of receipts, with the Adelphi as the worst offender doing 'very material damage indeed'.[20] By 1827 its patent theatre rival Drury Lane, having struggled from crisis to crisis for years past, had virtually ruined Elliston and was about to do the same to its new manager, Stephen Price. The crisis of the patent theatres, aggravated by huge payrolls, ruinous rent – the sums which, in Planché's view, the committee 'were screwing out of their lessees rendered any chance of enduring success hopeless'[21] – and conflict with not only the minor theatres but between themselves, lasted into the 1840s. Nothing seemed to work, neither retrenchment nor expenditure, competition nor alliance. As James Winston wrote in his journal at the end of Stephen Price's first season at Drury

Lane, the new manager 'has sown the seed of future destruction
to the theatre. The season has been carried on with a parsimony
unknown in a London theatre and as opposite to liberality as Mr
Elliston's was to prudence.'[22] Alfred Bunn considered Price
wasn't a gentlemen and totally devoid of real interest in the
theatre; but Bunn's own despotic reign over the two patent
theatres for a couple of pretty miserable seasons after 1834 only
confirmed the blight that seemed to have settled so thickly over
patent theatre management.

The deterioration of theatrical finances is reflected in the altered
fortunes of the dramatic author well before 1830. In the second
decade of the century, despite the downward spiral of receipts,
the patent theatres attempted to maintain traditional rates of
remuneration for their authors. But during the 1820s the
established rules began to break down. As James Boaden put it
in 1825, '[t]he dramatic writers of the present day, repressed by
the more prominent claims of the *equestrian* order, are narrowed
to a badly paid £300; or, as the spirit of some lawyer arranged it,
£33 6s. 8d for nine nights: there was a tradition, that a one-and-
twentieth night once ensured a further benevolence, "But
WHEN,/ Extends beyond their catalogue".'[23] Indeed, by the end
of the decade there were even a few cases of the patent theatres
being unable to honour contracts with their authors.

The patent theatre managers tried to put a brave face on
things at the 1832 enquiry, but the assertion by David Morris of
the Haymarket that 'authors are better remunerated now than
they . . . were 20 or 30 years ago; they are more sure of the profit;
they go on safer grounds' was less than honest.[24] In respect of
authors' reliance on fixed payments instead of the receipts of
benefit nights it was true, but actual income was less, in most
instances considerably less, even for top-liners. The claims of
Samuel Beazley (who was 'very well satisfied') and Richard
Brinsley Peake ('[u]pon the average' content with his
rewards),[25] were not confirmed by the rest of the active dramatic
contingent present as witnesses, including Planché, John Poole,
William T. Moncrieff, James Kenney, T. J. Serle, and Douglas
Jerrold.

As one of the proprietors of Covent Garden, Capt. John Forbes assumed the role of apologist for the two winter theatres by arguing that, despite all the difficulties put in their way by the minors, Covent Garden and Drury Lane were still capable of properly remunerating their authors; especially when compared with minor theatres like Davidge's Coburg, which paid a maximum of £50, or the City (under John Kemble Chapman), which he alleged offered a mere 10 shillings a play and then defaulted on payment. Excluding translations and short after-pieces, which were said to attract on average, and dependent on merit, between £200 and £400 (in the former case) and £100 or less (in the latter), standard terms for authors at Covent Garden, unless there was a 'special contract' – which might offer as much as £500 for a full-length tragedy or comedy – were £100 on each of the third, sixth, ninth and fortieth nights of representation. In the event of a piece exceeding forty nights, he claimed, authors 'are always very liberally dealt with', but Forbes admitted at the same time that 'very few pieces' could be expected to go so far.[26] This was, of course, for a main piece in four or five acts, and he did not draw attention to the fact that the £100 formerly payable on the twentieth night (sometimes the twenty-first) of representation had been quietly dropped some time previously, probably around mid-decade. In effect this reduced an author's expectations during the late 1820s from £500 to £400 on a full-length play running for forty nights or down to a bare £300 for anything less. Given the resistance of tragedies to long runs, unless there was a 'special contract' the lower figure was realistically the maximum that could be counted on.

The two patent theatres were said to have each paid out to authors an average of £1,500 every year over the past decade, whilst in 1832 Covent Garden had disbursed £1,750 in authors' fees, matched by a figure 'nearly the same' at Drury Lane.[27] But though there is some truth in Forbes's claim that the patent theatres tried to maintain reasonable rates of remuneration during the 1820s, prices were substantially depressed in comparison with earlier decades. The higher rates mentioned for each category were rarely attained. As contracts were negotiated on the basis of projected returns and on the incidental state of the theatres' finances at the time, there is a wide spectrum of payments even within the same class of play. To an increasing degree the financial state of Covent Garden was used as an excuse to cut some rates to the very bone.

At the bottom end of the scale were after-pieces. These were usually farces, modestly remunerated by fixed payments but at unstable rates. For a short farce (or 'interlude', as it is often described in the account books) the rate could be as much as £50. At Covent Garden this is what Joseph Lunn had for *Lofty Projects* (1825) but he received only £20 for *Three Deep* (1826). John Poole had similarly variable payments for his farces: £50 for *The Scape Goat* (1825) but £25 for the earlier farce *The Two Pages of Frederick the Great* (1822). For more substantial farces placed higher up the bill better prices were to be had. R. B. Peake managed £100 for *The Duel* (1823) and the same, with an extra £30 for the copyright, for *The £100 Note* (1827).[28] Most profitably of all, Thomas Morton secured the generally accepted maximum fee of £200 for authorship and copyright of the musical farce *The Invincibles* (1828). Indeed, for all its financial difficulties, Covent Garden still had the edge on the Haymarket, where Morton was able to wheedle no more than £150 (including copyright which Morton reckoned was of 'no value') out of the parsimonious manager David Morris for the farce *Separation and Reparation* (1830), which was £50 less than his normal expectation for a Haymarket farce under the former manager George Colman junior.[29]

For comedy, the median level of payment at £200 was equivalent to a main programme farce, which is what Peake, usually a very dependable kind of author, received for *Chancery Suit* (CG 1830), although as it turned out it was acted for only 'a few nights'.[30] Indeed, comedy was an altogether unpredictable genre. In terms of fees, it swung between extremes of miserliness and prodigality. John Howard Payne was persuaded to part with his comedy *Charles the Second* (1824) at the rock-bottom rate of £50 because not only was Covent Garden alleged to be in a condition of dire poverty but the author was himself 'too hard pressed to wait for a better opportunity'.[31] Yet in the same year the Revd George Croly, whose dramatic experience was limited to the unacted tragedy *Catiline* (1822), was offered a very generous £300 for his comedy *Pride Shall Have a Fall* (1824). Remarkably, since five-act comedies at this period were hardly more reliable in terms of the box-office than tragedies, Croly's play cleared twenty nights and as a reward a grateful management gave him a £100 gratuity.[32] At the upper end of the scale was Thomas Morton, who seems also to have benefited from a 'special contract'. Though he had not written a play of any description for seven years and no comedy for twice that time, his reputation must have been a sufficient guarantee for the exceptional sum of £500 which he was paid for the comedy *A School for Grown Children* (1827).[33]

Because of their increasing fashionableness, operas tended to attract fees which bore a fairer and more consistent relationship to the genre's ability to generate better-than-average business. William Dimond had £200 for his opera *Native Land; or, the Return from Slavery* (CG 1824) and £410 (which probably includes an allowance for copyright) for *The Seraglio* (CG 1827). Late in the decade, when finances were becoming very tight indeed, Michael Lacy secured a surprising £300 for his adaptation, *The Maid of Judah* (CG 1829). But on balance it was Planché who reaped the most regular higher-paid work in opera under Charles Kemble's management of Covent Garden after 1822. He received £300 for the libretto of *Maid Marian* (1822) and a similar fee for *Cortez* (1823), which was less an opera than a drama with music. Even more lucrative was the libretto of Weber's *Oberon* (1826), which he sold for £400; but this included £100 for copyright.[34] Planché's other work for Covent Garden, where he was a sort of unofficial house author, paid less handsomely but well enough. He received £150 for *The Woman Never Vext* (1824), adapted from William Rowley; and the same sum (in two instalments, both unusually in advance) for his work on a pageant representing the coronation of the new French King, *Charles X* (1825). For alterations, payments ranged from £10 for remedial work on J. H. Payne's *Ali Pasha* (1822) to £20 for changes to the same author's *Clari* (1823). Planché was also receiving continuing payments on revived pieces. The opera *Carron Side; or, the Fête Champêtre* (1828), for instance, brought him an extra £20 for two nights' performance in the 1829–30 season.[35]

The benchmark of dramatic literature was still the full-length tragedy. Encouragement of the genre under increasingly difficult circumstances was the patent theatres' best defence against attack by the minors. But it is apparent that in the 1820s authors of tragedy had a difficult time of it – more difficult indeed than perhaps any other class of dramatic writing – because the majority were forced into contracts which cut the accepted standard remuneration for tragedy by as much as a half. Only James Sheridan Knowles, against the trend, made a healthy profit.

In 1820 Knowles was still a virtually untried quantity, but Macready took up *Virginius* (CG 1820) and negotiated a better-than-usual bargain with Henry Harris, who accepted the play some time in late April or early May. Under normal conditions of success, the play would have produced the usual £300 total for nine nights but, as the imminent conclusion of the season would deprive Knowles of the additional £100 payable for the twentieth night, it was Macready's special 'stipulation' that the run should be continued during the following season, thus ensuring the author the extra fee.[36] Because of the success of *Virginius*, Knowles was courted for his next play, his remodelled tragedy *Caius Gracchus* (first performed Belfast 1815), which Robert Elliston bought for Drury Lane in 1823 at a rate which was £50 higher than normal. Even the arrangements for payment were unusual: apparently Elliston agreed to pay £200 in two equal instalments before the play was performed, then another £100 spread over the twelfth, fifteenth and eighteenth nights, a further payment of £100 'as usual' on the twentieth, and a final £50 on the twenty-fifth night,[37] making a grand total of £450. Knowles became the theatre's only reliable serious dramatist and his reputation for attracting good houses followed him into the early years of the next decade at Covent Garden.

All tragic dramatist were risks and, apart from Knowles, unacceptably high ones, given the kind of investment that tragedies generally needed in props, scenery, and costumes. As victim of managerial opportunism and parsimony at both major theatres, Payne was as unlucky in tragedy as he was in comedy. At Drury Lane, where his first tragedy *Brutus* (1818) provided a fine role for Kean and proved to be a much-needed stimulant for the precarious finances of the theatre, he is said to have been 'lured into an improvident bargain' through reversion to the old benefit system of payment. After deduction of house charges, his four authors' benefit nights left him with a grand total of £183 6s. Payne protested by letter to the management committee, insisting that his success merited not only making up his fee to the 'established sum' of 400 guineas for a five-act play running for twenty nights but, again as was customary, 'an *additional* remuneration, which has varied, in different cases, from one to five hundred guineas'. In his own case, he pointed out, he had in fact received less than might be expected for a farce ('at two hundred guineas for twenty nights'). Payne's sense of unfairness of treatment was genuine enough, as his play had survived for forty-one nights. As a gesture the committee offered him an additional benefit, 'but the terms were fixed so high and the season so far gone', that Payne was obliged to decline for fear of falling into further debt.[38]

In spite of his proven reputation carried forward from Drury Lane, the rival patent house seemed just as tight-fisted when he offered them his new drama *Richelieu* in 1823. On instructions from the committee, Henry Robertson wrote to explain that the managers liked his play and were willing to produce it:

but in consideration of the circumstances of the Theatre not permitting them to pay so liberally as formerly, and the piece being an adaptation from another they regret that it is not in their power to offer you more than two hundred guineas to be paid by 3 instalments for the 3rd 6th & 9th nights – the present circumstances of the Theatre will not justify their giving more now but they hope that they shall have a further opportunity of being able to remunerate your talent better.[39]

This was half the usual rate and Covent Garden's only concession to Payne's proven worth was to name a fee in guineas rather than pounds. At the same time, a first-time tragic author like Mary Mitford was obliged to settle for £200 for her first tragedy *Julian* (CG 1823)[40]; and she managed no better for her second tragedy *The Foscari* at the same theatre three years later, even though it had been contracted for at the full price. Indeed, by this time the half rate almost became the norm for tragedy – certainly for first-time authors – and Fanny Kemble, flattered by the apparent equality of treatment with Miss Mitford, professed herself proud and delighted at the offer of £200 for her tragedy *Francis the First* in 1827 – 'if it succeeds'.[41] Even the proprietor's daughter, it seems, could expect no better than half measures. In truth, Miss Mitford's experience over *The Foscari* was shabby and thoroughly discreditable to the Covent Garden management. With her father as negotiator, the play was accepted on full-rate standard terms of £400 payable in four instalments on the third, ninth, fifteenth, and twentieth nights. Halfway through its run the proprietors panicked and withdrew it from the stage. Henry Robertson was detailed to explain to the author that the receipts of the play 'having latterly fallen so far short of what they had anticipated . . . [the proprietors] regret it will not be in their power to continue it to the 15th night'. And in the same letter came the humiliating proposal that in the event of Miss Mitford's being 'disposed however to waive [her] claim for £100 for the 15th night', the management might be able to revive the play at some unspecified point later in the season, presumably when their finances were stronger.[42] Her response is not recorded but may be inferred from the fact that the play was not re-staged and she never wrote for Covent Garden again.

The variety of contracts negotiated during the 1820s at Covent Garden and Drury Lane shows the finely tuned relationship which existed between authors' remuneration and the state of theatrical finances in general. The security and confidence of 1800 had gone. In their place was uncertainty, the ever-present threat of bankruptcy, and even the occasional touch of dishonesty. In such circumstances the negotiating positions of even well-established authors were severely constrained. At the beleaguered theatres of the 1820s a successful play was a rare phenomenon and necessary enough for it to be seized upon as an opportunity to repair depleted finances rather than fairly to reward its author. This is what Covent Garden did with Thomas Morton's musical farce *The Sublime and the Beautiful* (1828), which was reintroduced into the repertoire late in the following year. Morton's request for additional payment was brushed aside on the grounds that the committee did not consider it 'advisable' to vary the terms already agreed on: a total of £100 for fifteen nights made up of £10 a night for the first five nights and £5 for the following ten.[43] In other words, Morton was deliberately excluded from any further share in his play's success.

To some extent the theatres had long walked a financial tightrope. Even during better times, around 1800, it was usual practice at both Drury Lane and Covent Garden to remunerate their authors by promissory note, redeemable at short periods, rather than in hard cash. In the 1820s very few authors were paid in advance of performance and, in a large number of cases, probably the majority, payments on the contract did not begin until about two months after the first night. Planché was treated slightly more favourably than others in this respect, even though in some cases he might have had to wait almost a year for full settlement. For *Maid Marian* (CG 1822), for example, he was paid in four instalments: two-thirds of his £300 fee had been paid within two months of the first performance, but the final £100 was split into £30 paid in April and £70 in October 1823.[44] Gradually the intervals for settlement became longer and at Covent Garden began to overrun their time-limits. In 1822, Dimond and Morton were owed money and in the latter's case a bill of £50 due in October 1821 was still not settled in full by the following January.[45] The theatre must have gained some notoriety for slackness in meeting bills because in October 1826 John Poole insisted on terms for an unnamed comedy – probably *The Wife's Stratagem* (CG 1827) – in which the advance agreement actually specified dates for payment of the £250 total, made up of three instalments in sums of £125 (including an allowance for copyright), £50, and £75. By the following year the theatre's regular pantomime-writer Charles Farley was owed £500 (most of it from the two previous years' pantomimes) and arrangements were made to pay off the debt at £10 a week. On behalf of the proprietors, Robertson proposed that Farley should be remunerated for the new Christmas pantomime 'at the rate of £5 per night to the 40th Night inclusive, the payments to be made in the course of the ensuing season'.[46] Farley objected that the risk should not all be on his side, but Robertson responded that the proprietors

do not think it right that they should agree to pay £150 even though the Pantomime should be a complete failure & therefore prefer a more equitable mode of payment[,] a certain sum nightly as expressed in my letter of yesterday's date by which as in the case of other dramatic pieces the remuneration is in some measure dependent upon the success of the piece.[47]

On the whole Covent Garden's contracts at this period were decidedly in favour of management rather than authors.

Well might Capt. Forbes claim, in defence of the monopoly, that at the patent theatres there was, in general, 'no want of encouragement to authors'. But under pressure of questioning at the 1832 Committee, he was forced into the embarrassing admission that Covent Garden's finances were so bad in the 1831–2 season that the management had chosen to pay salaries of performers in preference to authors' fees.[48] Authors like James Kenney accepted the need to tailor their demands to the prevailing economic circumstances of the theatre but, although he had consented to sell *The Irish Ambassador* (1831) to Covent Garden 'on much less terms than I had been accustomed to receive', his contract had still been defaulted on, owing to the theatre bankruptcy: he had only £50 out of the promised £125 for the play despite its having been performed for thirty nights. The arrangement was that he should be paid £100 whatever the success or otherwise of the play, plus £25 if it ran to twenty nights. Kenney had good cause for his resentment, especially when he discovered that Fanny Kemble received preferential treatment by collecting full fees on *Francis the First* only six months later. Even worse was that Kenney was still awaiting payment for a piece staged at Drury Lane more than three years previously in May 1829, and with every indication that the theatre disputed his claim. The agreement for the opera *Masaniello* (DL 1829) specified £50 every third night of acting up to a total of twenty-four nights, but he had actually received nothing at all, ostensibly because in the middle of the ensuing season the lessee had gone bankrupt and the management of the theatre had fallen to a caretaker committee. Nonetheless, *Masaniello* continued to be staged and proved a very substantial success. By July 1832 Kenney estimated that it had been acted more than 150 times and the profit to the theatre 'must have been very great indeed'.[49] But he had already had a kind of revenge for his treatment in his embittered preface to the published text of *The Pledge* (DL 1831), in which he denounced the management's behaviour: 'I have found in this theatre', he wrote, 'an obtuse, an intractable and an unblushing insensibility to the claims of authors.'[50] It is clear that with cases like Kenney's still unresolved the patent theatres' bankruptcy was as much moral as financial.

With smaller overheads than the patent houses it was at least in theory easier to make a success of minor theatre management. Even so, many of them were running close to the wind and were certainly not immune from the processes of decline suffered by the patent houses during the second and third decades of the century. Thomas Dibdin claimed to have been £18,000 in the red at the conclusion of his management of the Surrey; but this was £9,000 short of what Glossop was reputed to have lost at the Coburg. Sadler's Wells also hit a bad patch around 1817, the result of the price inflation of the Napoleonic war period coupled with the subsequent peace settlement, which emptied the theatres of the profitable soldier element in the audience.[51] In contrast, the two great success stories were the Adelphi in the 1820s and the Olympic in the 1830s.

In at least one respect minor theatre writers were for the most part better off than some of their patent theatre contemporaries in being paid for their efforts. The Surrey was in general one of the better payers. As a matter of policy, Elliston consistently tried to offer higher terms than his rivals and it seems that £50 was the going rate there for melodrama in 1829.[52] The Coburg was less generous on the whole. George Davidge, claiming that £50 was in theory possible for a piece, had to confess to the 1832 Committee that £20 was more usual. This was a fixed sum and the author was not entitled to any further payments. Davidge also operated an occasional alternative system, whereby the author was paid between a half and one guinea for every night his play was performed up to the maximum sum agreed. Thereafter the author had no further claims on the profits of his play, however successful. At the same period, David Osbaldiston for the Surrey Theatre also claimed a degree of flexibility over contracts with authors: either 'a nightly sum during the run of the piece, or a bargain agreed upon between the manager and writer for the piece entirely'.[53] The former scheme offered the playwright the chance of a better deal if his play was a success; but, despite the manager's assertion that either method was equally likely to apply to Surrey authors, it seems that the latter was much more common. As a rule, authors were victims of a changing theatrical climate which gave total control into the hands of managers, who justified their parsimony as the natural, if unfortunate, consequence of their struggle for survival. The minor theatres as a whole were hard schools. In actual cash terms they were responsible for exploitation of an extreme kind, illustrated by the experience of William Bayle Bernard, who is said to have received only £3 for one of his earliest dramas (probably his first), a nautical piece entitled *Casco Bay* (Olym 1827), seasoned by a further £2 on the one-hundredth night of a run which eventually lasted another forty. This was proportionally comparable, if not inferior because of the abnormal length of the run, to Jerrold's composite fee of £20 for four successful plays written for Sadler's Wells at the start of his dramatic career in 1821.[54]

No doubt Douglas Jerrold, whom Elliston poached as house dramatist in 1829 at a salary of £5 a week from the Coburg – where since 1825 he had been writing whatever farces, burlesques, melodramas, and sketches the management required – was a classic victim of the fixed payment system. Nautical dramas were all the rage in the late 1820s and in his famous *Black-Eyed Susan; or, All in the Downs* (1829) Jerrold provided the Surrey with its most triumphantly successful play in its history. His fee was just £50, to which a further £10 was added from the sale of copyright. In its extraordinary success for the theatres – 150 consecutive performances at the Surrey (restoring Elliston's fortunes), together with another 250 spread over Sadler's Wells, the Pavilion, other minor theatres, even Covent Garden – and for the leading actor T. P. Cooke, who played Long Tom Coffin not only at the Surrey but elsewhere in London and for years afterwards throughout Britain, its author had no further share.[55] Jerrold's application to Covent Garden for compensation for performing a play which didn't belong to it was dismissed with the patronising suggestion that he should be well enough satisfied at the benefit to his reputation from having his play performed at a patent theatre. But the alleged advantage was merely theoretical and was of no help in his gaining a foothold at Covent Garden during the following season. Nevertheless, he did do rather better financially at the rival patent theatre with his next play *The Rent Day* (DL 1832), though its relatively long run and profitability for the theatre again showed up the inherent injustice of the fixed-payment system. William Dunn, the theatre's treasurer, described it as, apart from the lions, 'the most profitable of anything that was played' at Drury Lane. Jerrold reckoned it had been acted for either forty-three or forty-four nights, but he received no more for it than the £150 agreed to be paid on the twenty-fifth night.[56] Wisely, he made no immediate attempt to dispose of the copyright, thus securing for himself some small but continuing income from the piece. It was still a popular play in the mid-1830s: and even Covent Garden paid him for permission to act it, along with an earlier minor theatre farce called *Law and Lions* (Sur 1829), at a total fee of £20 for twelve months from October 1835.[57]

As perhaps the most adventurous of the minors in the 1820s, the Adelphi began to attract a more fashionable kind of audience and, with writers like Planché in its employ, became one of the strongest rivals of the patent theatres. Planché wrote as many as ten pieces for it in the 1820–1 season and from the summer of 1821 entered into an agreement to write exclusively for that theatre, only to quarrel with the management shortly afterwards over their insistence on his adapting for the stage *Life in London*, Pierce Egan's popular and rumbustious novel of sporting life. Sooner than submit to what he regarded as a prostitution of his talent, he tore up his contract and decamped to the opposition at Covent Garden. His successor at the

Adelphi, W. T. Moncrieff, had no such scruples and the resulting drama of *Tom and Jerry; or, Life in London* (1821) – produced before the last instalment of the novel on which it was based had made its appearance – became a resounding success. It was the first play in the history of the British theatre to exceed 100 nights and eventually ran to almost 300, thereby netting the Adelphi proprietors a small fortune. Moncrieff claimed to have had about £200 for the piece and at the time believed himself 'very well paid' for it.[58] Indeed, by comparison with the general level of minor theatre fees he had every right to be pleased; but Moncrieff realised in retrospect that he had been shamelessly abused by nearly every theatre manager in the country, each of whom appropriated his play entirely free of charge. As he remarked with grim humour in the preface to the published version, since 'every Theatre in the United Kingdom, and even in the United States, enriched its coffers by performing it . . . the smallest tythe portion of its profits, would for ever have rendered it unnecessary for the Author to have troubled the public with any further productions of his muse'.[59]

In the eyes of contemporaries anxious to support and preserve the legitimate drama, the dramatist who seemed to matter most in 1832 was James Sheridan Knowles. Since William Hazlitt had heaped praise on him in *The Spirit of the Age* in 1825, Knowles was universally seen as the upholder of all that was strongest and most valuable in the tradition. His latest play *The Hunchback* (CG 1832) by filling the theatre demonstrated that, despite appearances, the public's taste for legitimacy was, as Charles Mathews indicated, 'only scotched, not killed'.[60] According to George Bartley, stage manager at Covent Garden, Knowles touted the MS to both main patent theatres, even before it was finished, in an attempt to raise the price by competition. He is said to have asked £500 for the play; but what he actually received was £400, which was in effect a standard patent theatre contract for a full-length legitimate piece running for up to twenty nights, that is, a total of £300 for the first nine nights and £100 on the twentieth.[61]

Knowles was such a valuable property in the distressed

theatre of the 1830s that when Alfred Bunn took over the management of the patent theatres, he was most anxious to secure his services as the one dramatist of the period who, in his opinion, could 'never be paid too much for his works'. He tempted him with special terms completely separate from and unrelated to contracts given to lesser authors. 'It is not my desire', he wrote in June 1833,

to confine the terms of remuneration to those which are usually given to dramatic authors for successful productions; but . . . I will advance, in your case, in the ratio of two-thirds – *viz.*, that inasmuch as the customary price for a full tragedy, play, or opera, has been three hundred pounds, so shall you be entitled to receive FIVE HUNDRED; and in all private treaty for your dramatic works which may not be on the scale of full pieces, the same consideration shall be made in your individual case, without reference to other authors.[62]

Knowles resisted the bribe, at least for a time, by pleading solidarity with his fellow dramatic authors – his 'co-mates in exile' as he called them – who, united in their opposition to the theatrical monopoly as operated under Bunn's joint manager-ship of Drury Lane and Covent Garden, refused to write for the patent theatres in protest against Bunn's amalgamation of the acting companies.

Macready's success with Knowles's *Virginius*, apart from substantially enhancing his reputation as an actor, had the effect of making him sought after as authors' friend and he continued to take an interest in any author (like Knowles, Bulwer Lytton, or Browning) whom he imagined might be able to provide him with a suitable acting role. Sometimes his involvement was more disinterested, as was the case with George Lovell's tragedy *The Provost of Bruges* (DL 1836). Though never convinced of its dramatic worth, he tried his best as a negotiator with Alfred Bunn on behalf of the author and sought terms which, if approved, would have given the author £20 per night for the first fifteen nights ('instead of the customary nine'), £50 for the twentieth night and a further £20 if the play reached twenty-five nights. Having no reason to be generous, Bunn stood out for a nightly fee of £20 only for the first nine nights. In the event, the play expired after eight performances, ostensibly because it had drawn unsatisfactory house receipts averaging just £159 per night, which meant (so Bunn contended) that when the author was paid his 'not unreasonable' nightly fee, there was insufficient left in the Drury Lane treasury even to cover house expenses.[63] The dismayed author even offered to forgo any further payment rather than have the play stopped prematurely; but, as Macready well knew, Bunn's rascally opportunism was at work and the costumes had already been cut up for the next production. Even then Bunn prevaricated over payment for the play and it was only by the threat of legal proceedings that Lovell eventually received his proper dues at the end of May 1836.

The theatrical climate of the mid-1830s was even less well disposed towards serious drama than that of the previous decade. Melodrama, spectacle, and opera made money; legitimate drama on the whole didn't. Bulwer Lytton, with an already established reputation as a novelist, was foolish enough to believe that that was sufficient in itself to ensure acceptance of his first play *The Duchess de la Vallière* (CG 1837). With Macready as negotiator, Bunn was expected to take it unseen. As Macready noted, 'the price down was for *his name*' and not surprisingly Bunn rejected the proposed terms, which included a stipulation for limiting copyright in the theatre to three years and an advance to be paid on submission of the MS (this to be returned should the play fail).[64] Bunn, who suffered from vaingloriousness himself, was no respecter of the same vice in other people, nor of the kind of theatrical naïvety he discerned in Lytton. But Osbaldiston, having recently graduated from minor theatre management to become the new lessee of Covent Garden, was more easily impressed and even paid Lytton an advance of £100 on the play.[65] This generosity he had cause bitterly to regret a few months later after the first few performances, when the play failed to live up to expectations and Osbaldiston was obliged to plead with Lytton – though without success it seems – to vary the terms on which the play had been taken. Bunn said smugly that the production was 'dramatically speaking, a failure, and a positive loss to the treasury of the theatre'.[66]

Osbaldiston made a similar error of judgement over Robert

Browning's first drama *Strafford* (CG 1837), which he seized upon so eagerly that he even agreed to the strengthening of his dramatic company purely for the privilege of staging it. Cast again in the familiar role of negotiator, Macready managed to elicit from Osbaldiston a surprisingly liberal set of terms, despite his own growing lack of confidence in the play's suitability for the stage. Browning was reported to be 'very happy' at news of the agreement 'to give the author £12 per night for twenty-five nights, and £10 per night for ten nights beyond'.[67] For Browning to earn the standard fee for a five-act tragedy his play would have had to run for the full twenty-five nights (which would bring him £300) or thirty-five nights (for £400). Such a run was in truth well beyond the bounds of practical possibility, as Macready admitted the night before its première, and his worst fears were confirmed when Osbaldiston took it off after only four nights. As the first night was allocated to Macready for a benefit, Browning's remuneration was restricted to three performances. Just over a month later he received from Covent Garden's treasury the sum of £36.[68]

The active theatrical lives of Browning and Bulwer Lytton cover substantially the same period, but only Lytton actually made any money out of dramatic writing, even though to begin with at least Lytton's ostensible concern was artistic rather than financial. His second play *The Lady of Lyons* (CG 1838) was presented *gratis* to Macready in the hope of its rescuing his reputation as a dramatist after the dismal failure of the previous year. Its success, though modest, showed that even in the late 1830s it was still occasionally possible to make the serious drama pay both author and theatre. Macready actually sent him a cheque for £210 (made up of payment at the rate of £15 per night for fourteen nights) – this was proportional to a fee of £600 over forty nights – but Lytton returned it on the grounds that their partnership had been made for the sake of dramatic art, not money. Solemnly, he reminded Macready that 'our compact was not of an ordinary nature, and on consideration, you will see that it is impossible to lower it into a pecuniary arrangement'.[69] Nevertheless, with his next play, *Richelieu* (CG 1839), Bulwer Lytton became the most successful playwright of the late 1830s, challenging and eventually out-running Sheridan Knowles in the revenue he collected. Although Knowles was still a name to be reckoned with and was offered as much as £600 for *Love* (CG 1839) by Vestris and Mathews – probably the largest sum he ever had for a single work – he could not compete on level of income with Lytton. The terms for *Richelieu* (CG 1839) were left to Macready, who confirmed his confidence in Lytton's abilities by offering a top fee of £600 on a forty-night run. This, together with similar fees exacted from Ben Webster at the Haymarket for *The Sea Captain* (1839) and *Money* (1840),[70] brought Lytton a grand total of £1,800 in just under two years and made him far and away the best-paid dramatist of this period.

Yet for Lytton in the early 1840s even such substantial returns as these were considered to be on the economic margin. Writing to Macready, he confessed that 'no play can pay me in a pecuniary sense' because it took up at least half the time and effort of writing a novel and yet '[t]he utmost pay it can receive is not half the profit derived from a fiction'.[71] The defeatist terms of his letter held a depressing message for the prospects of the drama in general. Douglas Jerrold couldn't have had Lytton in mind when in 1832 he commented that Knowles's income from *The Hunchback* was less than half of the £1,000 that could be made by a gentleman writing a novel, since Lytton was at that time receiving from Richard Bentley only £400 a novel, exactly the same as Knowles had for his play. But the commercial superiority of the novel was positively demonstrated in the following year when Lytton secured a further contract for a novel with the same publisher for more than double the earlier price, at £1,100.[72]

On strictly financial grounds Lytton was right to give up the theatre. Between roughly the early 1840s and the late 1850s almost no dramatist made any money out of plays as the long process of economic decline in the theatre reached its nadir. Because of the desertion from the theatre of moneyed society managers were forced into a continual pruning of admission prices so that it was actually cheaper to go to the theatre in 1850 than in 1800.[73] But crowded threepenny and twopenny galleries could not make up for lack of patronage in the more expensive areas of the theatre and in response to ever-decreasing house receipts authors' fees fell to rock-bottom by mid-century. As a relative newcomer, however, Dion Boucicault must have been especially gratified at his £300 fee received from Vestris and Mathews for his five-act comedy *London Assurance* (CG 1841). Although this was half the rate paid for Lytton's *Money* in the previous year, in comparison to others Boucicault had little cause for complaint. Stalwarts like Sheridan Knowles did no better. There was potential for a substantial income in his agreement for *Old Maids* (CG 1841) on the basis of £15 per night with the stipulation that his fees should not be stopped after the fortieth night,[74] but as the play did not last beyond the twentieth, it must be assumed that his income was limited to £300 instead of the more than £600 for which the contract catered. Thereafter Knowles's prospects did not improve and Boucicault's even declined. Three years after his brilliant success with *London Assurance*, he was rudely brought back to some sense of the economic reality of his profession by the offer of only £100 for a play – possibly *Old Heads and Young Hearts* (Hay 1844) – by the manager of 'a principal London Theatre'.[75]

If the 1840s were bad for the dramatist, the 1850s were the financial doldrums. As the value of dramatic property plummeted the expectations of playwrights such as Tom Taylor, Shirley Brooks, and even a veteran like Planché were limited to the 'wretched sum' of £50 or £100 per act.[76] Charles Reade, in collaboration with Taylor, had a mere £150 to be shared between them for their costume comedy *Masks and Faces*, produced at Webster's Haymarket in 1852. Even original drama did not attract appropriate returns. Reade and Taylor's *Two Loves and a Life* (Adel 1854), which was unusual in not being an adaptation from the French, produced for the two collaborators just £50 each.[77]

Low as these figures are, they pale by comparison with the unhappy fate of playwrights compelled to sell at or near the bottom of the market. A pantomime by Edward Leman Blanchard was worth £10 a time to the Surrey, Marylebone and Sadler's Wells theatres in 1851 but only 2 guineas to George Conquest at the Grecian in the East End.[78] At the Britannia

Theatre George Dibdin Pitt as resident drudge collected only 30 shillings for burlettas like *The Cricket on the Hearth* (1846). Pantomimes, melodramas, and domestic dramas of the period at the same theatre rated slightly better at £3 apiece, but by 1850 this was apparently reduced to £2.[79] Hack writing at and below this general level was common at East End theatres like the Pavilion, Grecian, and Britannia. Indeed, rates at the minor theatres were invariably no higher (and possibly sometimes lower) than an author might expect in writing for one of the superior portable theatres, like 'Old Wild's' that travelled around the northern counties. About 1846 Sam Wild paid Charles Somerset 2 guineas each for a series of three-act canine plays based around 'Nelson', the proprietor's famous performing dog.[80] These were specially commissioned pieces but, since Wild also claimed to be in regular correspondence with other minor playwrights and to have been an occasional purchaser of new melodramas, it may be assumed that his rates were competitive with those of London's East End theatres. Somerset, described by Edward Stirling as a 'clever and well-educated' playwright, supplied the Surrey, Adelphi, and Olympic with popular melodramas through the 1830s; but by the following decade he was reduced to writing for the Grecian and the lowly Bower Saloon at the rate of 25 shillings for a two-act drama. Stirling said his last sight of him was 'standing before the Mansion House, with a printed label hung round his neck, inscribed thus: "Ladies and Gentlemen, I am starving"'.[81]

CHAPTER 3

The profit-sharing revolution

I

Although for the greater part of the period under discussion the drama tended to compare unfavourably in financial terms with the novel, its natural competitor in the nineteenth century, the disparity between the two has sometimes been overstated. Questioned on the relative economic status of the novel and the drama at the 1866 Committee of Inquiry, Charles Reade agreed that the former was still on balance more remunerative for authors, mainly because theatre managers, unlike publishers, were not in the business of offering large advances.[1] As Reade and others were prepared to recognise, however, the economic fortunes of theatre were in the process of improvement. During the 1860s dramatic authorship slowly begins to recover its financial viability.

From about 1840 to 1860 the drama was incapable of producing high returns for any author and, as has been discussed in the previous chapter, that was one of the reasons why Bulwer Lytton recognised that his future lay with the novel. In the highest reaches of the novel market large advances (sometimes of the order of £2,000–£3,000) became relatively commonplace. Anthony Trollope ceased to sell his novels outright in 1860 and switched to a profit-sharing system which brought him a very comfortable average yearly income of about £4,500, while George Eliot in the early 1870s made £9,000 out of *Middlemarch* alone. Away from the upper extreme, the gap between the earning power of the novel and the drama diminishes. Just as the theatre had its share of wily managers out to make a killing by excluding dramatists from the profits of their work, so the world of Victorian publishing harboured occasional sharp operators who manipulated the system so as to deprive novelists of their rightful income. In the 1840s Charles Lever described himself as 'rogued and robbed' by his Irish publishers; and many later writers saw little improvement. From Hurst and Blackett W. G. Wills received £120 down for his novel *The Three Watches* (1865) – he actually did better writing plays – and even R. L. Stevenson, out of a total income of £465 for 1883 (his best year to date) had only '[a] hundred jingling, tingling, golden, minted quid' for his highly popular *Treasure Island*; while Hardy's first novel *Desperate Remedies* (1871), on a half-profits' agreement with William Tinsley, cost the author £15 out of his own pocket.[2]

Although writing novels or plays continued to entail risks, especially for the beginning author, from the 1860s onwards the drama wasn't necessarily the poor relation any more, at any rate at the theatres of London's West End. At the height of his powers Dion Boucicault was capable of earning £1,000–£1,500 in a week. And at the Princess in 1879 Reade, at the tail-end of a writing career which began with drama, graduated to the novel and then alternated between the two, made a staggering £20,000 out of *Drink* (an adaptation from Zola), in the production of which he was sensible enough to take 'a large share of the risk, and a proportionate share of the profits'. This compares with a best of £4,000 for his novel *Put Yourself In His Place* in 1870.[3] By this time the most astute members of the playwriting fraternity demonstrated that the revenue-earning capacity of the drama was potentially as great as, and in many instances superior to, that of the novel.

For hack playwrights in the East End theatres and saloons, where there was a rapid turnover of plays to satisfy frequent changes of programme, no improvement in conditions or in pay took place, but at the more prosperous end of the market there was an amelioration in the fortunes of the dramatic author. To a large extent this was the result of the energy, resilience, and determination of the playwright who, in the quantity of his plays and their qualitative range, seems to sum up so well the diversity of the Victorian dramatist, Dion Boucicault. In the first twenty years of his career he knew the temporary fame of a brilliant debut as well as the grubbing life of a hack dramatist from the mid-1840s to the early 1850s, the hardships of bankruptcy as much as the joys of affluence. But as a result of his first sojourn in the USA between 1853 and 1860 he learnt the rules for true success as a pot-boiling melodramatist. Of all nineteenth-century playwrights Boucicault became one of the most business-like, and, what was more important, intensely aware of the immense power he could exert on managers through his ability to create a desirable commodity. Boucicault was his own man, fired by the conviction that no one could look after his interests better than he. On his return to London, in the process of proving his ability to squeeze as much money out of managers as they could be persuaded to part with, he reversed the terms of the traditional relationship between manager and author and exerted a profound and lasting, though not immediate, influence on the general economic status of the late Victorian playwright. Boucicault is too easily characterised as a showman who happened to have a special talent for giving audiences what they wanted, but he was really more than that because his negotiating strength with theatre managers helped to turn the theatre from the habitat of the amateur, the hack, and the gentleman-dramatist into the lucrative, commercial theatre of Arthur Pinero and Henry Arthur Jones. In economic terms the theatre of the 1860s belongs to Boucicault because he is the prime example of the dramatist as entrepreneur.

The ground of Boucicault's economic success was profit-sharing. He operated on the principle that the buoyancy of theatrical profits in the 1860s was such that no dramatist capable of writing successful plays could lose. That theatre management had begun to be an increasingly attractive financial proposition was obvious when even theatre managers acknowledged it to be so. In evidence before the 1866 Committee Horace Wigan of the Olympic agreed that theatres were making considerably more money than twelve or fifteen years previously, and this view was confirmed by John Hollingshead's general analysis that theatre management was 'as lucrative a business as any', the profits of which 'are far above those of ordinary trades'.[4] What Boucicault did was simply to exploit that fact and the certainty of his own talent.

Boucicault worked in the theatre of two continents and the

lessons learned in one were applied to the other. The system which he imported into the London stage was mainly founded on his experience gained in North America, though Boucicault also had some familiarity with the French system of author remuneration, in which author payments were reckoned on a scaled percentage of house receipts. Either way it brought the drama closer to the novel in respect of its potential earning capacity. The New York run of *The Colleen Bawn* in 1860 made him sufficient money to buy two houses and to embark on an ostentatious lifestyle; and he was determined to make as much, if not more, in London. The agreement eventually pressed upon a reluctant Ben Webster at the Adelphi was heavily weighted on Boucicault's side. It was designed to produce a reasonable return if the play was only a modest success or an extremely large one if it achieved the level of business enjoyed during its American run.

In a sense there were two separate or parallel agreements. One related to Boucicault as actor (which was perfectly standard) and the other as dramatist (which was exceptional). In the first respect Boucicault and his wife Agnes were to receive fixed fees as 'stars' in their respective roles as Myles na Coppaleen and Eily O'Connor. But as author Boucicault was permitted to make his choice, depending on circumstances, between a fixed weekly payment of £50 (subject to deduction for house expenses) and a share in any takings of more than £80 a night, an arrangment which 'would last as long as the weekly returns exceeded £600 and would run, in the first instance, for a year with an option to renew after six months'.[5] As a well-filled house at the Adelphi could be expected to produce £150 per night (or about £900–£1,000 a week), and the run of *The Colleen Bawn* (over 300 nights, though not consecutive) consistently attracted packed houses, Boucicault naturally chose the second alternative, with the result that he and Webster did extremely well out of the deal. The difference was that instead of the real money being made by the manager alone, the dramatist was entitled under contract to equal shares with him. With Webster's agreement, Boucicault also tapped East End audiences by allowing the Britannia Theatre to run the play in parallel with the Adelphi production. The precise financial arrangement is not known; but it may be assumed that it was to Boucicault's advantage and based on some form of profit-sharing – its first appearance in the East End theatre and limited to Boucicault.

Out of the agreement with Webster Boucicault enjoyed a very comfortable weekly return of several hundred pounds; but he was shrewd enough to realise that there was also an unexploited and potentially very sizeable source of revenue in the provinces. In February 1861 he set up two touring companies (Boucicault employing the actors for the main parts), which then performed at provincial venues with what was in effect the officially authorised version of *The Colleen Bawn*. From these touring performances of the play Boucicault drew about £500 a week on top of his London earnings which, in the first year, amounted to £10,000.[6] Never before had a dramatist made so much money out of a single play.

Because of his extensive profit-sharing schemes in London and provincial touring on basically similar arrangements, Dion Boucicault was by 1866, as he readily acknowledged, of all dramatists the one with the largest pecuniary interest in the theatre. His system was organised for maximum profits:

I produce certain works in London at one or more of the theatres, on which I share the profits of the theatre while the work is being played. I can send a piece into the country sometimes, with one or two actors employed for the purpose of the principal parts; and then that drama going round the country acts as a star; and I receive a clear half of the net profits in all those theatres, by which means it sometimes appears in five or six theatres at the same moment.[7]

In mid-1866 while Boucicault's hack play *The Streets of London* (1864) was running on a profit-sharing basis at the Princess's, he set up another version of it entitled *The Poor of the London Streets* by agreement with Benjamin Conquest at the Grecian Theatre (in a second instance of the introduction of unfamiliar profit-sharing into the East End). These were unashamedly opportun-ist sensation-dramas, spawned out of *The Poor of Liverpool* – an earlier 'bob tail piece', as he described it to Edward Stirling[8] – itself the offspring of *The Poor of New York*, dating back to 1857. Boucicault had rightly foreseen a capacity for considerable profit in this sort of play, owing to its easy adaptability to a variety of locales. Of the Liverpool piece he reported that the development of this 'new vein in the theatrical mine' was making him £100 a week, on the basis of sharing profits in excess of £30 a night; and from further localised versions (such as those at Leeds and Manchester) he was able to make as much again.[9] When *The Streets of London* was first offered to the Princess's in 1864 Boucicault refused to entertain a reversion to the simple royalty system as proposed by the manager, George Vining. Instead Vining, desperate for a money-making play, was obliged to agree to a half-and-half division of the profits over and above £100 a night. As his house expenses were set at £70 a night, the terms of the agreement did allow a small concession to the management side by allowing Vining some leeway before profit-sharing began to take effect. Theoretically Boucicault's was the greater risk, but his confidence was such that he considered the whole arrangement as yet another licence to print money. In the event *The Streets of London* directly benefited both parties to the contract: the Boucicault–Vining partnership was reported by John Hollingshead to have been chiefly responsible for the Princess's net profit of £32,000 in just one year. When *Arrah-na-Pogue* (Dublin 1864, P'cess 1865) replaced it in the bills in the following year, the level of income generated was said to have been almost as much.[10]

With thrilling plays such as *The Streets of London* and its spectacular conflagration scene, just as in the sentimental Irish melodramas like *The Colleen Bawn* and *Arrah-na-Pogue*, Boucicault was safe and, despite the author's uncompromising stand on terms, his theatre managers content. Straight comedy was, however, economically speaking, a rather more contentious area and even Boucicault could miscalculate public taste. His 'pure and simple' comedy (Boucicault's own description) *How She Loves Him* (PoW 1867), written for the Bancrofts, though it survived for forty-seven nights, was counted a box-office failure and, revealing a more attractive side to his usual aggressively mercenary nature, Boucicault magnanimously elected to forgo all fees.[11] But it really wasn't his usual style.

At this period Boucicault was in a class of his own. His technique was to set manager against manager and to play on the resulting competition. As Horace Wigan (who had a taste of Boucicault's acquisitive attitude to profit margins in abortive negotiations over a play for the Olympic) observed in 1866, there was no other playwright who could demand such 'very exorbitant' terms and get away with it. Apparently Wigan's offer of a contract likely to produce about £120 a week was not good enough. Boucicault argued that it was far below what he was accustomed to receiving, which amounted to nearly £200 a week from the Manchester and Glasgow theatres, between £240 and £400 from George Vining for *The Streets of London* and *Arrah-na-Pogue*, and another £500 a week in fees from New York for the past eleven weeks. By way of compromise, he expressed readiness to consider a sharing arrangement above an arbitrarily determined house expenses level of £35 a night. 'These are not your expenses', he wrote grandly, 'but you will, I hope, pardon me if I say they should be.'[12]

The London theatre that Boucicault returned to in 1860 with such panache was still the old, economically uncertain, world dominated by cheap adaptations from the French; a theatre that for decades had undervalued original work simply by making it too expensive and labour-intensive for dramatists to write or for theatre managers to buy. Although there were a few playwrights who still seemed to make a little money – a relatively old farce like John Maddison Morton's enormously popular *Box and Cox* (Lyc 1847) was still running in the country theatres and, thanks to reasonably efficient collection of fees by the Dramatic Authors' Society, was said to bring the author 'never less than £500 a year' and possibly a good deal more[13] – the majority of his contemporaries were still struggling under a system in which outright purchase was the rule rather than the exception, generally at the rate of £50 an act. Tom Taylor's experience demonstrates the kind of injustice often suffered by authors of money-making plays. A year after *The Colleen Bawn* he received just £150 for the highly successful play *Our American Cousin* (Hay 1861), which was expected to have a life of only six weeks to two months but in fact ran for over a year, brought fame to the principal actor Edward Sothern, and to Buckstone's theatre an income of £20,000. Indeed, Taylor counted himself fortunate to have had anything at all for the play: there was a question mark over his rights because it had been first produced in the USA in 1858. Though Buckstone grudgingly paid Taylor his £150, he took 'care, naturally perhaps, to let me know I had no right to it'. Taylor was apparently content enough to accept the same rate of '£150 down' a couple of years later for *The Ticket-of-Leave Man* (Olym 1863)[14] which ran for 407 performances, making it one of the longest-running and most successful melodramas of the period.

The Boucicault revolution was relatively slow to spread owing to the natural resistance and conservatism of the West End theatre managers and, it must be said, of dramatists themselves. But by the late 1860s there is some evidence that things were slowly changing for the better. Horace Wigan of the Olympic Theatre spoke in 1866 of the arrival of a new system of author remuneration, which had supplanted but not entirely suppressed the traditional outright-purchase scheme: '[p]lays are sometimes paid for down; but more frequently that is made conditional on the success, and so much per night is paid for them during their run'. According to Charles Reade, although the new system (which in fact he saw as a form of reversion to the older system of benefits) was 'not universal', no manager in his senses would now, as formerly, consider making a down-payment of £400 or £500 on a play, but would allow the author to participate in the risks involved in production and share in what profits, if any, accrued.[15]

Tom Robertson's method was to operate on the basis of a fixed nightly fee – what may now properly be called a royalty, since there was no ceiling on earnings. Though more limited in returns than full profit-sharing (a system which it's clear Robertson was aware of but seemed not to favour), it was in effect a form of profit-sharing as income was directly proportional to the length of the run. While Robertson's career in the 1860s was contractually less adventurous than Boucicault's, the rate at which he was paid per night was influenced by the level of income enjoyed by his colleague. That Robertson did better than most of his other contemporaries was not only the result of the steady climb in the nightly rate per play but because his pieces had relatively long runs and he was allowed a continuing share in revivals, some of which were more extended than the original runs.

Robertson began from a low base but at the Prince of Wales the Bancrofts' rising confidence in his powers was reflected in the rates of payment: £1 per performance for *Society* (1865), £2 for *Ours* (1866), and £3 for *Caste* (1867).[16] As the average run for the three plays was just under 160 performances, any increase in his income at this period depended exclusively on the rate per night. An attempt was made to persuade him to take an increase on the original fee agreed for *Ours* at its highly successful revival in 1870, but Robertson demurred. As he explained to Marie Bancroft:

I cannot reconcile it to my sense of justice and probity to take more than I bargained for. An arrangement is an arrangement, and cannot be played fast and loose with. If a man – say an author – goes in for a certain sum, he must be content with it, and 'seek no new;' if he goes in for a share, he must take good and bad luck too. So please let *Ours* be paid for at the sum originally agreed on.[17]

The revival ran for 209 performances, ending in August 1871. At the same rate as its first run price of £2 a night it would have realised £418 in fees. The Bancrofts indicated that their top rate for Robertson was £5 a night. If this rate applied to *School* (PoW 1869), which enjoyed a wholly exceptional run of 381 nights into the spring of 1870, the play must have produced an income of £1,905, well in excess of anything Robertson had made previously or was to make afterwards on any single play.

One of his earliest biographers took the view that Robertson was well satisfied with his fees, but this is belied by his friend Burnand's insistence that Robertson was well aware, in his later years at any rate, of managerial exploitation. Repeatedly he told Burnand 'with Savage-Club earnestness, that "when his turn should come he *would* make the managers pay"'. While Robertson's cordial relationship with the Bancrofts would have prevented him from speaking his mind, he was under no such constraint with Sothern at the Haymarket, from whose pocket he coaxed his highest fee of £10 per night.[18] Ironically this was for one of his last major plays, *Home* (Hay 1869), a relative failure at only 130 performances. Nevertheless, his total income of £1,300 was nearly three times as much as he had made out of *Caste* only two years earlier.

On balance, Robertson would seem to have benefited slightly more from the phenomenon of the long run than from the gradual increase in his nightly fees. Of course, the long run was a moneyspinner for Dion Boucicault as well. But by contrast, during the very same year, Boucicault, still holding on firmly to the inestimable advantage afforded by direct profit-sharing, was clearing £1,500 out of *Formosa* (DL 1869) in just one week.[19] And this was from (in Boucicault's terms) a relatively unsuccessful play, much abused by the critics, who complained of its unpleasant and salacious subject-matter. Robertson's total income for 1869 – probably his best year financially – was just under £4,500, but in the following year it had declined by £500 to £3,960 (including monies due but not yet received).[20] Respectable though these earnings were, they were not even remotely in Boucicault's league.

Under Boucicault's direct tutelage Francis Burnand's career however assumed an altogether different course. As a complete novice 'with not a soul to advise [him]', Burnand considered that with a royalty of £1 a night and £25 down in advance for his burlesque *Dido* (St J 1860) he 'had distinctly made a fair start as a dramatic author'.[21] In the late 1860s, however, Burnand was initiated into the more aggressive techniques of Boucicault, whose advice he carried out to the letter. Burnand's burlesque *Black-Eyed Susan* (Roy 1866) was first touted to the Surrey Theatre (the home of the original Jerrold version), where the managers Shepherd and Creswick laughed at his request for a nightly royalty of 3 guineas and offered him 10 shillings as absolute maximum. Over at the Royalty, now managed by Patty Oliver, where Burnand had already achieved more than modest success with *Ixion* (1863), he determined to take a bolder stance in negotiations. The result was a sharing agreement – not a percentage on gross receipts, which was the other option arising out of the Boucicault system – on nightly takings, less house expenses (including rent to the landlord). This last expense

Burnand estimated amounted to about £20 a night on a house capacity of between £60 and £70, though the final bargain was struck on the basis of sharing above £23 a night. There were also certain deductions from gross receipts (including one on the sly by the theatre manager which Burnand was unaware of until completion of the run); but the burlesque ran for over 200 nights and, assuming it played to near capacity houses yielding an average of £65 per performance, it seems that Burnand's share of the profits amounted to somewhere in the region of £3,000.[22]

Dion Boucicault, as Francis Burnand put it, 'let in the light on the relative position of author and manager'.[23] The revolution in the system was of most immediate benefit to those few authors who were at or near the top of the dramatic profession and had access to London's West End theatres. Charles Reade, who had been writing plays since the early 1850s, easily adapted to the new regime because it so much resembled the sort of contract he had been used to as a novelist. For short pieces (presumably one-acters) he declared himself as 'the cheapest author going'; but for more substantial plays, as he explained to John Hollingshead in 1874, only 'the big game' (that is, sharing 'after a sum' in the Boucicault style) would do.[24]

Newer recruits into the drama like W. S. Gilbert were equally adept at learning how much profit could be made out of plays. Indeed, in his business acumen and his unconcealed desire to make money, Gilbert was just as forthright as Boucicault. Although his naïvety in the ways of the dramatic market-place led him to sell what he identified as his earliest piece, an adaptation from the French entitled *Dulcamara* (St J 1866), outright for just £30, Gilbert never repeated this error of judgement.[25] Even before the flowering of his long partnership with Arthur Sullivan, he was a highly successful playwright and a profit-sharing veteran, though he began on the more limited returns of the fixed royalty. But by continually insisting on raising the stakes, he was, by the early 1870s, making large sums out of his fairy plays in verse at the Haymarket. For *The Palace of Truth* (1870), Gilbert sought an agreement which more properly reflected the status of the author and the improving economic environment in which he worked: fixed payments of 4 guineas for every performance during the first three months of the run, dropping to 2 guineas thereafter, except in the provinces, where 3 guineas a performance would apply throughout. A similar agreement was in force for *Pygmalion and Galatea* (Hay 1871). Indeed, such was the popularity of the play that Gilbert successfully negotiated an increase in his nightly fee arrangement. Writing to Buckstone in January 1872, Gilbert, stressing the time and effort he intended to devote to his next piece, requested his fee be raised to 5 guineas per performance for up to 100 nights and 3 guineas thereafter for a longer run. From this point in his career Gilbert never looked back. Numerous revivals of this piece (notably at the Lyceum in 1883 with Mary Anderson as Galatea) ensured him a steady and highly satisfying income; in all, it is said, about £40,000.[26] This figure obviously represents fees accrued over a long period of time, but it could only have come about by profit-sharing. Certainly he made more money out of *Pygmalion* than from any of his other dramas outside the principal collaborative operas with Sullivan. Gilbert was also aware of the rich pickings sometimes to be had out of adaptations from the French, much though he despised the activity. He was not particularly proud of the fact that *The Wedding March* (Crt 1873), again presumably on some form of share agreement, brought him 'considerably more than £2000', yet was the product of merely two days' labour.[27]

However slow most of the rest of his fellow dramatists, apart from Burnand and Gilbert, were to follow Boucicault's lead into full profit-sharing, one indirect consequence of his enterprise was that it helped to generate a greater awareness of the value of dramatic property, whether by profit-share or fixed royalty. Advising Albery as fledgling playwright in 1870 on the desirability of what he called 'Sharing terms' (the inverted commas suggest that the notion was still not fully integrated into the theatrical vocabulary), the drama critic Joseph Knight detailed the conditions necessary for success from the author's point of view. The theatre, he insisted, should be small (hence in the event of success the play would run that much longer to satisfy audience demand), the company 'tolerable', the manager 'safe', and the play a comedy (as more likely to succeed than tragedy or other serious drama).[28] It was sound advice to a dramatist capable, as Albery later showed, of sustaining long runs. He fulfilled most of Knight's criteria, finding 'safe' managers in H. J. Montague and Charles Wyndham and using theatres like the Vaudeville (1,000 capacity) and the Criterion (660) which were small enough to exploit the advantage of relatively low audience capacity against high box-office demands. But none of Albery's agreements were full sharing agreements in the proper Bouci-caultian sense; they were really modelled on Tom Robertson's – whose artistic disciple he was – though with wider effect since, unlike Robertson, he drew a steady income from American fees. That said, his terms were sufficiently lucrative to give Albery a reasonably comfortable income from authorship in the 1870s.

At the Vaudeville Theatre Albery's agreements for nightly royalties normally ranged between £2 for the two-act comedy *Tweedie's Rights* (1871) and £4 for the more successful *Apple Blossoms* (1871). For his most famous play, *Two Roses* (1870), which received performances all over the English-speaking world, Harry Montague paid him at a rate of £3 a night. This implies a total income of £882 out of the 294 performances of its first run. There were also provincial fees at about 30 shillings a night when Montague took the play on tour. Apparently it was still earning money as late as 1885, when 'fees for a provincial tour and for occasional performances [brought in] over £100 in one year'.[29] Its success encouraged the higher rate of payment for later plays like *Apple Blossoms*, which ran for 100 nights and produced an income of £400. Albery enjoyed a continuing income from his successes: *Two Roses*, for instance, was revived in London no fewer than five times by 1881 and the American theatre also provided welcome additional revenue. For performances of *Two Roses* and *Coquettes* (renamed *Two Thorns* on appearance in Britain) he received a total of £243 19s 1d; and in South Africa he was even offered a share agreement at 5 per cent on gross receipts at the Theatre Royal, Cape Town,[30] though given the limited run and the expectation of low audiences, this probably didn't amount to any large sum.

Albery's highest fee seems to have been 6 guineas a performance when Irving resuscitated *Two Roses* in 1881–2.[31] This figure for the revival of an eleven-year-old play presumably reflects enhanced values in dramatic property since 1870 – but even so it was a high rate compared with the general level of Irving's payments to authors; possibly it shows Irving's gratitude for Albery's having written him such a good character part in Digby Grant. Until his decline in the early to mid-1880s, Albery's financial strength lay in fees generated from his almost continual presence in first runs or revivals on the London stage, fairly extensive touring commitments in the provinces, and steady representation in the USA and British Dominions. Except in this one instance there was nothing remarkable about the royalty rates; what counted in his case was the consistency of stage exposure.

Despite his extensive experience as theatre manager with the Bancrofts and elsewhere and as a highly popular playwright for a quarter of a century, H. J. Byron was a late convert to any form of sharing profits. As manager of the Criterion in 1874 he feigned mild surprise (during soundings with Albery on the possibility of his writing him a play) at the author's request for a nightly fee, though he did agree that such an arrangement 'places author and manager on his mettle'. Maybe this awareness, however, had an effect on his negotiations over his own comedy *Our Boys* (Vaud 1875) because instead of selling it outright for an agreed sum – his usual practice – he opted for a weekly fee of £20, which roughly equates to 3 guineas a performance and put him on a similar level to Albery.[32] No one could have foreseen the exceptional run (unprecedented even in the overworked hyperbole of the theatre) which *Our Boys* enjoyed, eventually closing four years later in 1879. On the London run of 1,362 performances (assuming that this represents 227 weeks' playing time) Byron must have made just over £4,500. This was supplemented by a slightly more advantageous contract for provincial performances, but the greatest benefit accrued to the country manager William Duck, who, having initially leased the provincial rights, was said to have subsequently purchased them outright for £1,000. The relative smallness of Byron's share of the overall earnings of the play illustrates how meagre were the returns on a fixed-royalty system compared with the fortune Byron might have realised under a percentage-based profit-sharing agreement – possibly as much as ten times his actual income.

Even in the face of all the evidence about the superior advantages of profit-sharing and royalty agreements, the instinct to settle for a lump sum (so avoiding all risk in production) was still deeply engrained amongst a number of older dramatists and even some new ones. Old hands like Edward Blanchard, for instance, continued to write pantomimes for Drury Lane at £50 a time. Cash on the nail was naturally always a tempting proposition to the impecunious and George R. Sims later sorely regretted having parted with his highly successful first play, the alarmingly titled comedy *Crutch and Toothpick* (Roy 1879), for only £150. As he noted in 1884, it had run for 240 nights in London 'and has been played in the provinces uninterruptedly to the present time'.[33] His next major drama *The Lights o' London* (P'cess 1881) he valued more highly – on the fixed-fee system he reckoned it to be worth £1,000 (though 'less for cash') – but by default rather than design it introduced him to the even greater advantages of profit-sharing. Wilson Barrett accepted it but wasn't at all interested in making a cash-down payment in case the play was a failure, so at his suggestion it was agreed that the risks should be shared.[34] This first excursion of Sims into the territory of profit-sharing is important because it is one of the earliest examples of the kind of sliding-scale percentage system which soon became a standard feature of contracts for other dramatists like Henry Arthur Jones and Arthur Pinero:

It is agreed between us that you cede to me and I take from you the sole right of producing your new play, now entitled (provisionally) *The Lights o' London*, in all English-speaking countries on the following terms: I agree to produce the said play at the Princess's Theatre and elsewhere, and will pay you the following fees as consideration of this agreement:

In London. If the sums taken as receipts do not exceed £600 per week of six performances, £2 2s. per performance.
If over £600 up to £700, 5 per cent. of the gross receipts.
If over £700 up to £800, $7\frac{1}{2}$ per cent. of the gross receipts.

If over £800, 10 per cent. of the gross receipts.
In the Provinces. Five per cent. of all sums up to £50 per night, and 10 per cent. of sums after £50 per night have been taken by the theatre. This agreement to remain in force for three years after the first production of the play.[35]

The interesting feature here is that a fixed royalty operated up to the receipt threshold of £600 per week (that is, average takings of £100 a night), at which profit-sharing proper took over. By such an arrangement Barrett was covered for production and house expenses and Sims profited if business was good. It may be that this is the very model of a Boucicault agreement. Most assuredly it was the kind of contract that Burnand urged his fellow dramatists to adopt. In the event, the profit-sharing part of the agreement was brought into effect and Sims made £150 in the first week. In the year before the lengthy run of *The Lights o' London* his income (from 'casual journalism' and 'a few commissions to polish up old burlesques') was £1,400, while in the following year it jumped tenfold. Years later the *Era* reported that Sims's fees from this one play had amounted to £30,000.[36]

II

By the early 1880s, when West End theatres were enjoying prosperity from large middle-class audiences, authors were far less likely to be exploited than in the past. But the same was not true of London's East End theatres, where admission prices were low, the audience exclusively working-class, and the playwright in consequence operated in an entirely different economic world. Indeed, the trend in the last two decades of the century was for the two worlds to move even further apart as one stood still and the other allowed the successful professional playwright increasingly better rewards. The rates for a new play in the East End could be anything from £2 up to £10, but often house dramatists (such as George Roberts, who worked at the Elephant and Castle in the late 1880s) beavered away for salaries of no more than 30 shillings a week.[37] For the playwright, the contrasts between East End and West End theatres were so marked because in the former, apart from Boucicault's enterprise in the 1860s at pressurising managers at the Britannia and Grecian theatres into taking some of his most popular plays on his own terms, profit-sharing was unknown and the outright sale of MSS for a pittance was the universally accepted practice.

Even in the West End there was no common agreement on the value attached to a dramatist's work and for a new writer the rates could be depressingly small. Representative of what might be realistically expected by a beginning author was Wilson Barrett's offer to Henry Arthur Jones on *A Clerical Error* (Crt 1879): 2 guineas per week up to a maximum of £50, when the play would become the manager's sole property. Jones settled for broadly similar terms for all his early plays until about 1882.[38] For authors like Jones, who gave up secure employment to begin life as full-time dramatists, the prospects might not have appeared very encouraging; for them, it might seem that the Boucicault revolution had not happened. But, in fact, with steadily increasing audiences, the theatre of the last two decades of the century turned out on the whole to be more commercially successful for authors and managers than at any time since 1800.

The trend in the 1880s and, with some exceptions mainly for new authors, the norm in the 1890s was for London's West End theatres to employ profit-sharing as the preferred method of remunerating authors. This was almost always to the author's advantage and his improved financial status helped to further his professional status. Almost as important, as a result of changes in the copyright law, was the gradual decline in the reliance of managers on cheap plays derived from the French, and the consequent accelerated growth of a strong repository of native talent, properly valued in the diminished competition from foreign adaptation. Profit-sharing ceased to be the preserve of the privileged few and became the rule for the majority. In general terms, the mid- to late 1880s mark the transition between the old order of playwright managing at best a reasonable but unspectacular living out of dramatic authorship and the representatives of the new order, many of whom made comfortable fortunes out of it, thanks to the acceptance of profit-sharing by innovative managers like Charles Wyndham and George Alexander.

The exception was the Lyceum, where Henry Irving resisted profit-sharing for more than twenty years. His authors suffered by it, even though W. G. Wills, who was resident dramatist in all but name and spent most of his later career writing bespoke plays for Irving, never considered Irving's terms as anything but 'liberal'.[39] Henry Arthur Jones, on the other hand, aware that Irving's propensity for large-scale spectacle cost a great deal of money – Wills's version of Goethe's *Faust* (1885) actually cost £15,402 – maintained that his priority was to obtain 'cheap plays' and that he 'would probably have grudged a thousand pounds to an English author as an extravagance'.[40]

Irving's managerial success at the Lyceum was achieved through a skilful policy of mixing old-fashioned melodrama with grandly staged spectacle and Shakespeare. For this reason, as Jones and others continued to point out, he had a reputation for ignoring new, native talent. But it was not wholly deserved. In fact, Irving laid out quite large sums of money in buying up rights on likely plays (some by untried authors) and in commissioning suitable vehicles for his own acting talents. During his first season at the Lyceum he spent around £900 in commissioning fees and by the end of four years this figure had risen to more than £3,000, but there was not a great deal to show for it. One of Irving's long-term projects was an Arthurian play (based on Tennyson's poem *Idylls of the King*) which the industrious Wills began to prepare around 1884. By 1890, the year of his death, Wills appears to have received as much as £650 on what Irving still considered an unsatisfactory script. Comyns Carr, who took over the task, had by 1892 received an additional £350 and there may well have been further payments before *King Arthur* finally took the stage in January 1895.[41] Amongst a number of abortive long-term commissions, Irving gave Frank Marshall a large advance of £450 for a play on the Irish patriot hero Robert Emmet – £250 by July 1880 and another £200 by July 1883 – only to find his plans for production frustrated by the censor at the Lord Chamberlain's Office, who indirectly made known the official view that the play 'might have a dangerous effect on a people seething in revolt'. During his management of the Lyceum Irving laid out in excess of £9,000 on commissioning plays, but a surprising number of them (including four of Wills's, two of Burnand's, and one of Barrie's), for various reasons, never reached the stage.[42]

Behind the innovatory acting technique and the splendour and expense of Irving's productions was a manager who was, in his system of payment to authors (depending on one's point of view), either an atavist or a skinflint. At any rate, by the standards of his contemporaries at the St James's, the Criterion, and elsewhere, it was an out-dated system. Authors for Irving generally came cheap. He relied either on outright purchase of all rights or, alternatively, on the fixed royalty. The majority of Lyceum authors Irving paid at rates no higher (and in all but a few cases quite a bit lower) than the Bancrofts had given Tom Robertson in 1869.

The finances of the Lyceum Theatre were conducted amidst the greatest secrecy – with what Bram Stoker (who alone with Irving himself and the accountants was privy to the details) called 'a very strict reticence at headquarters'.[43] As no one else knew the full picture it cannot have been easy for Lyceum authors to make comparison either with each other on royalty earnings or against the financial position of the theatre. In an off-the-cuff remark in 1886 Irving implied that it was possible for a successful dramatist to earn '£10 and more a night'[44] but the evidence for this at his own theatre is very small. Admittedly, as shown in the accounts, Irving's son Laurence received this amount for *Peter the Great* in 1896 (a total of £380 over thirty-eight performances); but it seems fairly clear that this claimed top rate of £10 (let alone 'more') was the exception, not the rule, for Irving even in the 1890s. Amongst Lyceum authors the only two ever to exceed £10 a night were Tennyson (very marginally) and Victorien Sardou (very substantially).

For special reasons connected with his name and the regard in which he was held by Irving, Tennyson was numbered amongst this select band of Lyceum dramatists in respect of a production which he never lived to see. In 1892, after an extended gestation period of fourteen years, Irving finally decided that he was in a position to stage *Becket*, the play which in 1879 he had been forced to decline on the grounds that it was a certain loss-maker for manager and author alike. Irving was always very careful to weigh business against reputation. As he explained to Hallam Tennyson in 1879, given the heavy financial commitment he sustained on entry to the management of the Lyceum, he simply could not then afford to mount a production purely for reputation's sake:

> That à Becket should have a long run is not I believe probable, & that it should be acted to more than £150 a night is not I believe possible. The expense would be nightly at the least £135, not including any royalty fee for the author – and with an outlay of two thousand pounds upon the production you may calculate the position of the manager at the end of a run of one hundred nights.
>
> Need I repeat what a delight to me it would be to produce a play of your father's, and I frankly believe that a less remarkable work than à Becket would have a greater chance of success.[45]

When *Becket* was eventually performed on 6 February 1893, about four months after Tennyson's death, the family received a royalty of 10 guineas for every performance including matinées.

Tennyson was inexperienced in the commercial world of the theatre. He trusted Irving implicitly but on the face of it this was a bad bargain. In fairness, the fee was proportionate to the nightly royalty of £2 a performance which Tennyson had received from the Kendals and John Hare for the one-act play *The Falcon* (St J 1879); but it was only the barest improvement on the £10 per night royalty Tennyson received for his first play *Queen Mary* (Lyc 1876) (under the previous management) nearly twenty years earlier, which failed after only twenty-three nights.[46] Certainly for Tennyson it was the Lyceum or nothing – no one but Irving would have shouldered the risk of staging *Becket* and Tennyson probably wouldn't have agreed to anyone else doing it – but what was generous and at the top of the market in 1876 was pretty niggardly for a man of Tennyson's reputation at the end of his career.

Fortunately Irving was saved from embarrassment by the exceptional run of the play, which far exceeded all realistic expectations by logging 112 performances. In fact, *Becket* produced the highest royalty return of any of Tennyson's plays, amounting to £1,165 by the end of Irving's seventeenth season in June 1893.[47] This was more than twice what Tennyson achieved from his earlier drama *The Cup* (Lyc 1881) – written in response to Irving's curious suggestion that 'a less remarkable work . . . would have a greater chance of success' – which, as it was not a full-length work, attracted a lower royalty of £4 a night, amounting to £508 on a run (Tennyson's best) of 127 nights. Under a profit-sharing scheme or a sliding-scale of royalty the financial picture for both plays – *Becket*, for instance, averaged £300 in nightly receipts – would have been very different. But Irving's contracts were simply not designed to reflect any direct relationship between the profitability of productions and author's income.

In comparison, however, with most other authors at the Lyceum under Irving's management Tennyson was well paid. At the lower end of the scale, the accounts show that a one-act version of an old Charles Reade piece (re-jigged by and for Ellen Terry in collaboration with Bram Stoker as *Nance Oldfield*) merited 1 guinea per performance in the early 1890s; but the royalty on Arthur Conan Doyle's *A Story of Waterloo* (1895), which Irving thought of very highly, was still only 2 guineas a night. At this period Irving's payments to authors generally offered no improvement on scales in force ten years previously. Even when he appeared generous he invariably emerged from negotiations with the financial advantage. As a new author J. M. Barrie was offered a choice on *The Professor's Love Story* (Com 1894) between £100 as retainer on the play for six months, followed by a further £400 should he wish to continue the option (that is, £500 in total 'to include all rights'), or a simple royalty of £6 a night payable if and when Irving decided to stage it. Unable to resist the lure of ready money, Barrie not surprisingly accepted the first suggestion, which was almost certainly Irving's real intention.[48] It was evidently his preferred method of authorial payment and likely to turn out less expensive for him in the event of a successful run, though in this case Irving never staged the play as it did not fit his plans, and he was obliged to forfeit the advance.

Bernard Shaw would have been the first to admit that his record as a staged dramatist by 1896 was rather short on substance. Nonetheless, he can't have been impressed at the £3 per night royalty (paltry by standards prevailing elsewhere) which Irving offered him during negotiations for *The Man of Destiny*. Although the two eventually came to an understanding about terms and conditions of performance – essentially Shaw's rather than Irving's – there was no written agreement nor firm stipulation on the date of production, and Irving eventually pulled out of the contract altogether. Shaw pointed out that he had given Irving 'the power to behave like a confidence-trick man if he liked, which he has accordingly done'.[49]

If he had known the whole truth Shaw might have felt even more cause to be aggrieved. The extremes of Irving's policy on royalty payments are well illustrated in the contrasts between Shaw, whom Irving undervalued, and Victorien Sardou, whom he overvalued. Both had written plays on the subject of Napoleon. For *The Man of Destiny* Shaw was being offered a royalty which was actually smaller than the 3 guineas Irving paid on each performance of the vintage melodrama *The Lyons Mail*, whose origins dated back to 1854, and which still appeared occasionally on the Lyceum menu throughout the 1890s.

Sardou, on the other hand, had a potential earning power which made him one of the best-paid playwrights in Europe, and Irving's agreements with him were forced to reflect that status. No one, during Irving's tenure of the Lyceum, was paid more. On *Madame Sans Gêne* (Lyc 1897) – contrary to what might be expected from a dramatist whose whole career was based on profit-sharing – Sardou accepted a fixed royalty on every performance of £14. The theatre accounts show weekly payments of between £56 and £84 (depending on the number of performances). Although this was Irving's highest rate since the commencement of his Lyceum management, the results were only moderately lucrative and over eighty-five performances the total royalty bill amounted to £1,190. Sardou's reasons for abandoning profit-sharing are not clear, but perhaps he accepted that the Lyceum was not that sort of theatre and that in any case Irving as Napoleon would be a sufficient compensatory attraction, likely to result in a long run. The relatively poor showing of the play at the box-office however perhaps deter-

mined Sardou's reversion to profit-sharing for his next contract
with Irving on *Robespierre*, which was written expressly for him.

According to the original agreement drawn up between
author and manager for the as-yet-unwritten play, *Robespierre*
(Lyc 1899) was to be remunerated on a profit-sharing basis. As
such it would have been the sole example of profit-sharing in
Irving's career. But it is extremely doubtful that it was ever put
into effect as the theatre account books tell a quite different
story. Irving apparently offered £500 for the scenario, another
£500 on receipt of the script, plus a further £1,000 in the event of
his deciding to take it to the USA (which he did). In addition to
the advances there was to be 5 per cent on gross receipts.
Evidently this being new ground for Irving, he expressed serious
doubt whether sharing terms were in the best interests of the
theatre. At the same time he was aware that the percentage
being offered might seem grudging, especially to a dramatist of
Sardou's standing, and he endeavoured to explain that '[t]his, in
the main, is more than it seems if you compare our business with
ordinary business, as since we cannot, with our vast expenses,
afford to play to mediocre business . . . the result of percentage on
our takings is more than ordinary'.[50] When *Robespierre* (translated by Irving's son Laurence) eventually took the stage, it
drew fuller audiences than for a few years past and at the end of
its 93-night run Sardou's royalties amounted to £2,604, paid in
weekly instalments of between £168 (in weeks when there were
six performances) and £198 (when there were seven, including a
Saturday matinée). The payments are too regular and consistent to suggest profit-sharing. They seem to bear the mark of the
normal Lyceum system of fixed royalty payments, albeit in this
case at the vertiginous rate of £28 a performance (twice what
was paid for *Madame Sans Gêne*). (Although it is just possible that
the fee was fixed on the basis of a percentage of notional – rather
than actual – average receipts, the effect is in any case equivalent
to a simple royalty.) In taking the play on tour to the USA in
1899, Irving incurred the additional fee stipulated in the
contract, amounting to an advance royalty payment in May
1899 of $5,000 (or £1,028 16s 1d at the prevailing exchange
rate).[51] Even without profit-sharing, in terms of royalties paid

out on it, *Robespierre* was by a large margin the most expensive play Irving ever purchased.

The late Victorian playwright tended to do better financially at the other leading West End theatres, despite the virtual monopoly of control by the actor-managers. Competition was keen. Every manager sought plays which offered the best chance of a long run, the generally accepted touchstone of success, and some of them were prepared to pay handsomely for the right material. Even more than Irving, Charles Wyndham was an inveterate buyer of plays and so was George Alexander, but the latter was generally reputed to be more generous in his payments than the rest because his policy was to obtain the best plays on the market.

Nonetheless, the system was not tailored to the best interests of the dramatist. Those who tried to break away from it had hard lessons to learn. On the whole, Jones suffered much more than did Pinero from the artistic tyranny of the actor-managers. Through hiring the Avenue Theatre for the unsuccessful production of *The Crusaders* in 1891, he lost more than £4,000, though this was partly accounted for by the extravagance of having his friend William Morris design and make the furniture and draperies.[52] The commercialised theatre of the 1890s was tougher than ever on the lame-duck play and managers moved quickly to remove from the bills any play whose receipts fell below the line generally understood to be fixed at about £100 a night. Pinero, whose comedy *The Benefit of the Doubt* (Com 1895) had just been taken off because of falling houses, complained to William Archer of the severity of the economic pressures on modern management. At their worst, receipts had never dipped below £700 a week 'but so high are the salaries that one is compelled to pay even to indifferent artists, that such a sum is not sufficient nowadays to enable a manager to keep a play in his bills'.[53] Because of a substantial fall-off in receipts Jones had a similar experience with his controversial drama *Michael and his Lost Angel* (Lyc 1896) under Forbes-Robertson and Frederick Harrison, but he was less disposed to sympathise with what was in his view a precipitate decision by the managers to withdraw it after only ten nights. During its run receipts had twice fallen marginally below £100, but by the tenth night they had recovered to £231 7s and Jones protested 'that no piece has ever been taken off with returns amounting to over £231 on the tenth night'.[54] Jones always contended that it was his favourite play; but it was in fact also his biggest failure.

With few exceptions, the pressure on theatre management was relentlessly in favour of the safe play. Sydney Grundy reported privately to William Archer that his adaptation *A Marriage of Convenience* (Hay 1897) made him £2,155 in six months and was 'still going on at the rate of £200 per week, in fact only beginning'.[55] (Grundy's purpose in making this revelation from his ledger – it had to be regarded, he warned Archer, as 'confidential & only for your private reflection' – was to illustrate the huge disparity between receipts on adaptations compared with an original drama like *The Greatest of These*, which played at the Garrick in 1896 after a try-out in Hull, the total fee income on which amounted to only £46 17s 8d.) At the St James's R. C. Carton was greatly encouraged at the level of his returns on his comedy *Liberty Hall* (1892) and wrote to tell Alexander of his great delight at the amount (unspecified) of his first royalty cheque.[56] At the end of the century Haddon Chambers was drawing a very comfortable 10 per cent royalty on Charles Wyndham's production of the comedy *The Tyranny of Tears* (Crit 1899), which was regularly producing gross receipts of up to £1,600 a week.[57] Though it provided him little comfort in his efforts to have his plays preferred over popular successes like Carton's or Grundy's, Bernard Shaw adopted a realistic attitude to the theatrical economics of the late 1890s in his recognition of how thin was the margin between success and failure, how receipts could fall from £100 to nothing in a matter of days, and how managers were 'kept so desperately sharply to business by the terrible drain of from £500 to £1000 a week going remorselessly on all the time'.[58]

Alexander at the St James's could generally be relied upon to deal fairly with his authors by offering contracts based on the percentage system, but there were exceptions, one of whom was Henry James. Though well respected in the field of the novel James still had to earn his colours as a dramatist. Even so,

Alexander's initial offer of £5 a night for the historical drama *Guy Domville* (St J 1895) in the summer of 1893 seemed surprisingly tightfisted, especially as Alexander had suggested his writing it in the first place. Advised to hold out for £10, James was reluctant: 'I am too modest', he wrote, 'or perhaps only timorous to ask Ten . . . I am informed (by G[eorge] A[lexander]) that Irving gives the Tennysons Ten (on account of their name – no pun!) for *Becket* – and I don't dream of approaching *Becket*.' Agreement was however eventually reached on the basis of a royalty of £7 per night, though whether Alexander resisted modifying his original proposal that there should be a ceiling of £2,000 on the royalty earnings (which James was particularly unhappy about) is not clear.[59] But in any case, when Alexander was in a position to stage *Guy Domville* in January 1895, it made no difference. It barely survived its anguished first night (which etched itself into James's memory and put him off the theatre altogether) and then struggled its way through thirty-two performances, including weekly matinées, over the next month. His total income from the London performances was £224, though some extra provincial matinées in Brighton at £5 per performance succeeded in raising this figure to £275.[60] Given James's desire not to compare himself with Tennyson, this figure ironically just about matches Tennyson's income from *Queen Mary* back in 1876.

Arthur Pinero and Henry Arthur Jones tended to inhabit a different sphere from most other dramatists of the period because they came to occupy a position whereby they could virtually dictate their own financial terms. The latter's total fees over his 38-year writing career (1879–1917) amounted to over £150,000.[61] By any standards this was very big money indeed. As top dramatists their incomes eventually approached the exalted levels enjoyed by Dion Boucicault, but like their predecessor they had to work their way up from the bottom. For one of Pinero's earliest pieces, *Two Can Play at That Game* (Lyc 1878), written while a member of the Lyceum company and to which Irving later took a fancy, he was paid a token sum of £5, while his second, a comedietta entitled *Daisy's Escape* (Lyc 1879), was sold for £50 '"all at"'.[62] Such rates were pitifully low, yet for an embryonic dramatist Irving's interest in and encouragement for his playwriting skills were far more valuable than money. By 1884, when Pinero gave up acting to concentrate exclusively on writing for the stage, he already had sixteen plays to his name; but he had to wait another year until his comedy *The Magistrate* (Crt 1885) provided him with his first really substantial commercial success in Britain and the USA. Henry Arthur Jones, on the other hand, having turned full-time professional five years earlier than his colleague, was by this time already enjoying the financial fruits of his sensational melodrama, *The Silver King* (P'cess 1882), written in collaboration with Henry Herman. Such indeed was its impact that in the words of his daughter, it freed him 'from financial anxiety . . . and although in the last twenty-five years of his life he was often overdrawn at the bank, he was never other than well off from 1882 to the day of his death'. The dramatic nature of the financial transformation is illustrated in the contrast between his fee incomes for 1881 and 1882 at just over £500 in each case and 1883 (the first year to include fees from *The Silver King*), when his income totalled £3,398 6s 9d.[63] The play ran initially for 289 nights and was often revived. Over a period – it was popular right through to the end of the century and beyond – Jones seems to have made about £18,000 from this play alone. A decade later this was eclipsed by Pinero's reputed earnings of £30,000 from *The Second Mrs Tanquerary* (St J 1893).[64]

Incomes of that level were only made possible by the introduction of a sliding-scale of royalties. It enabled the playwright to draw the fullest financial advantage from a really successful play, since his percentage share was allowed to grow in direct proportion to business at the box office. Pinero was suggesting 'a per centage on the receipts' in negotiations with American managers as early as mid-1883, so presumably he was already used to such contracts in London. And Henry Arthur Jones certainly took advantage of such a scheme. On *The Middleman* (Shaft 1889), which did 'magnificent business' at well over £200 a performance, he drew a straight 10 per cent of gross receipts, giving him a weekly fee of about £130. In general his rates were said to have been 'very rarely . . . less than ten per cent, rising to

15 per cent. or more'.[65] As is clear from the way in which other dramatists sought his advice, he became an expert on the matter. Thomas Hardy consulted him in 1896 on the terms he had been offered at a theatre of 'average size' (actually the Lyceum, temporarily leased by Forbes-Robertson and Frederick Harrison) for a possible London production of a dramatised version of *Tess*, a project which had been long urged by Mrs Patrick Campbell and other actresses anxious to tackle the role of the heroine:

> Houses under £100 – nothing.
> From £100 to £130 – 5 per cent.
> £130 to £170   – 7½ –
> Over £170   – 10 – [66]

Although Jones's reply is not recorded, it may be said that such terms were about right for the period. Of course they were below what Jones at his best was able to command, but issues of the Society of Authors' monthly journal *The Author* during the 1890s confirm that customary scales for dramatists ranged from 5 to 15 per cent. Although there was obviously room for flexibility on rates at the higher thresholds, the base-line on which the percentage scale operated at £100 per performance (or £600 in a week of six performances) was, it seems, a more or less commonly agreed standard. It was really a safety-net against the complete flop. As far as the main West End theatres were concerned, gross receipts of £100 a night were regarded as being on the breadline.

For Oscar Wilde, who was chronically short of money, the size of advances was always what interested him most. But he also had a well-developed taste for profit-sharing derived from his experience with his first successful play *Lady Windermere's Fan* (St J 1892). There was considerable risk attached to his rejection of George Alexander's tempting offer of £1,000 in favour of a percentage on receipts, but Wilde was utterly convinced that the play would be a glittering triumph. He was right, of course, and during the first year it earned him royalties of no less than £7,000.[67]

Although the precise terms of Wilde's contract with Alexander for *Lady Windermere's Fan* have never been disclosed, they are likely to have shared a broad similarity to the agreement Wilde entered into some months later in 1892 with Beerbohm Tree for the British and Irish rights of *A Woman of No Importance* (Hay 1893). Indeed, as Wilde was by then fully aware of the considerable economic value of his dramatic property it is possibly that for the latter play he was able to demand more favourable terms. At any rate, Wilde's businesslike attitude and his insistence on a fair, properly witnessed contract incorporating a sliding-scale is evident enough. The contract specified that

when the gross receipts for six performances are under £600 you shall pay me nothing, when the gross weekly receipts are over £600 and under £800 you shall pay me 6%, when the gross weekly receipts are over £800 and under £1000 you shall pay me $7\frac{1}{2}$%, and when the gross weekly receipts are over £1000 you shall pay me 10% of such gross receipts.[68]

Wilde carefully stipulated that in the event of more than six performances in a week a further £100 per performance should be added to the sums specified. And if Tree took the production on provincial tour he expected to be paid a royalty of 5 per cent on gross receipts. Business was excellent, and years later Wilde recalled that from this play 'I used to draw [in royalties] £170 to nearly £200 a week.'[69] If his memory was accurate, this made Wilde's income from *A Woman of No Importance* comparable with that derived from *Lady Windermere's Fan*.

Potentially Wilde's most lucrative play was *The Importance of Being Earnest* (St J 1895). For its production, because of scheduling difficulties with Charles Wyndham, he reverted to his former managerial ally George Alexander, who, according to Shaw, in addition to 'substantial advances' consented to a sliding-scale of royalties 'up to 15% for full houses'.[70] This placed it firmly at the very top of the market. Its successful run was, however, unexpectedly cut short (as was that of *An Ideal Husband*, running more or less concurrently at the Haymarket) by Wilde's initiation of a libel case against the Marquess of Queensberry and his subsequent trial and conviction on charges of homosexuality. Nonetheless the royalties derived from these productions (which

ran on borrowed time for a few weeks, initially with Wilde's
name excised from the bills, before being withdrawn altogether
under pressure of the scandal attached to his arrest) certainly
confirmed, as he indicated to his solicitor from Reading gaol,
that 'if one makes money at all by plays, one makes a good deal'.
His royalty income 'for the *week* preceding my fatal and idiotic
step of beginning an action at law' – those 'halcyon days' at the
end of March 1895 – amounted to an eminently satisfactory
total of £245.[71]

In a highly competitive world which had become increasingly
international in scale since Boucicault's excursions to the farther
reaches of the British Empire – he even took his plays to
Australia in the mid-1880s – all the mainstream dramatists of the
period were keen to negotiate percentage-based profit-sharing
contracts for the lucrative USA market and even further afield.
In the early 1880s George Sims reported having concluded
'arrangements with American managers which have made my
pieces excellent properties in the States'.[72] Pinero's American
terms were usually between 7 and 8 per cent of gross receipts. For
the New York production of *Lords and Commons* (Hay 1883), he
sought 'eight per cent on the gross receipts, with an advance, say
of £150', for which sum Pinero would supply the set and
costume models (by William Telbin) and a printed copy of the
original MS so that Augustin Daly might make an informed
decision on whether or not he wanted the play. Pinero, always a
cautious negotiator, insisted he would not release the prompt
book (which contained 'such cuts, alterations and general
improvements as long and careful rehearsal under my own
direction have produced') until a proper agreement had been
reached. Daly did stage the play in New York in November
1884, but it seems on compromised terms of 7 rather than 8 per
cent (an agreement which was repeated for the New York
production of Pinero's next play *The Magistrate* during the
following year). Nevertheless Pinero declared himself 'delighted
with the returns': a cheque for £119 7s (which took account of
his £150 advance and other debts to Daly) in May and an extra
£291 3s 6d for royalties on New York and Boston productions up

to 24 October. By 1885 he was confidently asking for a higher percentage ('where the business rises above a certain amount, so that I may benefit in case we get a good success') on Daly's production of *The Hobby Horse*.[73] Henry Arthur Jones had expectations of even better results. Having the edge on Pinero in terms of American reputation, he sometimes managed to push his rates in the USA in the late 1880s to 15 per cent, the top of the scale.[74]

American rights were quite separate arrangements and the sums involved were potentially very high. Wilde claimed he had received 'very good offers' for *The Importance of Being Earnest* even before its London première – presumably from Charles Frohman, who staged the play in New York in 1895 – and he contemplated with relish the prospect of his earning 'at least £3000' in American fees.[75] To ensure best profits, it was essential to deal with one of the leading American managers, like Frohman (who by the late 1890s headed the Theatrical Syndicate, which controlled the biggest theatres in the large cities), Daly, or Albert Palmer. But if the returns were substantial, so were the risks of errors of understanding. Though Pinero and Jones happily made their own contracts, some of their contemporaries learned the advantages of instructing a literary agent on the spot. Wilde burnt his fingers badly over the US rights of *The Duchess of Padua* (New York 1891), by allowing sentiment to overcome his business judgement. From a three months tour by the American actress Minna Gale, he was astonished to receive royalties (which had been deliberately fixed at a 'ridiculously low' level, 'so as not to hamper [her] at the outset') for only eight performances. Such cavalier treatment for his play, Wilde objected, was 'absurd and annoying'.[76] To prevent future mistakes of this kind, from 1893 onwards he employed Elisabeth Marbury, an agent based in New York but with European offices in London, Paris, and Berlin, to manage his plays. Shaw did likewise some time in the following year, though in his case she dealt only with royalty payments – he preferred to handle all his contracts directly with the theatre managers, since '[a]n agent's commission would be sheer loss to me'.[77]

As a newcomer to theatrical economics in 1894, Shaw was

totally unfamiliar with the kind of arrangement he could expect from the sale of American rights. The London production of *Arms and the Man* (Ave 1894), on a graduated royalty scale of 5, 7.5, and 10 per cent, proved a financial disaster – gross box-office receipts amounted to only £1,777 as against production costs of £4,000[78] – but its potential was recognised by Richard Mansfield, whose wife persuaded him to negotiate with Shaw for production in the USA. Suspicious of the terms being proposed, Shaw wrote to Henry Arthur Jones for advice, explaining that the contract offered £100 down and a sliding royalty beginning at 5 per cent, rising to 10, and eventually 15 per cent on receipts above $6,000 a week. His instinct, however, was to play safe and ask for £150 down and a fixed royalty of 10 per cent 'all round'. 'Can I do better?', Shaw asked. 'Am I being had?' Jones probably assured him he wasn't; the results, at any rate, were better than Shaw might have hoped for. Combined London and US fees during 1894 of £341 15s 2d prompted him to open a bank account for the first time; and the play provided Shaw with further returns of £246 5s in 1895 and £139 10s 6d in 1896.[79] Although these earnings were in reality very low in comparison with strictly commercial propositions like Pinero and Jones, they proved a very acceptable supplement to Shaw's modest salary of £312 per annum as dramatic and music critic of the *Saturday Review*.

By the end of the decade Shaw's recognition that his plays were different and hence not commercially attractive to theatrical managers was belied by the dramatic turnabout in his earnings from the USA. Mansfield's production of *The Devil's Disciple* earned so much money that Shaw, writing to Ellen Terry, playfully represented himself as a voracious capitalist living on the fruits of others' labour: Mansfield had 'by bodily labour' made £25,000 out of the American public, while Shaw, having spent 'about a couple of months pastime' in writing it, had already made £2,500 and had every expectation of doubling his money.[80] Shaw's 'pastime' in dramatic composition had for the first time yielded dazzling financial results. At this relatively early point in his theatrical career, apart from a small sum in royalties on the published plays, almost all Shaw's dramatic income came from the USA. In *The Devil's Disciple* he had his first indication that he had real commercial potential in the theatre. By the end of the century he was already numbered amongst the steadily growing band of dramatists who could confirm the truth of Francis Burnand's observation on the post-Boucicaultian theatrical world: 'You may fail three times out of four perhaps; but let one play catch the public, and straightway you will become a comparatively rich man.'[81]

CHAPTER 4

Piracy and the defence of dramatic property

The two issues which most exercised those dramatists called as witnesses before the 1832 Select Committee were the notorious patent theatre monopoly and the want of a system of dramatic copyright protection. The first was resolved through the establishment of free trade by the Theatre Regulation Act of 1843 but the second, though it was the subject of immediate legislation in 1833 and again in 1842, proved much more resistant to remedy. Nineteenth-century dramatic copyright was regulated not only by Acts of Parliament but through case law, which seemed to confuse an already exasperatingly muddled issue and in some ways to work against the interests of dramatic authors.

For effective copyright protection, the drama requires a formula which covers not merely the words on the page but the representation of that text in public performance on the stage. Drama and literature in the nineteenth century shared a common ancestor in the copyright legislation enacted in 1709 (8 Ann. c. 19), which granted protection for published works for fourteen years, extended by a similar number if the author was still alive at the end of the first period. Over a century later this term was revised in 1814 (54 Geo. III c. 156), when authors were provided with twenty-eight years' protection from the date of publication or for life (whichever was the longer). Under both statutes the drama was subsumed under the general provisions for published works; and the disastrous omission as far as the playwright was concerned was that in neither case was any recognition given to dramatic performance. It was an ideal prescription for piracy: shady publishers who illicitly printed versions of plays still in MS and managers on the make who freely exploited both published plays and unpublished MSS for stage performance.

As one of the campaigners for reform observed in a pamphlet on the rights of dramatists in 1832, the great evil of the current state of affairs was 'the injustice which *now sanctions as a right* the piracy which managers of the theatre commit on dramatic authors by the performance, without the consent of the author, of any play as soon as published'.[1] Indeed, it was common practice to regard as public property any drama published legitimately or otherwise. Effectively, once a play was printed the author's property passed out of his hands into the public domain and he lost or relinquished all further rights in it. For different reasons managers like George Bolwell Davidge (of the Coburg) and David Morris (of the Haymarket) believed this to be so; the former as a general principle and the latter on the grounds that minor theatres (since they did not exist in law) were therefore not entitled to consider any play as their property.[2] For the unfortunate playwright, remedy at law for copyright infringements was so cumbersome and expensive that the general view of dramatists was that it was just not worth the effort. Moncrieff's popular minor theatre drama *Giovanni in London* (Olym 1817) was, against all his wishes, purloined by Elliston for use at Drury Lane in 1820. With Madame Vestris in the breeches role it won enormous popularity. Only the songs had actually been published, but since Elliston had first staged the play during his management of the Olympic, he felt he had a claim to it and challenged the impoverished playwright to apply for an injunction against him. In evidence to the 1832 Committee, Moncrieff disclosed that to have done so would have cost him £80, eight times as much as he claimed to have made out of the play.[3]

As early as the latter half of the eighteenth century, provincial managers like Tate Wilkinson at York had already begun to complain that the reluctance of dramatists to publish their plays (which he describes as a modern fashion) 'is of infinite prejudice to us poor devils in the country theatres, as we really cannot afford to pay for the purchase of MSS'.[4] In reality, as Wilkinson was perfectly aware, it was only too easy for an unscrupulous manager to obtain at little or no cost an unauthorised copy of any play once it had been performed. The methods were tried and tested ones, some of them dating from Elizabethan times. Traditionally, the method of reconstructing a text was to settle a group of longhand writers in the audience over a period, each with instructions as to which character or characters to record. This was the manner adopted by Thomas Holcroft, who pirated in Paris Beaumarchais's unpublished comedy *The Marriage of Figaro* (1794) in preparation for a Covent Garden production. In ten days, it was claimed, Holcroft, with the help of a companion, 'brought away the whole with perfect exactness'.[5] Most modern pirates, as Charles Mathews confirmed in 1832, tended to practise their craft by 'send[ing] shorthand writers into the pit of the theatres now, and instead of the prompter getting that which was formerly considered his perquisite, they steal it without any ceremony at all, and it has become a kind of property among booksellers and adventurers'.[6]

As a security against piracy London managers tended to hoard copyrights in the belief that a play which existed only in MS would be less vulnerable to attack. Theoretically it was protected under common law and by gentleman's agreement among the more responsible of the London managers; but it was usually in the managerial interest to buy up copyright both for immediate protection of the script and for the long-term investment it was likely to represent. It was common, though not invariable, practice for a theatre manager to make an offer, retain the copyright for as long as it suited him, and then to re-sell at a profit to a publisher when the time was ripe, thus effectively depriving the author of the real value of his property. Thomas Morton's hugely successful comedy *Speed the Plough* (CG 1800) was kept in limbo by the management for more than a year after its first performance, until the copyright was sold to Longman for publication.[7] Some theatres retained copyrights over much longer periods; especially the Haymarket, which was notorious in this respect. Several of John O'Keeffe's plays dating from the last two decades of the eighteenth century were still in MS there as late as 1832, and the theatre's proprietor David Morris had the resources successfully to defend his interests by obtaining Chancery injunctions prohibiting performances of four of them: one at the English Opera House and the others at the rival patent houses.[8] While a few managers, like Osbaldiston at the Surrey, made it a practice not to acquire copyrights,[9] most authors were compelled to part with them under the terms of their contractual arrangements with the theatres. William Dimond's comic opera *Brother and Sister* (CG 1815), popular enough to have been acted seventeen times, was not printed until 1829, the author having sold off the copyright to Henry Harris 'at his particular request'.[10]

Whilst those London managers shrewd enough to purchase as many copyrights as came their way could be reasonably certain that no other theatre in the immediate area would risk staging the plays involved, copyright infringement of this nature was not unknown. Charles Mathews, as part-proprietor of the Adelphi, observed in 1832: 'we have no protection whatever now, for there are four instances before the town of pieces that I have purchased the copyright of, that are acted at Sadler's Wells and the Queen's Theatre'.[11] For this reason within the London theatres (and to some extent outside) an informal system of spying on one's competitors was a standard strategy. James Winston of Drury Lane records having been instructed to pay John Howard Payne £40 (with the promise of a further £10 if it sold more than 1,500 copies) for the copyright of *Therese, the Orphan of Geneva* (DL 1821); but at the same time, owing to the billing of a piece with a suspiciously similar title – evidently sharp practice was suspected – he noted in his diary that on the night of the first performance 'Carr and Tyson [were] paid to go the pit of Coburg to take note of *Therese*. Payne also went.'[12]

Piracy was so widespread that it became almost an accepted hazard of theatrical life. It operated everywhere: in London itself, in the provinces using scripts obtained from London, and even by means of plays first performed in the provinces and then unceremoniously transferred (without payment) to the London theatres. Some managers were both victims of piracy and perpetrators of it. Tom Dibdin's experience illustrates a classical case of piracy which was as remarkable as it was shameless. His adaptation of Scott's *Kenilworth* (originally performed at the

Surrey Theatre) was conditionally lent to the Bath theatre in 1823, with Mrs Alfred Bunn taking the part of Queen Elizabeth. Unexpectedly, however, it was announced for January 1824 at Drury Lane, where her husband happened to be stage manager. An outraged Dibdin went to see Bunn's production with some friends, who all agreed 'with what the evidence of my own senses convinced me of, – namely, that it was *bona fide* my version, with some little additions'. Bunn denied the similarity, emphasising that, although there were certain parts taken 'with little deviation, from the Bath copy', 'the general feature has been re-written, and so altered, as to bear very little resemblance to the play you allude to'. He added by way of postscript, as if to legitimise his theft: 'You are, of course, aware that the play, as acted at Bath, is in print by a piracy in Edinburgh.' In revenge Dibdin promptly printed a circular addressed to the public, explaining the provenance of the Drury Lane version, in which, as he put it, his labour as author had been so 'unceremoniously appropriated'.[13] It was certainly a cheaper method than recourse to the law and although it brought Dibdin no financial satisfaction, it did at least go some way to mending his injured pride.

Playwrights' control over their own property was minimal, even for authors such as Byron who claimed to have no intention or desire of stage performance. His tragedy *Marino Faliero* (DL 1821) was staged expressly against his wishes by the wily Robert Elliston, who, being aware of the play's imminent publication, managed to obtain a copy as it came off the presses and this was swiftly manufactured into a text for rehearsal purposes at Drury Lane. On the day of publication he bought two further copies (his receipt carefully dated so as to avoid the imputation of using the text before publication), cut them, and then, retaining one for promptbook, cheekily sent off the other copy for licensing at the Lord Chamberlain's Office. Byron's publisher John Murray (who had a big financial stake in the matter, having paid Byron an exceptional £1,050 for the copyright) sought an injunction against the performance of the play, but Elliston's possession of the Lord Chamberlain's official licence for it put him in a strong position. Indeed the court, in accepting defence counsel's plea that Elliston's version (advertised as 'altered and abridged') constituted a new work totally separate from the original literary version by the addition of scenery and actors,[14] not only reconfirmed the old distinction between publication in print and stage performance, but actually made it even more clear-cut.

By 1832 dramatic piracy had virtually become institutionalised with the appearance on the scene of putative dramatic agents who, for a modest fee, would procure on demand, previous to publication, a skeletal copy of any London play for use at the provincial theatres. Douglas Jerrold revealed that a certain 'Mr [William] Kenneth, at the corner of Bow-street, will supply any gentleman with any manuscript on the lowest terms.' Such black-market MSS were readily available for between £2 and £3 and, as Moncrieff claimed, agents like Kenneth made 'a very considerable profit, often much more than the author of the piece himself'.[15] Certainly Jerrold was in a position to confirm this, since his most recent comedy *The Rent Day* (DL 1832) was on the boards of the country theatres within a fortnight of its London première: 'I have a letter in my pocket', he told the 1832 Committee, 'in which the manager said he would very willingly have given me 5*l.* for a copy of the piece, had he not before paid 2*l.* for it to some stranger.' In this respect, Jerrold continued, authors receive 'a double injury': they have no financial return and are 'represented by the skeletons of their dramas', so that they are 'not only robbed but murdered'.[16]

In the reforming climate of the early 1830s dramatic copyright was an obvious candidate for legislative attention. The initiative for the first (and, as it turned out, abortive) attempt at reform in 1830 was claimed by Planché, who in his autobiography takes credit for rallying the dramatic profession to the cause, following his shabby treatment at the hands of the lessee of the Theatre Royal, Edinburgh. Apparently Murray wanted to stage Planché's acclaimed and as yet unpublished drama *Charles XIIth* (DL 1828) but, pleading that like other provincial theatres his was on the poverty line, refused to pay 'the very moderate sum of ten pounds' for the privilege. 'This was all very well', as Planché records, 'but Mr. Murray had the audacity to obtain surreptitiously a MS. copy of the piece, and the effrontery, in the face of the above excuse, to produce the piece, without my permission, at *whole price*, leaving me to my remedy.' Instead of seeking legal redress, which would have been expensive and offered no guarantee of winning, the injured author called together a group of 'working dramatists of the day' (said to have included John Poole, James Kenney, Joseph Lunn, and Richard Brinsley Peake), who resolved on taking steps to secure a new Act of Parliament on dramatic copyright.[17] The Hon. George Lamb obligingly took up the matter in the Commons and a bill was introduced, only to be lost at the third reading when the House went into Easter recess. Nonetheless this failure was not an end but the beginning of a sustained, sometimes dispiriting, but always keenly fought, campaign for progressive reform of dramatic copyright lasting for the rest of the century.

In outline, what came to be known as Bulwer's Act (officially the Dramatic Copyright Act) represented all the features recommended by the 1832 Select Committee's *Report*, which recognised that dramatic authors were 'subjected to indefensible hardship and injustice' compared with all other branches of literary endeavour. Among its recommendations was 'that the Author of a Play should possess the same legal rights, and enjoy the same legal protection, as the Author of any other literary production; and that his Performance should not be legally exhibited at any Theatre, Metropolitan or Provincial, without his express and formal consent'.[18] Undeterred by the recent defeat of his bill to abolish the patent theatre monopoly, Edward Bulwer Lytton's appeal to the Commons was unusually strong and passionate. Amongst the members of the 1832 Committee, he declared, 'there was not a single dissentient voice as to the injustice of the present system', in which monies from a successful play 'filled the pockets of the managers, [but] not a single penny might accrue from its performance, however successful or however repeated, to the unfortunate author'. For this bill it was proposed 'to allow the dramatic authors the same copyright that was, by the existing law, given to all other authors'. It was the unfair distinction between dramatists and other authors which, Lytton argued, was at the root of the present 'striking decline in the modern drama'; and, in a high-minded flow of rhetoric, he asserted that the result of the proposed changes 'would be, that greater talents and a higher order of genius would be enlisted in the service of the stage, and that the dramatic literature of the country would once more regain that exalted position from which it had been degraded by want of the necessary encouragement and protection'.[19]

The 1833 Dramatic Copyright Act (3 Will. IV c. 15), the first piece of copyright legislation of any description since 1814, was hailed as a great victory for the dramatic profession. It was the first and only Copyright Act specifically to try to recognise the special problems of the playwright and the crucial difference between the publication of a literary work and dramatic performance. Its intention was to give authors sole rights in any unpublished play and the 'sole liberty' of permitting its representation – hence enforcing the notion of dramatic property – and in addition to extend copyright protection on published plays throughout the British Isles, that is, including Ireland (one of the main sources of dramatic piracy in the past). The period of copyright protection remained set at twenty-eight years from date of publication or the residue of the author's life; but a new feature was the retrospective operation of the law to any work published within seven years prior to the passing of the Act. Penalties for infringement of copyright were set at £50 plus double costs of suit.

Certainly the new Act was not perfect, but it was a welcome recognition of the growing maturity of, and respect for, dramatic writing as a profession. That sense of professionalism was further displayed by the foundation at the same time of the Dramatic Authors' Society with the aim of protecting those rights now established under the law, tackling the problems associated with collecting fees, identifying violations of the Copyright Act in London and the provinces, and sponsoring the publication of plays under the Society's imprint.[20] Foremost amongst those aims was the collection of fees for performance, because for the first time it was possible to make a realistic attempt to enforce dramatic copyright in the provincial theatres.

Naturally enough many provincial managers bitterly resented the idea of paying for their plays. In evidence to the 1832 Committee William Wilkins, proprietor of six East Anglian theatres, including the Theatre Royal at Norwich, heatedly opposed any form of remuneration to what he called 'mere cookers-up of dramas', by which he meant those who were translators or adapters rather than original writers – original talent, as he observed, was very difficult to find, but Knowles's *The Hunchback* (CG 1832) constituted an honourable contemporary exception.[21] Managers like Wilkins, who had to be cajoled into compliance with the new law, were resistant to change. For those who had long been accustomed, as Planché observed, 'to ignore the rights of authors, the recognition of them by the law of the land was anything but palatable . . . and it was really as pitiable as ludicrous to observe the mean shifts and dishonest practices to which many resorted to escape the payment of a few shillings to a poor dramatist'.[22]

The new legislation did have some force, even in the matter of words for songs and arias for operas. The principle of copyright protection for librettos had already been established in the early 1830s by Planché, who, disgruntled at the profits music publishers made out of songs, for which authors of the words were paid nothing, sold the libretto of his comic opera *The Mason of Buda* (Adel 1828) to John Cumberland for publication without the music in *Cumberland's Minor Theatre*.[23] In 1837 Planché, in what he later acknowledged as 'one of the most disagreeable recollections of [his] professional life', became one of the first dramatists to test the efficacy of the law through the prosecution of John Braham (manager of newly opened St James's Theatre) for infringing copyright on his libretto of Weber's opera *Oberon* (CG 1826). Rashly Braham had 'denied in writing' that his production used any of Planché's words; but it was obvious that the plagiarised version (constructed in burletta form on Braham's behalf by Gilbert Abbott à Beckett) actually employed verbatim some of the most striking arias of the original, including the widely known 'Ocean! thou mighty monster'. Numerous witnesses testified in Planché's support, though the clinching evidence of his 'brother-dramatists' John Oxenford and Charles

Dance (who had attended a performance with book in hand to mark up all direct borrowings) was disallowed as too partial. Nonetheless the case, as Planché said, was 'so clear' in his favour that Braham was obliged 'to pay very dearly for his experiment' at the rate of 40 shillings for every performance.[24]

While dramatists' expectations after 1833 were high, the reality was often rather different as Bulwer Lytton's Act began to reveal its shortcomings. Though Edward Fitzball recognised that there had been a genuine improvement in dramatists' affairs as a result of the new law, which he describes as having 'proved highly beneficial' to him, the principal beneficiaries from a financial viewpoint were the copyright-holders. Not infrequently these were not authors or even managers, but publishers. With hindsight, no one was more regretful than Fitzball at having sold off such a large number of his own pieces at knockdown prices to publishers like John Cumberland. What rankled more than anything was that it was Cumberland who first 'claimed upon his assignments the new privilege of nightly remuneration for dramatic pieces acted, either in town or country. This event, of course, was never contemplated by the legislature, whose intention was simply to assist literary (and too frequently necessitous) men, not publishers.'[25] The resultant transfer of fee income from the author to the publisher made authors wary of parting with copyrights too freely and also confirmed the needfulness of the Dramatic Authors' Society's scheme to publish members' plays under its own official auspices.

After 1833 dramatic copyright was never again legislatively divorced from the parallel issue of literary copyright. The debate on the injustice of a copyright term limited to only twenty-eight years widened to include novelists and poets, who recognised their common cause with playwrights. Among them, and prominent in agitating for change in the late 1830s, was William Wordsworth, who had long considered that the law severely inhibited publication and provided no guarantee of copyright income for relatives and descendants of deceased writers.[26] With the assistance of Serjeant Talfourd, a bill was introduced into the Commons in the 1837–8 Session proposing to increase the term of copyright protection to sixty years, beginning at the death of the author. Its principal concern, indeed, was to ensure that copyright should be treated as the property of the author, transmissible by bequest to descendants, and, in cases of intestacy, subject to the usual formula of distribution as for any other kind of personal property. Despite, as might be expected, serious opposition from publishers – Edward Moxon was a rare exception – and other interested parties, the bill made steady progress and might well have succeeded had not, by an unfortunate turn of fate, the death of the king intervened, resulting in its total loss. Its instigators tried again in 1839, 1840, and 1841 and were finally rewarded in 1842, by which time the dramatic authors had again mustered themselves and presented their own separate petition to Parliament, complaining of the general injury caused by the laws regulating the stage, including, of course, the still unresolved issue of the patent theatre monopoly.

As Viscount Mahon, one of their parliamentary supporters, put it, the 'loose state of the law' in matters of theatrical licensing precluded authors (and actors too) from enjoying the benefits of simple contract law when in negotiation with minor theatres which, even though sanctioned by a licence from the Lord Chamberlain, were held to be illegal in the courts. There were in consequence, he observed, several instances 'in which parties had been non-suited in courts of law' – of actors whose engagements had been broken, and of 'dramatists who had been defrauded of the stipulated sums for which they had sold their works'.[27]

Against stiff opposition from a clique who had for years based their argument on the allegedly monopolistic nature of literary and dramatic copyright and who, during the progress of the bill, seemed determined on setting the term of copyright at the minimum they thought they could get away with,[28] the supporters of copyright reform cut across party allegiances and included, amongst others, free-trader Conservatives like Lord Mahon and Whigs like William Gladstone. As drafted, the bill provided for a copyright term extending for twenty-five years beyond the author's death (with no term being less than twenty-eight years). Macaulay argued eloquently for a total period of forty-two years; but it was Sir Robert Peel's amendment that the term should run for forty-two years (or seven years after the death of the author, whichever was the longer) that finally found its way into law, and this provision remained unaltered until the Copyright Act of 1911.[29] The new Copyright Act of 1842 (5 & 6 Vict. c. 45) – usually known as Talfourd's Act in recognition of his dedicated championing of the copyright cause, though he had retired from Parliament in the previous year – was a sensible, consolidatory measure, a tidying-up of the laws on literary and dramatic copyright, which *The Times* (8 April 1842) regarded, with a few reservations, as 'a most liberal concession to the claims of authorship'.

For all their ambiguities and imperfections, the progressive reforms of Victorian copyright law marked important milestones in the growing status of the playwright in the nineteenth century. In this respect, case law was just as influential as the reforms initiated by parliamentary process. The important principle that copyright was the dramatist's personal property, vested *ab initio* in the author, and that it could not be taken from him except by his express written consent was established by appeal in the Court of Common Pleas against the potentially devastating judgment delivered in *Shepherd* v. *Conquest* (1856), which implied that the author of a play was not the copyright holder in those cases where he was employed to write at the particular dictate of a theatre manager.

The action was initiated by the manager of the Surrey Theatre against George Conquest of the Grecian Theatre in the City Road for performing on seventeen occasions John Courtney's melodrama *Old Joe and Young Joe* (Sur 1853).[30] The plaintiffs argued that the copyright belonged to them, since they had a verbal agreement with the author (who testified in court that this was so) giving them all rights of representation in London, with Courtney retaining copyright control in the provinces. The matter was complicated by two factors: the claim by the Grecian Theatre that the author had subsequently reassigned the copyright to them and the fact that the Surrey Theatre claimed it was still theirs, morally and legally, since they had paid Courtney, who was employed as their 'stock author', his usual salary of £2 per week and expenses to visit Paris in 1852 for the sole purpose of spotting suitable plays for adaptation, *Old Joe and Young Joe* being one of the results. Despite the absence of written evidence on copyright ownership, however, the court found in favour of the plaintiffs, who were awarded damages of £34.

But the case turned out to be more interesting for what it said about playwrights than about the rights or otherwise of theatre managers. On appeal, Conquest's counsel pointed out that '[t]he result of a decision adverse to the defendant in this case will be the utter annihilation of the law of copyright and the degradation of literature'. More than that, it would have effectively reduced the status of the playwright to that of mere servant to his master, in the manner (as was suggested in court) of one who invents some mechanical device while in the employ of his master, to whom any patent established as a result would then belong. After considerable deliberation the court found for the defendant on the grounds that the Surrey Theatre (or indeed any such employer of a house author) had no automatic right to the copyright of a play in which they had done perhaps no more than merely suggest the subject and taken

no obvious share in the design or execution of the work, the whole of which, so far as any character of originality belongs to it, flows from the mind of the person employed. It appears to us an abuse of terms to say, that, in such a case, the employer is the author of a work to which his mind has not contributed an idea: and it is upon the author in the first instance that the right is conferred by the statute which creates it.

George Conquest escaped the charge of violating copyright and Courtney perhaps kept his job since he had supported the plaintiff; but, more important, the judgement had far-reaching implications for dramatic copyright in general by demonstrating its superiority to patented inventions. It was clear that copyright belonged to the author whose mind had created the play, in effect reiterating the principle on which the original Copyright Act of 1709 was based. Copyright could not be divided and it could not be reassigned without proper written agreement, that is, by registration at Stationers' Hall in accordance with the general provisions of the 1842 Act.

Until the 1860s neither legislation nor case law did anything to alleviate an area of copyright obscurity which was the cause of much ill-feeling between novelists and playwrights, namely, dramatised versions of novels, which were in effect immune from the law on copyright. Novels had copyright protection neither from those hack dramatists who, recognising their complete defencelessness, plundered them for all they were worth, nor from managers who were tempted by their cheapness in dramatic form. All popular novelists from Walter Scott onwards were victims of this form of piracy, which eventually grew to alarming proportions. Oddly, Planché, earlier so prominent in the defence of dramatists' copyright, subsequently claimed in his autobiography that he failed to see what all the fuss was about. His experience, following his adaptation of Peacock's novel *Maid Marian* (CG 1822), when he had been inundated not only by novelists but by their publishers seeking his expertise in dramatisation, led him to the belief that stage adaptation was of considerable benefit to novelists in giving them free advertisements for their work.[31]

Dickens, who was not impressed by such arguments, suffered dramatic piracy from the earliest stages of his career. The activities of the 'literary gentleman' in *Nicholas Nickleby*, who dramatised any novel to order, was based on first-hand experience as victim. The portrait was commonly identified with William Thomas Moncrieff, who had adapted the novel in question (six months before Dickens finished it himself) for the Strand Theatre in 1839. Vigorously denying the charge, Moncrieff in a 'manifesto' to the public, dated 5 June 1839, asserted that *Nicholas Nickleby* had already been dramatised twice before (one of them having been published by Dickens's own publisher, Chapman and Hall) and he challenged Dickens to 'finish *his* "Nicholas Nickleby" *better than I have done*'. Dickens had accused him, he declared, of being 'a species of Novel Highwayman, an universal Robber of Romance' who had dramatised no fewer than 247 novels 'as fast as they come out, and very often, *Mirabile dictu*, even "faster than they came out", though I know not well how that could be'. Moncrieff pointed out that he hadn't invented the practice and that in any case 'novels have always been "fair game" to the Dramatist, without any complaint from their Authors'. While conceding that the piracy of novels was 'unfair and vexatious', Moncrieff went on piously to regret Dickens's descent into 'scurrility and abuse', which had made him 'lose sight of that sense which should ever characterise a man of letters'. In essence Moncrieff's defence was that he was doing no more than his job as a dramatist, just as Dickens did his as a novelist.[32] Moncrieff is an example of a hack playwright who spent his life plundering the works of others; Dickens of a novelist who probably suffered more from the activities of such pirates than anyone apart from Scott. No novelist was quite so outraged about it as Dickens nor dramatist so brazenly self-justifying as Moncrieff.

The remarkable thing is that Dickens waited so long – more than twenty years – before doing anything about it. But finally the trap was baited in 1860 with Dickens's short story *A Message from the Sea* (co-authored with Wilkie Collins and published in *All the Year Round*), which was also written up in a dramatic version and, as provided for in the 1842 Copyright Act, duly registered at Stationers' Hall. Then they simply lay in wait for the first unwary hack dramatist to come along, in this case Colin Hazlewood, whose adaptation was announced for Sam Lane's Britannia Theatre. On advice from Charles Reade, however – who argued that court action might be counterproductive in this instance as the outcome was uncertain and might, if things went against them, create an undesirable precedent where none hitherto existed – Dickens and Collins on this occasion settled out of court and sold Lane a performing right in the play for £50.[33] It was probably not the outcome for which they had quite hoped but it was safer than entanglement with the courts, which for Reade, with all his legal training, proved such a frustrating experience, even though in the end he helped to create important case law on novelistic and dramatic copyright.

Dickens's primary interest was to protect the copyright status of his novels; Charles Reade's was to protect both his work as a novelist and as a playwright. But it was a notoriously difficult area and progress was slow. Reade assumed, for example, that he was on safe ground in bringing George Conquest of the

Grecian Theatre before the Court of Common Pleas in 1861 in an attempt to secure damages for a play in regular performance at his theatre (written by his brother G. A. Conquest), which Reade claimed was based on his novel *It's Never Too Late To Mend*, based in turn on a play of his entitled *Gold* (DL 1853). The Conquest version, it was argued, infringed his rights in the novel; but the court refused to uphold his claim,[34] and Reade was forced into further litigation to prove his point. In the next round he secured an injunction against Thomas Hailes Lacy, publisher of another version of the same novel-play (using dialogue almost verbatim from the original play) by C. H. Hazlewood (and, by a nice touch of irony, Reade's own version of 1853) on grounds of infringement of rights in *Gold*. The judge decided that Reade's play was copyright and that he could not be supposed to have forfeited his rights in it merely on account of his legitimate use of the plot as the basis of a novel. The way was then open for a return match with George Conquest and in January 1862 Reade was granted damages against him of £160 on the same grounds as in *Reade*. v. *Lacy*.[35]

Lacy was again defendant in another case at the Court of Chancery in 1863, brought this time by fellow publisher William Tinsley. The latter claimed infringement of his copyright on Mary Braddon's novels *Aurora Edge* and *Lady Audley's Secret* by Lacy's publication of William Suter's dramatisations (performed at the Queen's Theatre), which included dialogue lifted from the novels and made substantial use of the most striking incidents in the originals. In court it emerged that Suter's errors were two-fold: in not professing his plays as abridgements of the Braddon novels and in allowing them to be published. Giving judgement, the Vice-Chancellor pointed out that '[s]o long as [the defendant] confined himself to dramatic representations he could not be interfered with; but when he printed his plays he brought himself within the letter of the law'.[36]

The decision was evidence, if any were needed, of the gaping loophole at the heart of copyright law; but at least it was now clear (absurd though it was) that in order to prevent dramatisation of a novel by anyone other than the novelist or an authorised adapter it was first necessary to write it up as a play. As a result, from the early 1860s onwards novelists attempted to assert their rights in this matter, usually by some form of public statement. One of the early exponents of the practice was Wilkie Collins, another popular target for the plagiarisers, who announced close to the conclusion of the serial version of *No Name* in December 1862 that he had 'caus[ed] to be written a dramatic adaptation' of his novel, 'of which he is the sole proprietor, and which has been published and entered at Stationer's Hall as the law directs'.[37] Other novelists who chose not to protect their work in this way never received a penny for anyone else's stage dramatisations of their novels: Mrs Henry Wood's *East Lynne* (1861), for instance, regularly appeared in new stage versions for well over thirty years after publication.

In view of the accumulating obscurities of the law on copyright and the devices to which novelists and dramatists were forced to resort in defence of their rights, the setting up in 1875 of a Royal Commission (chaired by Lord Manners and with Anthony Trollope as one of the members) to enquire into the law in Great Britain and the colonies was long overdue. When it eventually reported three years later, it was unequivocal in its condemnation of existing legislation as 'wholly destitute of any sort of arrangement, incomplete, often obscure, and even when it is intelligible upon longer study, it is in many parts so ill-expressed that no one who does not give such study to it can expect to understand it'. The essential distinction between literary copyright and dramatic (and musical) copyright was still sufficiently misunderstood to need re-statement and new emphasis: '[w]hile in books there is only one copyright, in musical and dramatic works there are two, namely, the right of printed publication and the right of public performance . . . These rights are essentially different and distinct.' It was the Commission's recommendation that printed publication of any play or piece of music should automatically confer 'dramatic or performing rights' and that, reciprocally, 'public performance should give literary copyright'.[38]

Unanimous though the Commission was in its recommendations for urgent reform, none of the suggested initiatives was taken up. Indeed, the old controversies were re-fuelled during the early 1880s by renewed claims that marauding bands of plagiarists and pirates were at work ransacking popular contemporary novels for dramatic purposes. To two of the cases a special interest was attached because of the eminence of the parties concerned. Arthur Pinero was the first target with the claim that his play *The Squire* (St J 1881) plagiarised Hardy's novel *Far From the Madding Crowd* (1880), a charge he vehemently refuted in a series of letters to the *Daily News*.[39] In the second case the novelist Marie Louise de la Ramée, under her pen name of 'Ouida', revealed in an outraged letter to *The Times* (3 March 1882) that her latest novel *Moths* was about to be dramatised without her permission on the London stage. With such 'pirates of the green-room' and 'Dick Turpins of the dramatic profession' on the loose, she declared, 'there is no work of fiction which does not suffer, and is not dwarfed and degraded, when misrepresented by association with the false taste, the ludicrous ignorance, the dull blunders, and the duller jokes which characterise the English playwright, who confesses his own miserable poverty of brain by his perpetual recourse to foreign inspiration and to stolen goods'. But even the *Times* leader writer (3 March 1882), sympathetic as he was to the general position, commented on the novelist's 'rhetorical exaggeration'; and a few days later (6 March) the correspondence flourished anew with W. S. Gilbert writing to protest at the slur cast on the whole profession of the playwright by 'Ouida's' supposed grievance 'against some dramatic pilferer'. Mischievously Gilbert suggested that any thief was surely to be congratulated if he could discover any material of dramatic worth in her novel. At the same time the 'pilferer' (identifying himself as Henry Hamilton) defended his position by claiming that he had acted within the terms of copyright law, that adaptations were good advertisements for the original piece, and that far from being devoid of imagination and industry he had worked hard to adapt 'Ouida's' novel to his satisfaction by 'endeavouring to adhere to its spirit and to do justice to its great and indisputable beauties, while removing what was objectionable and useless'. Herman Merivale's advice was that 'Ouida's' or any novelist's best defence against piracy (or being 'Pinerized') was to cobble together a stage version, 'however rough', and then secure copyright on it through a single, very token, stage performance, registering the result at Stationers' Hall – in consequence 'that odd thing the law will protect her play . . . and as practically her novel. Or such I believe the law to be.' What Merivale was recommending was generally known as the copyright performance, the origins of which are to be found in the complexities of international copyright.

This was a contentious as well as complex issue because it involved two distinct and often contradictory aspects: the rights extended to foreign authors by British copyright law and the rights extended to British authors by foreign countries. The degree of attention devoted to it over a period of fifty years was an index of its importance to authors in general and to dramatists in particular. All authors suffered from international piracy but dramatists were in the distinctive position of being both victims (mainly from the USA) and predators (mainly on the French theatre). In addition, a large number of dramatists were wrong-footed by American productions (authorised or not) which effectively nullified any copyright protection for their work in Great Britain.

Early Victorian legislation on international copyright actually inhibited the writing and production of original drama in the British theatre by actively encouraging adaptation from foreign models, which, for all practical purposes in the period, meant adaptation from the French. This flooding of the stage by castrated versions of French novels and plays was directly advanced by an Act on international copyright in 1852 so ill-drafted that it destroyed what it sought to promote. The intention behind the Act (15 & 16 Vict. c. 12) was to protect the copyright of foreign authors in Great Britain; but one clause specifically excluded from such protection any 'fair Imitations or Adaptations to the English Stage of any Dramatic Piece . . . published in any Foreign Country'.[40] In effect this was understood to give legal sanction to the practice of indiscriminate foreign adaptation. As Charles Reade, who spoke at length about the matter in evidence to the 1866 Committee put it, '[t]hat clause rendered the statute null and void entirely, because "fair adaptation" is colourable piracy'.[41]

To an uncomfortable degree the London stage became an outpost of the Parisian. Burnand commented in the late 1870s that as authors were generally underpaid 'it suits them better, far better, to adapt foreign plays provided by the managers than to devote time and labour to original work'. Indeed, the commercial instincts of theatre managers could hardly be better served. As Sydney Grundy observed, 'what plan can be safer than to put upon the stage a version of some piece which, in another country, has secured approval, which has been well advertised in all the English papers, and about which curiosity has been excited?'[42] The works of dramatists such as Augier, Sardou, and Scribe could be picked off at will by British adapters at no cost to themselves, because for most of the time theatre managers had their spies out in Paris with instructions to send home texts of all the latest novelties for instant translation. As Mr Crummles says to his new house author Nicholas Nickleby: 'Just turn that into English, and put your name on the title-page.'

For the British playwright by far the largest issue in international copyright was the total absence of protection in the USA. During the debate in the House of Commons on the Copyright Amendment Bill in 1852, Lord Mahon observed that '[i]n consequence of the affinity of race and of language, there was no country with which it was more desirable that they should come to a good understanding with regard to copyright, or any other subject, than the United States of America'.[43] Yet while it was generally recognised in Britain that some form of controlling legislation was self-evident and urgent, the process actually took another forty years because American publishers had nothing to gain by such an agreement and quite a lot to lose.

In the meantime, the American stage formed a rapidly expanding market for the British playwright. But for the unwary it was full of pitfalls. There was a marked discrepancy between the level of copyright protection offered to American dramatists in their own country compared with that granted to British playwrights in theirs. Dating back on a national scale to 1790, American copyright legislation, by a series of progressive reforms, gradually extended the terms of protection, recognised books and plays as the sole property of their authors and, by means of congressional legislation passed in 1856, granted dramatists formal rights in the stage performance of their plays. Dion Boucicault, whose American interests were extensive and who had been instrumental in the passage of the 1856 law through Congress, observed to the 1866 Committee that it was 'a much more stringent law' than existed in Great Britain.[44] Unfortunately, from the British point of view, it applied only to native authors.

The existence of two quite separate and mutually exclusive copyright laws in the USA and in Britain had damaging effects in both countries. Just as in Britain original drama was inhibited by dependence on French, so in the USA the ease of access to the productions of the London stage delayed, with one or two honourable exceptions (such as Bronson Howard, founder of the American Dramatists' Club), the emergence of a strongly based, native American drama. It was a great deal easier and cheaper for dramatists to steal plays from the British stage than to write their own. In Britain the inevitable loss of receipts through piracy was obvious enough; but much more disturbing was the fact that the American law also acted as a profound disincentive to the publication in Britain of plays by native authors. Such was the point made by Wilson Barrett to the up-and-coming Henry Arthur Jones in 1879. 'Are you aware', he enquired, 'that by printing your plays and publishing them, you forfeit your American rights? A play kept in MS. or printed in slip as MS. for use of actors only is to a certain extent protected in the United States. This is of great importance to dramatic authors.'[45] To publish in America was to be deprived of British copyright; to publish in Britain was effectively to lose all rights in America. By this simple expedient, British copyright discriminated against any native dramatist who, either by accident or design, permitted the first performance of a new play to take place in the USA. Stage performance in the USA was considered under British law to constitute publication, so that in the unfortunate instance of a play being pirated in, say, New York or Boston in advance of performance in Britain the author lost all copyright protection in the latter. As a result of this legislative unreasonableness Dion Boucicault's great money-spinner *The Colleen Bawn*, having been

exported across the Atlantic to London in 1860, was immediately stolen and played at many locations all over provincial
Britain entirely without fee. Tom Robertson suffered in the
opposite direction. None of his best-known plays was published
in his lifetime in an attempt to protect his copyright, yet in the
case of *Caste* (PoW 1867) he was defeated by old-fashioned
piracy in the guise of shorthand-writers placed at various points
in the Prince of Wales Theatre several nights in succession to
record the dialogue. This was accomplished, according to the
Bancrofts, 'so secretly and cleverly' that the complete text of the
play was soon being acted 'throughout the United States
without one cent of payment'.[46]

Although it was later discovered to have other uses, the so-called
copyright performance – more accurately perhaps, as Shaw used
to describe it, 'stagerighting' – originally grew up in Britain in
direct consequence of the uncertainties of the law in regard to
American copyright. Its efficacy was never properly tested in the
courts, but the ritual became established of holding one-off
performances, usually without scenery or costumes, in order to
establish rights in Great Britain on such plays as were first
performed in the USA.

The practice dates back to 1861, as a result of Boucicault's
outrage at the indiscriminate provincial performance of *The
Colleen Bawn* and his decision to resort to law as a means of
bringing the issue to a head. His chosen target, one of many
candidates, was Charles Delafield of the Theatre Royal at
Preston, who was prosecuted for piracy of the play. Boucicault
stood on shaky ground since he had technically forfeited his
British rights by having premièred the play in New York.
Although in the first instance the case went against him,
Boucicault persisted with his claim and attacked his quarry from
a different direction by suing him for damages of £2,600 (in
effect, the estimated value of the copyright).[47] Delafield, having
conveniently gone bankrupt in the interim, then counter-sued,
claiming Boucicault's injunction restraining his use of the pirated text of the play as the direct cause of his financial troubles.
He won token damages of 5 guineas but had to pay his own costs

because, although the judgement confirmed that Boucicault had indeed forfeited his British copyright, the law also recognised that the play was still morally his. It was with this experience in mind that Boucicault thereafter ensured that all American premières of his plays were preceded by a token copyright performance in this country or, in the case of those plays already performed, revised so as to render them as new works once again,[48] presumably thereby reclaiming British copyright protection.

Copyright performances became virtually standard procedure for any dramatist who contemplated first performance in the USA. But the same device was soon discovered to have wider application. It benefited a small number of dramatists – Shaw is the obvious example and Ibsen is another – some of whose plays were published before performance and a much larger number of novelists, who either intended to dramatise their own novels at a later date or to prevent others from doing so. Most versions destined merely for copyright purposes in the latter category would have been similar in status to the 'rough & crude' draft of his latest novel *The Christian* which Hall Caine submitted to the Lord Chamberlain for licensing purposes in 1897, immediately before the novel's publication.[49] (Despite their skeletal nature copyright versions were still subject to the normal requirements of the censor.) A dramatic adaptation of Rider Haggard's novel *She* was copyrighted (as the 'only authorised version') in May 1888, prior to its production four months later at the Gaiety, while in December 1890 the Opera Comique was used to secure copyright on an adaptation of Walter Besant's novel *Armorel of Lyonesse*.[50]

On the whole, copyright performances were performed on the cheap. Shaw's *The Devil's Disciple* in 1897 cost him only 30 shillings.[51] Although sometimes prominent theatres were pressed into service, the general practice was either to hire halls (like Ladbroke Hall and Kilburn Town Hall) or one of the lesser-known theatres on the periphery of the main theatre circuit (such as the Novelty, Elephant and Castle, or the Marylebone). It was at the last-named – in a rare instance of an American dramatist securing British copyright – that Bronson

Howard copyrighted *Young Mrs Winthrop* (September 1882), some three weeks before its American première in New York and more than two years before it appeared on the London stage. Copyrighting in the provinces, though rarer than in London, generally enjoyed an even greater degree of isolation from public attention. Northern venues seem to have been especially popular; in the 1880s and 1890s 'stagerighting' took place not only in large cities and towns like Sheffield and Barnsley, but relative backwaters like North Shields and West Hartlepool, where the hire fees were no doubt much cheaper and the risk of public attention even slimmer.

For reasons that are not altogether clear the copyrighting of *The Pirates of Penzance* at Paignton in December 1879 broke most of the normally accepted rules, in particular by announcing itself as a public performance and inviting the press. Gilbert and Sullivan had been dogged by serious piracy for about eighteen months, ever since predatory American theatre managers had stolen *HMS Pinafore* (OC 1878) within weeks of its London production. By the following year it was said to have been given unauthorised performances by no fewer than 150 US companies, only one of whom (a manager from Baltimore) had made any acknowledgement to the authors.[52] To challenge the pirates on their home ground it was decided that their next opera should receive its world première in New York, where piracy was most active. Richard D'Oyly Carte was despatched to handle the arrangements and a month before the projected first night of *The Pirates of Penzance*, at the end of December, he was joined by author and composer. In order to tap the substantial rewards they knew were available in the American provinces, the partnership established touring companies of their own, which took authentic performances to a number of American cities from Boston in the north to Charleston and Atlanta in the south.[53] In the USA the extensive precautions to guard the partnership's valuable property in the opera included the locking away of score and libretto in a safe after every performance.

Under these circumstances the need for a performance to safeguard British copyright was never in doubt. It took place at a two o'clock matinée on 30 December 1879 at the Royal Bijou Theatre, Paignton, just one day before its première in the USA. Apart from the provincial venue, the production bore none of the usual features of the copyrighting performance. Far from making a secret of the enterprise the playbill, announcing it as for one day only, specifically drew attention to its being the 'first production in any country'. Instead of the normal practice of having merely a token member of the public present, seats were sold at regular prices, ranging from 3 shillings in the 'sofa stalls' to sixpence in the gallery. Naturally enough, the production aroused intense interest and attracted a large audience to what was, to all intents and purposes, a full-scale performance with orchestra, and a fully professional cast drawn from the established *Pinafore* touring company, with Richard Mansfield in the role of the Major-General.[54] But it had been rehearsed under difficult conditions – part of the opera was actually written in the USA – and the drama critic of *The Theatre* considered the production difficult to judge fairly, since it was so 'imperfect[ly]' prepared. Nonetheless, when the opera had its first London performance (OC 1880) 'its airs and peculiar humour were already well known to many of the audience'.[55]

This particular device was not repeated in the same detail for subsequent Gilbert and Sullivan operas, but copyrighting was employed in conjunction with other anti-piratical measures. In the case of *Iolanthe* (Sav 1882) the title was a close-guarded secret even from the cast until the final dress rehearsal; and its première on 25 November took place simultaneously in both London and New York (or as near simultaneously as the time difference between Britain and the eastern seaboard of the USA would permit).[56] Nonetheless, frustrating battles with American pirates were an everyday feature of Gilbert and Sullivan's professional lives. All their operas during the 1880s were to some degree affected by pirating, but the principal victim was *The Mikado* (Sav 1885), the partnership's only large-scale success since *The Pirates of Penzance*. Its London première on 14 March was followed by negotiations between Richard D'Oyly Carte and two American managers, John Stetson and James Duff, for the rights to the authentic American production. Unwittingly,

D'Oyly Carte set up the scenario for an extraordinary bout of inter-managerial rivalry because Duff, unwilling to accept the former's terms, determined on a production of his own and when Stetson's authentic version, supervised by D'Oyly Carte, was announced in New York, Duff immediately brought forward the date of his.[57] Under extreme secrecy D'Oyly Carte arranged for a company of Savoyards to accompany him to the USA, causing Duff to make a further re-arrangement. Although both D'Oyly Carte and Duff were pre-empted by other pirated performances, the authorised production did finally steal a march on Duff's; but while D'Oyly Carte managed to obtain a temporary injunction in the American courts against the renegade's activities, he failed to have it confirmed. As might be expected, the legal view was that Gilbert and Sullivan, having published both libretto and vocal score in England, had forfeited their American rights. Determined to uphold copyright in *The Mikado*, D'Oyly Carte then embarked on a whole series of court actions, resulting in the absurdity of having the opera protected, for example, in Boston but not in New York. The process, though costly and time-consuming, did, however, have the effect of producing a number of legal decisions, many of them in D'Oyly Carte's favour, which then stood as legally binding precedents and which in the end helped to bring about desperately needed changes in the operation of British–American copyright.

The essence of almost all copyrighting performances – *The Pirates of Penzance* is the only outstanding exception – is that they were clandestine affairs, to the extent that the newspapers were as far as possible entirely excluded. For this reason they sometimes generated press hostility and accusations of underhand dealing, particularly when plays by prominent authors were being copyrighted. Any new play of Tennyson's, for instance, was certain to arouse substantial curiosity. As well as Tennyson, Frederick Macmillan, as his publisher, had a vested interest in protecting the stage-right of Tennyson's as-yet-unperformed drama *The Foresters, Robin Hood and Maid Marian* (published 1892). Macmillan was closely involved in preparations for its cloak-and-dagger copyrighting at the Lyceum Theatre (17

March 1892) before an audience of actors and at least one token member of the public pulled in off the street. After the appearance of a newspaper report in the *Daily News* alleging foul play Macmillan hastened to reassure the poet's son and secretary Hallam (worried whether all the supposed conditions for copyright performance had been satisfied) that everything was in order. The reporter involved was identified by Bram Stoker a Moy Thomas, the paper's dramatic critic, who, as Macmillan explained,

was annoyed because he did not succeed in being present at the performance. I do not think you need be in the least uneasy. There is no doubt that it *was* a public performance in the legal sense & the stage copyright or right of representation is fully secured (The book copyright is secured also, but there is no question about that).

The Theatre was opened at 9.45 a.m. on Thursday; a bill was displayed in a conspicuous place outside the doors & the box office was open for the sale of seats. Several persons paid for their seats, one of whom was an absolute stranger unconnected with the theatre. His name and address were taken so that he could be called as a witness if necessary. Moy Thomas could have been there himself if he had been sharp enough to be at the Theatre at the right time.[58]

As far as the *Era* (19 March 1892) was concerned, the most remarkable aspect of the affair was that it had been managed with such a total degree of secrecy, given that the play had been in rehearsal for no less than three weeks by a cast in regular contact with the Lyceum's vast labour-force, thought to number between 300 and 400 persons.

If anything, there was an even greater degree of secrecy attached to the copyrighting of some of Ibsen's plays. His was a special case, not only because of his often highly controversial reception, but because there was no British copyright agreement with Norway and Denmark. As a result, his early plays were completely unprotected in Britain (and, for that matter, in a number of other countries, including Finland, Germany, Hungary, and Russia). The few translations that did appear abroad were published without his authority and without fee. Archer's authorised translation and adaptation of *Pillars of Society* (Gaiety 1880) was published and performed (at a single matinée) in this country and Ibsen was aware of the existence by 1882 of at least two translations of *A Doll's House*.[59] Henry Arthur Jones, in collaboration with Henry Herman, adapted the still unprotected play as *Breaking a Butterfly* for the Princess's in 1884.

Ibsen was not a worthwhile commercial prospect for publishers under ordinary circumstances and the problems attached to copyright rendered him even less desirable. Even so, the youthful William Heinemann, more far-sighted than most, whose firm was established only in 1890, took up the challenge and as a first step published *The Master Builder* and *Little Eyolf* in 1892 and 1894 respectively. Special precautions were necessary to preserve all rights, including stage-rights. Since neither play had yet been published even in Norway, Heinemann in both cases brought out a limited edition in the original language and then, in order to make absolutely certain of the stage-rights as well, hired the Haymarket Theatre from Beerbohm Tree for morning copyright performances.

By their nature copyright performances in general were bizarre affairs, but there could have been few quite as unusual as that of *The Master Builder*. This 'curious little excitement', as described by Edmund Gosse, took place on the morning of 7 December 1892, heralded just before the performance was due to begin by a solitary poster outside the theatre, advertising a 'Special Matinée' of *Bygmester Solness*, its original Norwegian title. Admission, prohibitively expensive to deter unwanted spectators, cost the now customary guinea. At ten o'clock, before an audience of four people, the play was dutifully read through in Norwegian by a cast comprising the Norwegian Consul in the part of Solness, Amy Haldane as his wife, the actress Elizabeth Robbins as Hilde Wangel, with Gosse (his first and only appearance on any stage) as Dr Herdal and an equally inexperienced William Heinemann as Knut Brovik. Gosse, thankful that they had managed to escape notice in the newspapers, reported to a friend that a passing journalist who had thoughts of writing up the performance was 'promptly nobbled' (though precisely in what way this objective was achieved he does not say).[60] While guaranteeing stage copyright, Heinemann's charade had the useful further advantage of securing the plays from unauthorised translation and thus made possible the subsequent publication of the lucrative Archer–Gosse translations as the author ised 'Copyright Edition'.

For special reasons, as a dramatist with several key plays stil unperformed, George Bernard Shaw's career during the mid to late 1890s also relied heavily on the protection supposedly afforded by copyrighting performances. When in mid-decade he began to toy with the idea of publication the risk of possible forfeiture of his stage-rights in those plays called into question the whole enterprise. The law was still notoriously obscure and the results of Shaw's enquiries on the matter in 1895–6 with the publisher Fisher Unwin, who in turn consulted American opinion, only served to confirm his view 'that nobody does exactly know how the law stands'.[61] But the knowledge that copyright protection on some of Ibsen's early plays had been los by their appearance in translation before performance and that the later ones, under Heinemann's care, had been protected determined him to err on the side of caution and follow the precedent of pre-publication copyright performance.

Of the seven plays destined for inclusion in what was to become *Plays Pleasant and Unpleasant* (1898), the copyrights o three – *Mrs Warren's Profession*, *The Philanderer*, and *You Never Can Tell* – were still unsecured by 1897, by which time Shaw' intention to publish had taken definite shape. Not surprisingly the most problematical candidate for copyrighting was *Mr Warren's Profession*, written four years previously in 1893, but stil unstaged and with no immediate prospects of performance either in the USA or in Britain, where the censor had let it be known that it would not be granted a licence. To safeguard it fo possible future performance, copyrighting was, in Shaw's view essential before allowing its publication in the 1898 edition.

Shaw was now fully aware of what was required, having culled all the details from the copyrighting procedures adopted by Macmillan and Heinemann: the performance was to be given, without scenery, at an hour not usual for theatrical activity, when '[a] few people [would] gabble through the play reading the parts'. The absence of the press at the performance of such a controversial play was, as he explained, a first priority

No announcement is made except that half an hour before the play begins a very modest poster is stuck on the door in view of the passer-by with 'Admission: One Guinea' at the foot of it. One person (a confederate, of course) comes in and pays the guinea, of which a box office return is solemnly made. Legally, this constitutes a public performance & saves the stage right as effectively as if the play had been produced with full honours at the Lyceum.[62]

Shaw's eventual choice of venue for the copyright performance – the Victoria Hall, Bayswater (formerly the Bijou Theatre) – was, no doubt, satisfyingly removed from public attention, but it was still subject to the authority of the censor, to mollify whom he was forced to cut the play drastically, eventually to the point of reducing it from four to three acts. Nevertheless this castrated version (which absurdly leaves Mrs Warren's 'profession' unspecified) was regarded as legally protecting the full published text of the play.

Such performances sometimes furnished opportunities for friends (and occasionally even the author himself) to come together and read the play before a small audience. Shaw (using the pseudonym 'Cashel Byron') read the part of the Revd Anthony Anderson in copyrighting *The Devil's Disciple* in 1897, while two years later at Liverpool *Captain Brassbound's Conversion* had star quality with Lady Cicely being read by Ellen Terry. All the copyrighting arrangements were left in her hands: nominal advertising outside the theatre, obtaining a licence from the Lord Chamberlain and (above all) keeping the local press in ignorance of the project, which Shaw was very fussy about. At the copyrighting of *Candida* (South Shields), he reminded her, 'the Daily News published nearly a column of a horribly garbled account of it by somebody who got wind of it, and paid one guinea [i.e. as entrance fee] to earn two'.[63] As the now acknowledged expert in the field, Shaw confidently described the copyrighting business to Henry Arthur Jones as 'the hollowest fiction', assuring him that there was absolutely no necessity for actors actually to learn their parts.[64] To the uninitiated copyright performances had all the makings of Gilbertian burlesque, but they survived on custom and precedent as the accepted device for protecting the rights of dramatists, novelists, and their publishers.

Until the advent of secure international copyright protection nineteenth-century playwrights were reluctant to publish plays for fear of losing performing rights. The first major advance in this respect followed lengthy inter-governmental negotiations in the early to mid-1880s in Paris and elsewhere, culminating in the Berne Convention, signed in September 1885. The legislation giving effect to the new accord in Britain, the International Copyright Act (49 & 50 Vict. c. 33) of June 1886, secured rights for authors in all fourteen countries signatory to the Convention. It superseded those limited agreements already in existence with certain European states for reciprocal copyright protection and meant that dramatists and other writers had, for the first time, their work protected throughout much of the civilised world, though with the still vitally important exception of the USA. One major feature of the new Act was the repeal of the clause from 1852 permitting fair use of foreign material for dramatisation. Rights of translation were reserved to the original author for ten years after the date of first publication. No longer was it possible for the hack dramatist to feed indiscriminately off French drama. Indeed, some of the traffic went the other way as more and more of the popular successes of the London stage began to appear abroad in translation. Pinero's plays, for example, were much in demand on the continent. In 1890 he reported to Clement Scott that *The Magistrate*, having been translated into German some time previously, was now appearing on stage throughout Austria and Germany and was in the process of being translated into Czech for the Prague theatre. In addition, *Sweet Lavender*, having been performed in Germany, was in the course of translation into Italian, and *The Profligate* had been announced for an autumn production in Berlin.[65]

When the Americans were finally persuaded into signing a copyright agreement with Great Britain, no piece of legislation on international copyright was more welcome or more profound in its effects. The passage through Congress in 1891 of the American Copyright Act was a victory for common sense and it was the opening for which many dramatists had long been waiting. Indeed, it was a challenge for them to put their plays to the test, because, as the *Era* (10 January 1891) was quick to point out, '[w]e are never likely to have a native drama of much literary merit without the practice of publication'.

Throughout much of the nineteenth century dramatic copyright was an issue which exposed the extreme vulnerability of the playwright to exploitation. Its intricacies and shortcomings were the despair of those authors who saw the fruits of their work set at nought by unscrupulous managers, pirates, publishers, and the corps of small-time adapters who stole anything, novel or play, that they could lay their hands on. For more than any other group, perhaps, copyright actions filled the pockets of the lawyers. Although full protection of dramatic copyright was delayed until the 1911 Copyright Act, the long series of test cases and establishment of case law during the nineteenth century had at least shown up some of the inconsistencies, pitfalls, and dangers for the unwary dramatist which the complexity of copyright law harboured. It was by no means perfect by 1900 – though much reduced, the threat of piracy in both the USA and Britain had not entirely disappeared[66] – but the law had begun to offer the harassed playwright, for whose benefit and professional standing the legislation had been originally conceived, at least an odds-on guarantee of fair protection for his work both in print and in stage performance.

CHAPTER 5

Booksellers and dramatic publishing

In 1800 the modern world of publishing was still in its infancy. Most of the activity in drama was still in the hands of small syndicates of stationers and booksellers, who carried on the publishing traditions of the eighteenth century. But established partnerships on rather more modern lines like Longman, Hurst, Rees, and Orme, catering for a wide range of dramatic genres, and specialists such as John Murray, concentrating on serious drama, were also active in the field. These firms tended to cater for an educated and reasonably prosperous market for printed plays, publishing in relatively expensive octavo form, usually with paper covers, ready for binding up into leather-cased volumes to grace any self-respecting gentleman's library. During the 1820s, however, publishing began to change its character as the established firms surrendered their dramatic interests to a new generation of theatrical bookseller–publishers, who took full advantage of mass-production methods made available by the introduction of the machine press, cheap, low-grade paper, and the process of stereotyping, and later electro-typing, which made it possible to keep 'in stock' huge numbers of play texts and to sell them at very cheap prices. Small format 'acting editions' cornered the theatrical market in the series which bear the names of their respective publishers – Dolby, Duncombe, Cumberland, Lacy, French, and Dicks – almost all of whom published nothing but cheaply produced plays. For a large part of the century, except for closet dramas and occasional editions of a very small number of privileged major dramatists who still enjoyed the attentions of reputable publishers established in other fields, the ephemeral quality of most dramatic publication reinforced the widely recognised divorce between the stage and literature, which set nineteenth-century drama apart from all previous centuries since Shakespeare's time. Only towards the end of the century, mainly during the last decade, did the printed drama begin to return to the mainstream in a quality form designed to restore literary status to the drama and to capture an expanded reading public who, it was assumed, was ready to consider the play and the novel on equal terms.

Publication and dramatic copyright were always closely interwoven issues. Plays may exist either in performance or print or both and the failure of the copyright laws properly to distinguish between publication by performance and publication in printed form was, as has been discussed in the last chapter, at the root of the widespread dissatisfaction with dramatic copyright throughout the century. Indeed, the pressures on an author not to publish were at least as powerful as those which prompted him to do so. A significant proportion of nineteenth-century plays was never published. It may be safely asserted that by far the largest number of unpublished dramatists came from the ranks of those whose plays were first performed in London's East End theatres, since the majority of the plays taken by Cumberland, Lacy and their like were from West End theatres, whose audiences were better educated and more likely to be able to afford printed plays. A proportionally even larger percentage of plays from the low minor theatres, the gaffs, and from many of the provincial theatres, fairs, and booths, never proceeded beyond MS, if indeed they existed in such a dignified form. Few would have had any economic value to a bookseller–publisher.

The record of nineteenth-century dramatists in publishing is therefore, for all kinds of reasons, patchy. Until conditions changed at the end of the century, even in the case of manifestly popular writers none has anywhere near a full record in publication. Although it is difficult to make an accurate assessment (since it is clear that substantially more plays were published than have been recorded in the standard bibliographies), it is possible to establish general lines of comparison. On what must be a conservative estimate it would seem, for

example, that over half of John Buckstone's plays went into
print, and a similar proportion of W. T. Moncrieff's, but
probably rather less than half in the case of Edward Fitzball.
Dion Boucicault, who didn't care a great deal about published
texts, is probably somewhere in the middle at between a fifth and
a third of his prodigious output (which may number about 200
plays). At the bottom of the pile might be found a hack dramatist
such as George Dibdin Pitt, who published perhaps as little as 5
per cent of a total which rivals, or even well exceeds, Boucicault's
(though as a predominantly East End writer the identification
of his published plays is likely to be even less comprehensive than
for the others).[1] On Tom Dibdin's own admission, only about a
quarter of his output of 200 or so plays was published. But
Francis Burnand's estimate of between 80 and 100 of his pieces
having been printed implies a higher proportion of between a
half and two-thirds of his total of more than 150.[2] Almost as good
in relative terms was Planché's record of more than 100 plays
published out of a total of about 180; and it was supplemented in
1879 by Samuel French's unusually grand publication of the
Extravaganzas in five volumes.

I

In the early decades of the century London was well provided
with outlets for publication. The dramatist was supported by a
few larger publishers but in the main by a comprehensive range
of stationers, booksellers, and small-time printers all eager to
issue plays. Few playwrights were loyal to any single firm. Tom
Dibdin, for example, used (among others) Longman, Barker
and Son (of the 'Dramatic Repository', Great Russell Street),
Appleyards, Lackington and Allen, J. Hartnell, Robert Stodart,
Simpkin and Marshall, and John Miller of Bow Street. The two
last-named had fairly extensive dramatic lists including Isaac
Pocock and John Poole, and the former was also responsible for
the publication of *The New English Drama* (commonly known as
Oxberry's Edition). Others active in the same field were C.
Chapple, William Fearman, John Lowndes, and W. Smith.

Fearman and Smith were small-time printers but Chapple (of Pall Mall) and Lowndes (of 36 Bow Street, Covent Garden) were well-established booksellers and printers, whose lists embraced Pocock, Samuel Beazley, Fitzball, Charles Dibdin, H. M. Milner, George Soane, Planché, and Moncrieff.

At the beginning of the nineteenth century when copyrights still had a healthy value, larger publishers like Longman and John Murray found the publication of new plays economically worthwhile. Longman's list in particular was a varied one. In 1804 it was headed by Frederick Reynolds with eleven plays in print and John O'Keeffe with ten, together with representation from other authors like Thomas Morton, Tom Dibdin, and George Colman junior. In the second decade of the century John Murray's list, smaller and much less catholic than man's, tended to concentrate on tragedy, which, besides Byron and Maturin, included plays by Richard Lalor Sheil, and the works of the Revd H. H. Milman, afterwards Dean of St Paul's. Murray's reputation for generosity led Macready to apply to him on Knowles's behalf for the publication of *Virginius* in 1820, but by this time Murray's interest in dramatic publication was on the wane and instead the play went to James Ridgway of Piccadilly, who also took on Knowles's *Caius Gracchus* in 1823. Thereafter the acted drama was almost entirely ignored by John Murray, with the principal exception of Fanny Kemble's new tragedy *Francis the First*, which he enthusiastically added to his list in 1831. With £450 in her pocket for the copyright, Fanny Kemble wrote to a friend: 'Only think of it – was there ever such publishing munificence!'[3] At any rate the risk with such an untried dramatist seems to have paid off, since the play went to ten editions in London and New York.

Up to the 1820s the legitimate drama was regularly available in octavo editions of good quality and legibility, though at increasing prices. In the last decades of the eighteenth century, the traditional price of a new play was about 1s 6d; but prices were rising gradually and at the turn of the century Longman was charging on average 2 shillings, occasionally rising to half a crown, while older works like John O'Keeffe's comedies retailed at between 1 shilling and 1s 6d. From about 1800 onwards these higher prices were commonly applied by other booksellers and publishers of the period: not only Longman and his various partners, and the old-established John Bell of Oxford Street, who published Matthew ('Monk') Lewis's tragedy *Alfonso, King of Castile* in 1801 (unusually prior to performance at Covent Garden in January 1802), but smaller firms like Richard Phillips of Blackfriars and W. H. Wyatt of Temple Bar. Thereafter some prices went higher still. In the same year in which he was selling Jane Austen's newly published three-volume novel *Emma* for 21 shillings, John Murray charged an unprecedented 4s 6d for his edition of Maturin's highly popular *Bertram; or, the Castle of St Aldsbrand* (DL 1816), which Genest later protested was 'a scandalous imposition on the public'.[4] The same firm's edition of *Francis the First* in 1831 was priced at 5s 6d. Such relatively high prices – though still cheap in comparison with the contemporary three-volume novel, which rose to 31s 6d in 1821 and stayed there for the rest of the century[5] – tended to put printed plays out of popular reach. Although they were usually authenticated as acting plays by the inclusion of at least basic stage directions, their real purpose was as reading editions.

Until the early 1840s the continued publication in well-bound volumes of plays, including collected editions, of acknowledged leaders in legitimate drama such as James Sheridan Knowles and Edward Bulwer Lytton, endorsed the respectability of the legitimate drama and its condition as a branch of literature. Publication at the hands of growingly prestigious firms like Edward Moxon's of Dover Street secured favoured dramatists the literary distinction they craved. In the 1830s Moxon more or less had the field to himself. Longman was not really a serious competitor, having virtually withdrawn from dramatic publishing apart from a continuing interest in the works of Joanna Baillie. Their unsuccessful experiment with Browning's historical tragedy *Strafford* in 1837 at a time when Browning was not only an untried dramatist but had no great standing in the public eye as a poet either tended to extinguish Longman's interest in the theatre altogether.[6] Moxon was more cautious. Though he agreed to take on Browning's next stage play, *A Blot in the 'Scutcheon* (1843), it was issued at no risk to himself as the money for the project was put up by Browning's father. The play appeared as part of a series of pamphlets entitled *Bells and Pomegranates* (1841–6) – the texts printed in double columns cost a shilling each – in which Browning also included rejected dramatic pieces, amusing himself, as he wrote in a preface which was never printed, 'by fancying that the cheap mode in which they appear will for once help me to a sort of Pit audience again'.[7] Rushed into print at the author's special request so as to pre-empt what Browning, in a quarrel with Macready, believed was a mutilated version prepared for performance at Drury Lane, the full text appeared on the day of the first performance (11 February 1843). Remarkably, the whole process of printing and distribution to the theatre was completed in just twenty-four hours. The practice of making play texts available in the theatre on the first night had long been discontinued and it was not revived again until nearly fifty years later, when Heinemann brought out his edition of Pinero's *The Times* (Ter 1891).

Having built his reputation on quality, Moxon, though he loved the theatre dearly, was no sentimentalist: he applied to the drama as to poetry the principle of rigorous selectivity. In the drama he published only those examples of the legitimate stage considered to have some species of literary merit. Apart from Browning, he issued all three of Talfourd's tragedies (including collected editions in 1843 at 6 shillings and again in 1852), nine plays of Knowles's between 1832 and 1843, three poetic tragedies (not acted) by Richard Cattermole, and Henry Taylor's *Philip van Artevelde*, written in 1834 and also never intended for performance, but staged by Macready in 1843.

Above all, Edward Moxon was the publisher of James Sheridan Knowles, who, of all contemporary dramatists when Moxon entered the publishing business, was the unchallenged leader of the field. Among his earliest ventures were *The Hunchback* (1832) and *The Wife; a Tale of Mantua* (1833), each with preface and cast lists of the first productions at Covent Garden. But though he conferred status, Moxon was not a generous publisher at the best of times. These were the worst of times – following the shock of Constable's collapse in 1829 publishing in general had entered an uncertain phase – and by 1832 copyright values for plays, low enough beforehand, were close to rock bottom. It was Douglas Jerrold's belief that in the case of *The Hunchback*, universally praised as the greatest triumph of the season, Knowles 'was able to get scarcely anything for [the copyright]'.[8] And what was true of one was probably true of the rest of Knowles's arrangements with Moxon.

Although it is sometimes misleading to measure publishing success by the number of editions – some publishers resorted to frequent reissues in 'new' editons merely by reprinting the title-page to give the impression of public demand – Moxon was in this regard at least more scrupulous than most. The achievement of six editions for *The Wife of Mantua* and seven for *The Hunchback* by 1833 does testify to Knowles's popularity in printed form, even in a period of publishing recession. Knowles's works had become available in an earlier one-volume edition published in London, Baltimore and Calcutta with a four-page memoir by his friend and fellow Irishman R. Shelton Mackenzie, but it was a poor effort compared with Moxon's, who covered him with literary glory by issuing a two-volume edition in 1841, followed by a third, uniform with the others, in 1843, which printed the remaining works and Knowles's newest play, *The Rose of Arragon* (Hay 1842).

Yet by mid-decade Knowles was out of print both collectively and individually. Short of money and painfully aware that his plays were no longer producing revenue, he attempted to persuade Moxon to a 'cheap volume 8 vo' reprint in 1846,[9] but nothing came of it. The languishing copyrights were purchased as a group by George Routledge, who in 1856 brought out a two-volume edition of the dramatic works, essentially similar to Moxon's original formulation but with the addition of one new play, *The Secretary* (DL 1843). As the publishers asserted, this was an 'elegant and extremely cheap edition, of which the text has undergone a thorough revision by the Author', who must still be acknowledged as the leading dramatist of the day, deserving of a permanent place in the dramatic repertoire. Routledge were still printing Knowles's plays in 1883, when they were issued as a selection in the series entitled *Routledge's Poets for the People*.

Of all the literary dramatists of the nineteenth century the greatest publishing success was Bulwer Lytton. Because he was a novelist before he made a name as a dramatist, Lytton had readymade access to a publisher. Most of his plays up to and including *Money* (1840) were issued under the imprint of the publishers of his novels, Saunders and Otley, who also produced the first collected edition of the plays in 1841. After this date his allegiance switched to the new publishers of his novels, Chapman and Hall, who then printed a new collected edition of poems and plays – significantly the poems take precedence in the title – in 1852–4 running to five volumes.[10] Though much of his astonishing popularity was actually gained through the novels, the plays did not merely bask in their reflected glory. Many of them were sustained best-sellers in their own right for more than fifty years. Large-scale successes like *The Lady of Lyons* (1838), which went to a tenth edition only a year after publication, and *Richelieu* (1839), which enjoyed continued popularity through notable revivals in Britain and North America by Samuel Phelps, Barry Sullivan, John Vandenhoff, Lawrence Barrett, and Henry Irving, were the backbone of his published reputation in the drama. George Routledge took up the copyrights on a number of the novels for his *Railway Library* in 1854 for the incredible sum of £20,000[11] and later reissued five of the most popular plays in 1865. Lytton remained in steady demand for the rest of the century. Even John Murray was tempted into a temporary renewal of its old interest in drama by publishing *The Rightful Heir* in 1868 – the re-worked version of *The Sea Captain* (Hay 1839), which Lytton had withdrawn from sale – after its first production at the Lyceum. Nearly all the plays achieved separate play reissues by the main Victorian series publishers: Lacy, Samuel French, De Witt's of New York, and (when the copyrights had safely expired) John Dicks. During the 1870s George Routledge conceived, as a memorial to Lytton's reputation, the posthumous *Knebworth Edition*, which appeared over a period of years at 3s 6d per volume: the novels between 1873 and 1877 and the plays in two volumes, the first in 1876 (which included nearly all Lytton's best-known plays) and the second in 1883, advertised as completing the *Knebworth Edition*, available at 7 guineas for the 39-volume series. As late as 1887 another selected edition of the plays in cheap form for the mass market was published by Cassell's in their distinctive *Red Library* series at 1 shilling for stiff paper covers and 2 shillings for cloth binding.

II

The tradition of multi-volumed series of plays containing a variety of pieces, some old, some contemporary (or near contemporary), stretches back into the eighteenth century, notably to *Bell's British Theatre*, published in twenty-four volumes between 1776 and 1784. There were a number of imitations in the early years of the nineteenth century. In 1808 Elizabeth Inchbald undertook on behalf of Longman a 25-volume series called *The British Theatre*, which was so successful that it was followed by her 10-volume edition of *The Modern Theatre* in 1809 and a 7-volume *Collection of Farces* in the same year.

The 1808 collection is enhanced by the inclusion of Inchbald's biographical and critical remarks – 'two to four pages in the manner of preface' – to the individual plays chosen by the publisher. Many of the prefaces were written for older plays which still retained a place in the contemporary theatrical repertoire of the patent theatres. She had 60 guineas as a retainer for *The British Theatre* and £50 and 50 guineas respectively for the later collections. Neither was accompanied with prefaces as she detested the task and refused to comply with Longman's request to continue writing them. She had little faith in her competence and was dismissive of her 50-guinea fee which, as she explained to a correspondent, she had earned 'in five minutes, by merely looking over a catalogue of fifty farces, drawing my pen across one or two, and writing the names of others in their place'.[12] Nevertheless her editions sold well – she describes their sale as 'prodigious' – and they provided a useful model for later imitators of the acting edition, such as Tom Dibdin's 26-volume *London Theatre* (published by Whittingham and Arliss, Paternoster Row, between 1814 and 1818) and William Thomas Moncrieff, who edited the four volumes of

Richardson's New Minor Drama (1828–31). Publishers, it seems, recognised the commercial value attached to having a practising dramatist as editor.

Dramatic publishing from the 1820s onwards was a cut-throat business. Many of the purveyors of cheap series of dramatic texts were victims of takeovers by other concerns, who themselves later became subject to the same tactics. The longest-lived names in the theatrical publishing market were John Cumberland, Thomas Hailes Lacy and Samuel French. Lacy's business was pivotal. French subsumed Lacy on his retirement in 1873 and continues trading to the present day; but the genesis of Lacy's concern was a complex series of successful purchases of earlier publishers' lists – notably John Duncombe's and G. H. Davidson's, which Lacy acquired between 1852 and the early 1860s. Davidson's list was itself based on John Cumberland's lists and Cumberland's on Dolby's, which had been purchased following Dolby's bankruptcy in 1826.[13]

Thomas Dolby, who began issuing his series in 1823, was one of the pioneers in the market for cheap serial publishing, mixing old and contemporary acting texts. In the best nineteenth-century tradition, he was a self-made man, rising from provincial woodcutter and thatcher to stationer and eventually to bookseller, printer and publisher, trading from addresses in and near the Strand (latterly, as owner of the Britannia Press at 17 Catherine Street). He was a radical, and some of his early business in political material put him into conflict with the laws on sedition. Though his theatrical credentials were pretty minimal he had experience of series publishing with *Dolby's Parliamentary Register* (1819). Until he ceased trading in 1825, Dolby spent two years from 1823 issuing his 'superior edition of acting plays', which appeared at regular intervals in paper wrappers at sixpence per number. Only the later numbers printed new plays – Dolby's association ended with the eighty-fourth when Cumberland took over – but the series acquired an importance through the comprehensiveness of the stage directions and details of costume which made it into 'the model of almost all other "acting editions"' of the period.[14] Not all Dolby's plays, however, were published as part of the series or sold at cheap prices. Sheridan Knowles's *William Tell*, published in 1825, retailed at a price commensurate with the rarefied status of tragedy – 3s 6d – and in a superior octavo form, instead of the usual 12mo, the format which became the trade standard for nineteenth-century acting plays.

Pre-dating Dolby by a few years and of equal if not more importance because he issued cheap dramatic texts over a much longer period (more than a quarter of a century) was John Duncombe. Operating initially from 19 Little Queen Street in Holborn and later (trading as J. Duncombe & Co.) from 10 Middle Row, Holborn, he was responsible for an important series of texts variously inscribed as *Duncombe's New Acting Drama*, *Duncombe's British Theatre*, *Duncombe's Edition*, and *John Duncombe's Edition*, the last number of which seems to have been published about 1852. The novelty attached to his editions was that Duncombe chose to publish texts not already printed elsewhere, 'the Copywrights [*sic*]', as the paper wrappers announced, being purchased 'solely for this Collection'. In this way he gave encouragement to new authors, such as Douglas Jerrold, whose first play *More Frightened Than Hurt* (SW 1821) had the distinction of heading Duncombe's numbered series. Duncombe's texts were generally sold at sixpence a copy, though a shilling was sometimes charged, presumably in those cases where Duncombe had to pay over the odds for the copyright.[15] With the issue of his short collection of minor theatre dramas in 1834 the price fell to threepence.

One of the longest-lived names in the field was John Cumberland, whose extensive interests in dramatic publishing, having bought out the insolvent Thomas Dolby, began in 1826. Cumberland's editions followed the original formula. At first he issued Dolby's list under his own name as *Cumberland's British Theatre* 'with remarks biographical and critical by D.-G.' (the critic George Daniel). But the series was constantly added to and enjoyed an exceptionally long publishing history in some forty-eight volumes up until 1861. All his various editions commanded much popularity and in 1834 he declared a six-month amnesty on performing fees for selected plays – one being a melodrama by George Almar[16] – though his apparent magnanimity may in fact have been guilt. This is the period following the 1833 Dramatic Copyright Act when Planché, among others, objected that a recent legal decision meant that publishers were allowed to exact fees from managers that rightly should belong to the playwright and thereby 'rendered nugatory the benefit clearly intended for the author'.[17]

Until the late 1820s the minor theatres were not represented in the main serial collections. Nonetheless some outlets for minor dramatists existed, though disproportionate to the volume of minor drama, such as G. Herbert,[18] John Lowndes, and the larger enterprise of Simpkin and Marshall. Edward Fitzball enjoyed the special distinction of having his provincial 'melodrame' *The Innkeeper of Abbeville* (Norwich 1822) published in London by Lowndes of Bow Street (complete with coloured frontispiece) and Simpkin and Marshall produced the first edition of his nautical burletta *The Pilot* (Adel 1825). The first serial publishers to break with the tradition of printing only patent theatre texts seem to have been Thomas Richardson and John Cumberland, who began issuing minor drama collections at the end of the decade.

William Moncrieff, as biographical and critical preface writer for *Richardson's New Minor Drama*, neatly defended this new departure, undertaken, as he put it, despite 'the dubitations of critical friends', who had argued that the plays of the minor stage were 'not of sufficient importance' and that 'the Public would take no interest in them'. Yet, as he was keen to point out, the trend was already established whereby some of the more popular minor dramas had already been 'naturalized at the Royal Houses'.[19] At the same time John Cumberland began issuing *Cumberland's Minor Theatre*, in a series which lasted until about 1843. Its inaugurating volume was headed by a reprint of Fitzball's much vaunted success *The Pilot* – enthusiastically described by the author as 'Cumberland's beautiful edition'[20] – the first of a number of his plays which were published under the same imprint, mostly for the first time.

The minor theatre market was an important growth area in the early part of the century and in 1834 Cumberland was briefly joined in the field by his rival John Duncombe, who brought out *Duncombe's Minor British Drama*, a collection of about twenty-four plays representing a broad cross-section of minor theatre authors such as Moncrieff, Fitzball, C. Z. Barnett, T. J. Serle, Charles Selby, and George Dibdin Pitt. Nothing further was published however, probably owing to Cumberland's dominance in the same market. Yet Duncombe's minor drama collection was evidently useful and saleable enough to merit its continued advertising after Lacy bought out Duncombe's business in 1852.[21] Barth's series entitled the *Universal Stage* (formerly Pattie's) between 1839 and 1845 also published minor theatre dramatists, including George Dibdin Pitt, Leman Rede, Edward Stirling, George Almar, and W. T. Moncrieff.

From an author's point of view perhaps no publisher during the 1830s was more important than John Miller of 13 Henrietta Street.[22] Though small fry compared with Cumberland, he assumed a special importance in dramatic publishing in 1833 at that vital stage when the provisions of Bulwer Lytton's new Copyright Act were beginning to take effect. From this date onwards playwrights (at least in theory) were no longer risking their property as formerly and the simultaneous formation of the Dramatic Authors' Society helped them to achieve a sense of corporate identity. Miller was appointed agent to the society in 1833 and immediately started issuing members' plays. His responsibility as its first London agent is noted on the title-page of a number of dramatic texts published between 1833 and 1837. By 1834 some sixteen plays had been issued, with Jerrold's *Nell Gwyn; or, the Prologue*, published at 2 shillings listed as number one in the series, which was given the title *Miller's Modern Acting Drama*.[23] The pink wrapper (as distinct from the title-page, which is less informative) of number 16, Gilbert Abbott à Beckett's two-act farce, performed at the Royal Fitzroy Theatre in January 1834 reads:

The King Incog. / A Farce / Miller's Modern Acting Drama, / Consisting of / The Most Popular Pieces / Produced at the London Theatres. / Subject to the / Provisions of the Dramatic Copyright Act. / —— / London: / John Miller, Henrietta Street, / Covent Garden. / (Agent to the Dramatic Authors' Society.) / —— / 1834.

Most of the plays in the series, which included texts by Bunn, Poole, Peake, M. R. Lacy, and J. B. Buckstone – several of which are described in Nicoll as not published – were issued at prices ranging between 1 and 2 shillings.

Although Miller went on publishing into the 1840s (and probably later), in 1837 he surrendered his Dramatic Authors' Society agency to Chapman and Hall, who issued a new series under the title *Webster's Acting National Drama*, edited by Benjamin Webster. In Planché's dedication to Madame Vestris (dated 19 December 1836) of the first play of the series, *The Two Figaros*, he described the venture as 'principally, if not wholly, consist[ing] of pieces produced by members of the Dramatic Authors' Society'. To begin with this was substantially true. Besides Planché, the first volume included new plays by Webster, Charles Dance, R. B. Peake, J. M. Morton, and Edward Fitzball – all of whom were members of the society – and only one outsider, J. S. Coyne; the second printed two plays by Eliza Planché and Mrs S. C. Hall, who were classed as honorary members. About 1840, after ninety-three issues, Chapman and Hall in turn were replaced as publishers by Sherwood, Gilbert, and Piper of Paternoster Row, who continued publication until about 1843, when Webster and Co. of 20 Suffolk Street, Pall Mall East took over and steered the series to a conclusion in 1859. Long before this, however, the association with the Dramatic Authors' Society had begun to dissolve as dramatists like Planché found other outlets for publication, presumably on more attractive terms.

Smaller publishing firms, though overshadowed by the great series, were still available as alternatives. Up to the 1850s the London bookselling world was a comparatively close one, clustered in the main in two areas long connected with printing and publishing: Covent Garden and the neighbourhood of St Paul's, Ludgate Hill, and Blackfriars. Booksellers' imprints are frequently found in conjunction with associates in London or, in some cases, in Edinburgh, Dublin, even Paris. William Strange of Paternoster Row, publisher of editions of Thomas Bayly and J. B. Buckstone, and less regularly of others such as John Oxenford and T. J. Serle, dates from the 1830s, when he also began a series entitled the *London Acting Drama*; but it seems to have had only a comparatively short history.[24] His name (usually in company with S. G. Fairbrother, G. Berger, Lacy and others) was however perpetuated as a bookseller into the 1850s.

For a decade between 1842 and 1852 Fairbrother (31 Bow Street, Covent Garden), commonly in association either with Strange or with Berger of Holywell Street, was responsible for issuing, among other titles, a series of Planché's plays 'as they came out at the theatres, with uniform wrappers and titles'.[25] The paper wrappers indicate that they were part of an edition – *S. G. Fairbrother's Edition*[26] – and by 1852 it contained no fewer than forty-three Planché titles, mostly at a shilling or sixpence, together with five of Charles Dance's, and another forty-two texts described in the advertising under 'Miscellaneous'. About 1856 Fairbrother's stock was taken over by T. H. Lacy, who then issued the former's editions in his own wrappers.

Thomas Hailes Lacy was perhaps the most prominent and catholic of all nineteenth-century publishers of the drama for the masses. He traded as theatrical bookseller and publisher from rather seedy premises in Wellington Street, off the Strand in London, in 1849 and later from 89 Strand after 1857. Burnand describes him at this period in Dickensian terms as a bespectacled figure, with rumpled hair and 'dirty shirt sleeves . . . muddling about with books and papers in a very ill-lighted and grimy shop'.[27] Former actor and sometime theatre manager, he retired after a very profitable career in the spring of 1873, when his list was purchased in its entirety by Samuel French; a reversal of the process whereby Lacy had expanded his own business after 1852 through taking over Duncombe's entire stock. Lacy made a great deal of money out of his publishing enterprise. He was occasionally not averse to issuing texts to which he had no title, and on his death in 1873 the Dramatic Authors' Society tried to claim £700 out of the estate for unpaid fees, but settled for £250. He had a library worth £2,650, dramatic portraits which sold for £1,970, a number of properties in London, as well as a large capital sum. Through his will Lacy amply repaid his obligation at least to the acting profession by leaving his residual estate (including an £8,000 'Lacy Bequest' and the three properties in Garrick St) to the Royal General Theatrical Fund, on the board of which he had been an active member for some years.[28]

Nearly every Victorian dramatist of any note seems to have been involved in one way or another with Lacy, whose acting edition ran to over 100 volumes, covering 1,485 plays, with Samuel French (who added new titles to Lacy's list), or John Dicks – in many cases with all three – including those, like Lytton, Knowles, and Gilbert, who had had the privilege of more handsome treatment from earlier publishers. Closely printed in double columns (a three-act play was usually compressed into thirty or so pages) they sold at most for sixpence a copy. By the time John Dicks entered the same field in the 1880s the price for his famous *Standard Plays* was down to a penny.

Unlike his competitors, Dicks's business was not exclusively to do with the drama. He was also the publisher of *Reynolds News* and his fiction and general book list was extensive. His hall-mark was cheapness, built on a policy of handling only expired copyrights. The first series of plays, *Dicks's British Drama*, began publication in 1866 and was completed in twenty volumes, each containing from nineteen to twenty-three plays, but only a very few of them were being published for the first time. The second and longer series was published under the title *Dicks's Standard Plays*, beginning in 1875 and continuing into the first decade of the twentieth century. But again, Dicks was interested only in expired copyrights, especially any printed texts of non-copyright dramas acted before 1843. His biggest coup was the purchase of the theatrical library of the Adelphi Theatre and with it the texts of a whole clutch of plays by Buckstone, Webster, Oxenford, Lovell, Lemon, Fitzball, and Coyne, all of them, as he announced in his advertisements, 'valuable expired copyrights'.[29] But while he had no importance in publishing contemporary dramatists, there was some justice in his claim that his series had a function in preserving for posterity a whole host of dramas that would otherwise have been lost entirely or would have had no chance of existence beyond manuscript form, since, unlike the French drama, 'that of our country is sinking fast into oblivion, and if not speedily gathered by friendly hands, must perish irrevocably'. In all, Dicks's collections consisted of about 1,400 plays, which makes them equal in size, though not in importance, to *Lacy's Acting Edition*.

III

The sheer abundance of plays published 'in the form of miserable sixpenny pamphlets for the use of amateur clubs', coupled with the absence of quality texts, prompted William Archer to remark upon the completeness of the estrangement between literature and the stage.[30] Almost all the dramatic texts which he relied on as material for writing *English Dramatists of To-day* (1882) were available only in the flimsiest printed versions. Such better-quality editions as did exist for later nineteenth-century dramatists were generally reserved either for poets (like Tennyson) or novelists (like Lytton) who had claims independent of the drama on public attention. Indeed, W. S. Gilbert was the only example Archer could point to of a popular contemporary dramatist whose work was available in durable published form. Yet within ten years, dramatic publishing had been substantially transformed. The inconvenient format of the acting edition, full of stage directions printed in a technical language peculiar to the stage and thus incomprehensible to the majority of the public, more or less disappeared. In its place were readable, well-printed texts with meaningful stage directions, designed for a new market. On the assumption that the older form inhibited public demand, the new reading editions were an attempt to educate a novel-buying public into the purchase of plays.

At the forefront of the attempt to redraw the boundaries of dramatic publication during the 1890s was Henry Arthur Jones. In May 1890 he was advised to publish *Judah* 'as soon as the commercial reasons for withholding it are gone'.[31] Those reasons disappeared in the following year as a result of the security afforded to dramatists by the new American Copyright Act. In the event Jones chose for his first venture into dramatic publishing not *Judah* (which did not appear until 1894) but *Saints and Sinners*.

His publishers were Macmillan and Co., for whom the drama (apart from their continuing association with Tennyson)[32] was a departure from their usual field of interest. Given that Macmillan's experience with Tennyson's plays was not very encouraging – sales had never been high despite Tennyson's relative success on the stage – this was, on the face of it, an important expression from a well-established and reputable publisher of confidence in Jones as a playwright and in the marketing potential of dramatic texts in a well-bound uniform edition. At a late stage in negotiations during April 1891 Jones was evidently under the impression that Macmillan would, in the course of time, publish most of his work. He even suggested that a sliding-scale of royalty would need to be agreed upon 'in the event, which is not impossible, of some play reaching a very large sale'. One of the plays he had in mind was *The Dancing Girl*, then in the midst of its year-long run at the Haymarket.[33] Perhaps Jones tried to push them too far too quickly; in fact it seems that Macmillan had something less adventurous in mind and decided quite early on to restrict their initial commitment to only four plays (un-named) to be published at their own risk and expense. This accounts for their relatively slow, piecemeal issue.

By late May 1896 Macmillan had published only three of the four plays to which they were contractually bound – *Saints and Sinners* (1891), *The Crusaders* (1893), and *Judah* (1894). Although the appearance of *Michael and his Lost Angel* (Lyc 1896) was imminent, Jones was careful to stress that it should on no account be regarded as part of the contract because, in this instance, he had paid for the electrotyping plates himself.[34] Under normal conditions Jones withheld publication of his plays for at least two years (and sometimes considerably longer) after their first performances. This was, however, a special case and Jones was touchy about it, as he always was about failures. Macmillan were presumably reluctant to publish at their own risk a play which had not caught on with the public; but to Jones its publication was important as an assertion of his undiminished faith in it. No doubt he was encouraged in this belief by Shaw's remark in the *Saturday Review* that *Michael and his Lost Angel* had not deserved its ignominy and '[t]he sooner Mr Jones publishes it, the better for his reputation'.[35] Macmillan did not actually fulfil their contract for a fourth play until *The Case of Rebellious Susan* was issued in 1897, nearly three years after its successful run at the Criterion under the charge of Charles Wyndham.

In common with H. J. Byron, Tennyson, Gilbert, Pinero, and later Bernard Shaw, it was Jones's habit to print the texts of almost all his plays privately before even rehearsals began. Until the early 1880s he used John Tait of Ilfracombe and, though one or two of the texts from this source were taken up later for *Lacy's Acting Edition*, the majority remained unpublished. In the 1890s the task was made over to Charles Whittingham and Co. under the imprint of the Chiswick Press. Primarily intended for use at rehearsals and for prompt copies, they also served as gifts for valued friends like Ellen Terry and Bernard Shaw, and as the licensing copy submitted to the Examiner of Plays. As an additional spin-off they formed – with only slight emendation – copy for Macmillan's published editions.[36] Handsomely printed, complete with half-titles, titles, *dramatis personae*, and attractive devices separating the acts, they were texts of which any author might be proud. To all intents and purposes they were indistinguishable from formally published plays. Each private edition carries a warning notice on the title-page that '[a]ll its dramatic rights are fully secured, and proceedings will be immediately taken against anyone who attempts to infringe them'. The risk from piracy inherent in the existence of printed texts prior to performance and publication was presumably outweighed by Jones's sense of professional pride and his desire to fix his text before exposure to the revising instincts of actors and the vagaries of theatre managers.

Most of the *Macmillan Uniform Editions* of Jones's plays were issued with prefaces either by Jones himself or dramatic critics, such as William Archer and Joseph Knight. Jones's own preface (dated April 1891) to the first play in the edition *Saints and Sinners*, in which, as he told his publisher, he had 'some fresh matters of interest' to communicate,[37] was a rallying call for the rejuvenation of the English drama. The passage of the American Copyright Act he considered to be 'a fact of the highest import for English playwrights and for the future of the English drama, – that is, if the English drama has a future'. Now that publication could be fearlessly entered into, Jones argued in the preface, if 'a playwright does not publish within a reasonable time after the theatrical production of his piece, it will be an open confession that his work was a thing of the theatre merely, needing its garish artificial light and surroundings, and not daring to face the calm air and cold daylight of print'. For Jones, publication also served as an opportunity to revise earlier theatrical versions – such as restoring the original unhappy ending intended for *Saints and Sinners* or tricking-up plays like *The Silver King*, which had begun to date.

Jones's plays were shared between Macmillan and Samuel French. The former published eleven of the plays between 1891 and 1900 out of a total to that date of more than forty. *The Dancing Girl*, about which Jones had had such high hopes in 1891, was not among them; indeed, it never appeared under Macmillan's imprint. Samuel French issued it in 1907, the same year as Jones's most successful play ever, *The Silver King*, which for commercial reasons had remained unpublished for twenty-five years. During the previous year Samuel French of New York had taken over from Macmillan as publisher of the remaining plays; but this was a testimony as much to the considerable reputation that Jones then enjoyed in the USA – Harvard conferred on him an honorary MA in 1907 – as to the playwright's irritation at Macmillan's relative lethargy.

Arthur Wing Pinero entertained equally high expectations for published drama. As he put it in the introduction to the text of *The Times* in October 1891, his hope was that the new reading editions would play their part in 'dignify[ing] at once the calling of the actor, [and] the craft of the playwright'. The text of this play was the first of Pinero's to be brought out by William Heinemann, whose intention was to issue a new play every month. By January 1892 *The Profligate* and *The Cabinet Minister* had been brought out in their smart dark-red cloth bindings (priced at 2s 6d, with a paper-cover version available for a shilling less) and *The Hobby Horse* announced for issue in the following month. This edition was specifically designed to demonstrate the reading quality of the plays – the test which Jones had already suggested as the touchstone for the value of contemporary drama. Thus, when writing to R. M. Field (a regular producer of Pinero in the USA, who was interested in *The Times*) he was careful to stress that the copy of the play being forwarded was 'not a *stage copy*, but the work as prepared for the library; it forms vol:1 of a series of my plays which are being issued monthly to the reading public'.[38] The intention to publish monthly was not followed through but by the end of the decade Heinemann had brought out in uniform style and format nineteen of Pinero's plays, nearly twice as many as Jones had managed to extract out of Macmillan. Over the same period an identical edition was published by W. H. Baker of Boston, Massachusetts.

Though the sudden impulse to publish was for many dramatists irresistible, the practice was not without its critics. Both Pinero and Jones were attacked for publishing essentially actors' plays (like *The Profligate* and *Judah*) which, it was argued, demonstrated the flaws in their authors' literary pretentions.[39] A reviewer of *Saints and Sinners* in the theatrical press, though respecting the courage of its 'strenuous preface', remained unimpressed by Jones's claim that publication was really the only measure of dramatic worth. Though *Saints and Sinners* was as 'engrossing as a novel', it was felt, on grounds of literary quality, to have been a bad choice for beginning the series. In the same journal Cecil Howard, making a similar point about Pinero's *The Times*, argued that as a first choice it was 'perhaps unfortunate in the circumstances that have thrust it before the literary public as his representative work'.[40]

In sales terms the attempt to lure the public into the purchase of plays in large numbers was not an unqualified success. This was in some cases attributable to slack marketing techniques, as in the case of Bernard Shaw's *Widowers' Houses* (Roy 1892), published by J. T. Grein of the Independent Theatre Society in 1893, but which as Shaw ruefully pointed out had never once been advertised and had sold only 150 copies.[41] Macmillan deducted £1 from Henry Arthur Jones's royalties for every occasion on which they advertised his plays – an imposition which became increasingly irksome to Jones by the first decade of the twentieth century, when his revenue had dwindled to almost nothing. Indeed, given 'the smallness of the sales', Jones protested that it was 'an outrageous charge' and in 1912 finally urged Macmillan to stop advertising his plays altogether.[42]

Late in life Jones acknowledged to Sir Frederick Macmillan that he had always been 'a "worst" seller'.[43] But even a young, go-ahead publisher like William Heinemann was none too successful in his new venture. While Pinero declared himself 'not dissatisfied' with the enterprise – *The Times* in 1891 had sold out its first run of 5,000 copies and was into a second edition before the end of November[44] – the euphoria did not last as the market never properly extended beyond that of the amateur actor. The unexpected stage popularity of *The Second Mrs Tanqueray* in 1893 induced Heinemann to raise the price of his edition to 6 shillings, but, as Shaw observed, he was quickly forced to reduce it to the usual level. As Heinemann explained to Shaw – who enquired into the publishing potential of *Arms and the Man* – 'the general reading public [was] utterly unrepresented in sales of the library edition of Pinero, though Pinero was then beyond question the foremost English playwright'.[45] On a different level, appealing to a more intellectual market, Heinemann's edition of Ibsen sold reasonably well at 5 shillings. But Shaw's general enquiries with John Lane and Walter Scott only confirmed a generally disheartening picture, and for the time being he shelved the idea of publishing, fully recognising the substantially increased commercial risk he represented as an eccentric and largely unperformed dramatist.

In the meantime Oscar Wilde had better fortune. He was less of a risk and he already had contracts with Osgood and McIlvaine for prose work. Equally important, he was a practised negotiator. Admittedly, Macmillan rejected the offer of *Lady Windermere's Fan* (St J 1892) (possibly because of their experience with Henry Arthur Jones), but Elkin Mathews and John Lane, partners at the Bodley Head (with whom he also had previous connexions), accepted the play in 1893 on terms by which Wilde insisted on publication of some of his prose and poetry as part of the deal. In the same year the firm took on responsibility for the British sales of the original French version (printed in Paris) and in 1894 for the English translation of Wilde's controversial *Salomé*, which, because of its risky blend of biblical subject-matter and eroticism, had been refused a licence for stage performance by the Lord Chamberlain in the summer of 1892.[46] In the light of the censor's veto, publication assumed the guise of an act of defiance. Resplendent with sixteen specially commissioned illustrations by Aubrey Beardsley (some of which had been changed at the insistence of John Lane because they were considered too indecent), the published text of *Salomé* was the means by which Wilde could express his outrage, while Lane could happily reflect on the increased sales to be anticipated from printing a reputedly profane and immoral work. Indeed, a second issue of the first edition ran to a further 100 copies on top of the 500 which was Bodley Head's usual print run for the ordinary text of Wilde's plays. These were normally quite expensive at 7s 6d and 15 shillings for the large-paper version; but in the case of *Salomé* the prices were doubled in both formats. Wilde received a shilling royalty on every copy sold of the ordinary version and 3 shillings on the larger format.[47]

Later in October 1894 John Lane alone (his partnership with Mathews having been dissolved) also published *A Woman of No Importance* (Hay 1893), which Wilde anticipated might receive a boosted sale on account of its having 'formed a text for reckless sermons'.[48] After Wilde's arrest, trial, and imprisonment in 1895 *The Importance of Being Earnest* (St J 1895), potentially his most lucrative literary property, was impossible to publish and indeed no further Wilde plays appeared until 1899. This was almost two years after Wilde's release from prison, by which time he had met a new publisher, Leonard Smithers, who filled the gap created by the withdrawal of John Lane.

Lane's Bodley Head press, much involved in the publication of *fin de siècle* literature and eminently respectable, nonetheless occasionally dabbled in the controversial. In the drama, apart from *Salomé*, Lane was responsible for the publication of two other plays banned on moral grounds by the censor from stage performance, both ironically by his fellow publisher William Heinemann: *The First Step* in 1895 and *Summer Moths* in 1898.[49] Smithers, by contrast, was unconventional in a quite different way, having earlier made a name for himself as a purveyor of under-the-counter pornography. His general interest in the erotic – he published Ernest Dowson, Arthur Symons, and Beardsley – amused and attracted Wilde. They slid easily into a harmonious working relationship, though it has to be said that towards the end of Wilde's life Smithers took advantage of his weakened financial state by persistently delaying money that was due to him and forcing a humiliating contract on the author for the sale of copyright in his last two plays.

In 1898 Smithers and Co. exploited Wilde's notoriety by publishing, at first anonymously, *The Ballad of Reading Gaol*, which achieved huge sales, running into many thousands of copies. *Earnest* and *An Ideal Husband* eventually came out in February and July 1899 respectively, both of them being described as 'by the author of *Lady Windermere's Fan*'. By this time it might be plausibly argued that the copyright value in the plays (now four and five years old) had fallen but whether it had sunk quite as low as the miserable £30 which eventually secured Smithers all publication rights in them is open to doubt. As Wilde had unavailingly pointed out at an early stage in the negotiation, both plays 'have been great *successes*, have been admired etc, and belong to a series of published plays that were sold out almost at once'.[50] But by 1899 Wilde was in such straitened financial circumstances that virtually any offer in hard cash would have been accepted.

Although, as confided to a friend, he 'had lost the joy of writing', Wilde still retained a keen interest in all stages of the publication, including the binding designed for him, as with previous plays, by Charles Hazlewood Shannon, because, as Wilde told his new publisher, 'they form a series [and] I want same colour and treatment'.[51] Unlike some of his colleagues Wilde never went in for private printing of his plays, and so the text from which Smithers prepared the published version of *Earnest* was almost certainly a typewritten copy of the prompt copy from the St James's production with, as Wilde insisted, most of the stage directions deleted. In correcting his own proofs for *Earnest*, he also seized the chance to make some small textual revisions, many of which were based on the improvements (those that he could remember) which had been arrived at during rehearsal. Wilde also advised that the relevant back number of the *Era* should be consulted to provide an accurate cast list of the first production. Appropriately, one of the twelve presentation copies of *Earnest*, elegantly printed on Japanese vellum, was sent to Alexander for old time's sake.[52]

To Bernard Shaw the publisher as a species was his 'natural enemy'. Apart from the early play already mentioned, his dramatic work remained unpublished until April 1898, when Grant Richards – whom Shaw playfully described as 'the most incompetent publisher I ever heard of' – brought out the two volumes of *Plays Pleasant and Unpleasant*.[53] Richards, new to publishing in 1896, had been on the lookout for suitable customers but it took him six months' relentless badgering before he successfully persuaded Shaw to publish with him.

Once the decision had been made, Shaw embarked eagerly on the preparatory work. Fastidious as was Wilde in the supervision of the publication of his plays, Shaw easily surpassed him – confident in the knowledge that he was creating works of art for posterity which would set new standards for dramatic publication. No author was so demanding of his publisher; and perhaps no publisher but Richards would have been quite as co-operative, though he did manage to dissuade Shaw from some of his more eccentric notions, such as piebald printing of the two volumes in different colours and typefaces – 'Egyptian mummy color' paper and ugly type for *Plays Unpleasant* and white paper and 'the best Kelmscott style' for *Plays Pleasant* – and charged him an extra £10 6s for proof corrections, the result of Shaw's obsessive attempt to rid the text of its 'rivers of white'.[54] Nonetheless, Shaw's specifications (some of which were derived from his admiration of William Morris's book designs) on margin widths, the abolition of apostrophes, italicisation, on the binding and even the ink to be used for printing were all imposed upon the compliant publisher.

Shaw's intention was to appeal to an essentially novel-reading public. Everything which savoured of the old-fashioned, redundant acting edition was jettisoned. But he was also well aware of their potential as 'practical prompt copies'; and their dual purpose is reflected in stage directions which, while giving readers sufficient information to create the plays in the imagination, also directly inform actors and producers on positioning, gesture, and costume, but in a language which was utterly removed from 'Stabs her 2 R C; sees ghost up C (biz); and exit R.U.E'. His rule was 'never to mention the stage, proscenium or spectators; to discard all technical expressions and insert plenty of descriptive matter; to give sufficient guidance to the theatre management and information to the actor of *what* but not *how* to act – without spoiling anything for the reader'.[55] The public, however, was still not quite ready for it. For all Shaw's efforts – even his publisher admitted to the 'intense pleasure' which the look and feel of the edition gave him – it did not sell as anticipated. Grant Richards commented in retrospect that 'its rate of sale was entirely incommensurate with the amount of notice it attracted and with the reputation which it helped to make for its author'.[56]

If Pinero's published texts, like those of Jones and Wilde, are relatively spare in their appeal to the reader's imagination, Shaw's might be said to overwhelm it. But to Jones's complaint that the text was overloaded with stage directions Shaw retorted that 'to the ordinary reader [they make] all the difference between an intelligible and readable drama and a mere dialogue'.[57] Shaw tried to have the best of both worlds; but the conflicting demands between the acting edition and the reading play were not easily resolved. Jones and Pinero saw themselves primarily as practitioners of the stage with an important but secondary reading audience, while Shaw, who like Wilde set much store by the aesthetic appeal of the printed text, was keen to demonstrate his independence from the commercialised theatre and to cultivate a thinking, reading audience for plays which for the most part had only a limited exposure, or none at all, on the stage. Shaw and Wilde never doubted their place in literature and Pinero had his confirmed by his knighthood awarded in 1909, the first pure dramatist so to be honoured. But in Jones the desire for literary respectability was to some extent unsatisfied. Even the four-volume edition of *Representative Plays* edited by his friend and long-time admirer of his work Clayton Hamilton, published by Little, Brown, & Co. of Boston in 1925 – in fact a belated duplication of Pinero's *Social Plays*, also edited by Hamilton and published in the USA between 1917 and 1922 – wasn't quite good enough. Towards the end of the same year he confessed to his old publisher Frederick Macmillan that it was 'one of the vanities of [his] old age' to have the American edition published in Britain. 'I am so anxious', he noted on a postcard when he returned to the topic a few days later, 'to be a real literary man before I die, and I feel that your publication of the library edition of my plays will instantly secure that result.'[58] Macmillan duly obliged in the following year. Maybe Jones derived as much satisfaction from this final evidence of acceptance into the world of letters as his friend and rival Pinero had had in the award of his knighthood. At the very least, publication of a semi-collected edition under the venerable imprint of Macmillan helped to even up their respective literary accounts.

CHAPTER 6

From wings to centre stage

'If there is an occasion on which I loathe a theatre more than ever', Shaw wrote to Henry Arthur Jones, 'it is on a first night.'[1] Shaw had a general antipathy to footlights and greasepaint and to the whole paraphernalia of the theatre; but it is surprising how many dramatists of the nineteenth century seemed to share his prejudice, though not necessarily for the same reason. Audiences were fractious and unpredictable, frequently inattentive, sometimes dominated by claques, occasionally even given to rioting (as notably at Covent Garden in 1809 and Drury Lane in 1848), and by ancient custom and privilege possessed and not infrequently exercised the power, most terrifying to authors, of damning a new play on its first night. In the course of the century audiences tended to become less volatile and more refined, at least in the more fashionable theatres outside the East End – though there were still disturbances and the police were sometimes needed to keep order. As late as 1880 not only was the Haymarket affected by rowdy protest (over the abolition of the pit) but at the Vaudeville, during the première of Albery's *Jacks and Jills*, when what appeared to be organised opposition constantly interrupted the play, the author had to appear at the footlights and 'with gesticulations of menace and defiance' appeal for calm.[2] The trend, however, was for first nights to become ever grander affairs as the occasion for the assembly of men and women of consequence and fashion. At the St James's in the 1890s they were glittering evenings, though that still didn't stop them from sometimes being dismal failures as well. Perhaps no new author was more crushed by his audience's reaction than Henry James at the première of *Guy Domville* (St J 1893).

Following eighteenth-century custom, it was usual in the earlier part of the century for the manager to appear on stage at the end of the play to crave the audience's indulgence for 'giving out' the play for repetition on a subsequent night. Actors might be called for by the audience but authors weren't. Indeed, it was quite common for the playwright not even to be present. Thomas Morton claimed that he never liked seeing his own plays acted; and though Tom Robertson did attend his own first nights it was not to see the play but to observe the audience and its reaction.[3] Only in the second half of the century does it become customary for the author to be summoned in front of the curtain to accept the plaudits of the audience. And when there was the kind of ecstatic reception that Pinero experienced on the first night of *The Second Mrs Tanqueray* (St J 1893) the dramatist might even be called for between the acts.

Yet, despite the closer relationship that began gradually to evolve between author and audience, the professional dramatist had a natural tendency to wish to preserve his independence, specifically from any notion of patronage. Frederick Reynolds considered that audiences were generally inclined to be good-natured rather than ill-natured and that first nights were 'a fair fight between author and the audience'. Nonetheless the successful playwright had no one to thank but himself: 'a *dramatic writer* is no more indebted to the public for the *money he makes by them*, than is a merchant, banker, or any other active, honourable *speculator*'.[4] Edward Fitzball's belief that dramatists should be heard but not seen was not misplaced reticence; it was simply an aversion to the very idea of audiences calling for the author 'to have a *stare* at him', which, as he observed in his autobiography in 1859, was a recent, much to be regretted, innovation. Likewise, W. G. Wills abhorred as degrading to authorship all such bowing and smiling at the footlights merely to gratify the 'impertinent curiosity of those who want to see what manner of man has written the play'.[5] This self-sufficient view of authorship is perhaps no more graphically illustrated than by Oscar Wilde's appearance on stage at the first night of *Lady Windermere's Fan* (St J 1892), wearing a green carnation and languidly smoking a cigarette, to deliver a curtain-speech congratulating the actors for their charm and the audience for its intelligent, enthusiastic reception of his comedy, 'which persuades me that you think *almost* as highly of the play as I do myself'.[6]

Few authors had the nerve to be quite as sarcastic about audiences as Wilde, though there were admittedly scores of critics prepared to be even ruder about authors. 'Nothing injures an author, especially a dramatic author', Fitzball observed, 'so materially, as *luke-warm praise*'; but being a playwright required a generous thickness of skin and W. S. Gilbert was not alone in making 'a rule of never reading a "slate"'.[7] Most playwrights had no illusions about the dependence of their livelihood on audiences' approval and on that of the critics. At the same time as wishing to preserve or enhance his own integrity as an artist, the professional playwright could never escape awareness also of his interdependence, not only on his patrons at the box-office but on managers, managers' readers, actors, stage crew, and on the simple but vital requirement of the scenery not falling down on the first night. The pattern of authors' professional lives in the Victorian theatre is shaped by a greater understanding of the integrity of the author and, by extension, of what he creates. In terms of status he rises from being regarded as about equivalent to the stage carpenter to a level at least equal with that of his interpreters. Indeed, by the 1890s it might be said that in some cases he was even raised above it. In short, his progress is from unregarded obscurity in the theatrical wings to the glare of centre stage.

When Lord Byron sat on the management sub-committee at Drury Lane in the second decade of the nineteenth century, he was intrigued as well as dismayed to find the theatre's shelves piled high with dusty MS plays – Byron estimated there to be about 500 of them – all submitted by hopeful new authors and all of them unread. But upon investigation he declared 'I do not think that, of those which I saw, there was one which could be conscientiously tolerated.'[8]

In 1800, under the restrictive patent theatre monopoly, openings for new entrants into the dramatic profession were severely limited outside Drury Lane, Covent Garden, and (during the summer) the Haymarket. Over the next two decades the number of minor theatres grew fast. To Sadler's Wells and Astley's (which pre-date 1800) were added by 1820 the Olympic, Adelphi, Surrey, Lyceum (or English Opera House), and the Coburg (or Victoria/Old Vic). But the esteem still enjoyed by the majors (whatever their failings in their attempts to uphold the legitimate drama) was still an attraction to new and aspiring authors. As Tom Dibdin put it, 'a situation in a theatre royal, [was] the grand aim of my ambition'; and Edward Fitzball was no less committed to the idea that writing for Drury Lane was the only course for an author who wanted to write for posterity.[9] Authors complained about the lack of theatres – in 1843 after the ending of the patent monopoly there were twenty-five theatres licensed by the Lord Chamberlain, but by 1866 this number had increased by only one (exclusive of Covent Garden, which was given over to opera after 1847) – while theatre managements (with less justice) complained about the lack of authors. Despite the considerable increase in the number of theatres in London after 1866 – almost all of them in the West End and run on strict commercial principles (some financed by syndicates, which became an increasingly popular form of investment by the turn of the century) – there were relatively few opportunities either for the untried or radical dramatist. Moreover, the phenomenon of the long run, dating from the 1860s, took certain theatres out of the system for long periods and so restricted the field even further.

The resistance of the patent theatres under the monopoly to new plays was largely the result of their financial debility. Contemporary dramatists were not, of course, ignored but, apart from a few with special credentials as sure-fire box-office successes, were certainly undervalued. At Drury Lane under John Philip Kemble's management in the last decade of the eighteenth century so little importance was attached to their encouragement that, according to his first biographer James Boaden, he was reputed not to want new plays at all (except the occasional after-piece or farce), in the belief that the main business of the theatre could be satisfied by 'the treasures of our ancient authors, [which] were inexhaustible'. This was allegedly in marked contrast to Thomas Harris at Covent Garden, whom Boaden praised for having given 'steady encouragement' to new talent.[10] In the first decade of the century Tom Dibdin was Covent Garden's most prolific writer, providing a minimum of two plays per year, more often three or four and once as many as six. At the same time Thomas Morton and Frederick Reynolds were regular writers and between 1810 and 1821 (at the period when Dibdin had moved over to Drury Lane) they, along with a new writer, Isaac Pocock, were the theatre's best-paid authors. By the theatre's own account, from 1822 to June 1832 a total of eighty-two new plays was produced, with Pocock topping the list, closely followed by new-generation playwrights like Planché and R. B. Peake, then at a greater distance by John Howard Payne and Michael Lacy.[11] In truth the record of neither theatre is very impressive in the promotion of new writers for the stage. In the 1816–17 season, at a period when playbills were changed more or less nightly, Covent Garden applied to the Lord Chamberlain for licences for only thirteen new plays, while in the decade beginning in 1822 under Henry Harris (Thomas Harris's son) the average number of new pieces produced fell to just over eight per year. What new talent there was was mainly reserved by the more go-ahead minor theatres.

At the 1832 Committee enquiry, Capt. John Forbes, speaking for both principal patent theatres, stressed that '[t]he greatest pains are taken in every possible way to obtain the best plays', to which end MSS were usually read twice or three times by different readers; but he had to concede that new playwrights were less likely to be read promptly. Exceptionally, Peake, the better part of whose career was in minor drama, claimed that he had never had any difficulty whatever in having a good play accepted.[12] But Edward Fitzball expressed the more common view of 'how difficult it is even to get a play read, much more accepted, by the sometimes over-fastidious managers'. His own career he recognised was unusual in the sense that 'nearly everything which I had written for the stage had been produced'. That included one play from the middle of his writing career, which he was pleased to record finally took the stage some twenty years after completion.[13]

Most authors were irritated by the lengthy interval which almost always ensued between acceptance and production. Planché asserted that he had personally experienced 'a delay which I thought detrimental to my interests, and also to the interests of the theatre'; and T. J. Serle gave several examples of plays which had suffered exceptionally slow production processes, like Knowles's *The Hunchback* and Mary Mitford's *Rienzi* (eventually produced at Drury Lane), which 'lay four years in Covent Garden'. But this was slight in comparison with John Tobin's *Honey Moon*, which supposedly remained unread at Covent Garden for sixteen years.[14]

Play readers, whether professional like Thomas Morton at Drury Lane or more informal like Macready, found it a tedious job. In the early 1830s Morton was probably reading more plays than the Lord Chamberlain's Examiner. Literally hundreds of unsolicited MSS arrived at the theatre, of which only a handful were, in his opinion, worth a second glance. On retirement from the post in 1833 he sent the pile of rejected MSS he had accumulated to his employer, Alfred Bunn, who afterwards printed a selection of his deputy's uninhibited remarks on them in his memoirs: 'sad stuff', 'cannot be acted', 'quite unfitted for representation', 'respectably written – but what use to Drury Lane would a *respectable Saxon* TRAGEDY be?', 'nonsense', 'a bustling affair, but very dangerous'. Bunn commented that the list 'comprises but a small batch of the many I was favoured with from my facetious and yet discerning officer'.[15] Planché also did duty for a time reading plays for Madame Vestris at the Olympic and for Covent Garden, where Kenney nicknamed him appropriately as '*weeder*' to the management; but, like Morton, he found the task disagreeable. In one season at the latter he 'waded . . . through nearly two hundred plays and farces, without finding one I could conscientiously recommend'.[16]

In the first half of the century the reader of plays was an established institution in many of the larger theatres, though Macready was, in this as in other matters, an exception. In consequence of his acting reputation, since the 1820s he had habitually read and offered advice on countless unsolicited MSS pressed upon him by hopeful authors; as a patent theatre manager, however, he gathered around him a kind of 'kitchen cabinet' whose business it was to comment on and judge plays before they reached the green-room. Though Macready always took the final decision himself, he accepted that management was a collective affair. Likely prospects were first tried out on his family and then on a group which he called his council, comprising Charles Dickens and John Forster as regular members, sometimes augmented by others such as Serle, Blanchard, Talfourd, Bulwer Lytton, Browning, journalists like W. J. Fox and Albany Fonblanque, and the painter George Cattermole, who could always be relied upon to offer a disinterested opinion.

Macready's arrangements foreshadow the declining significance of the post of reader, which fell into disuse early in the second half of the century as managers relied more heavily on their own instinct and judgement. Nonetheless Fitzball, who succeeded Morton at Drury Lane, believed firmly in the usefulness of authors as managers' readers. Under the management of James Anderson at Drury Lane in the early 1850s, he describes himself as sitting 'like an owl in a cobwebby corner of the theatre, cogitating over incomprehensibilities'. No one else, he submitted, could properly judge the rhythm and tone of a piece except a practised author, as he was neither an actor looking for a good part nor a manager seeking 'money-drawing points'. When Tom Taylor came to comment on the office in 1879 it was already old-fashioned; yet he was not alone in lamenting its disappearance and with it the loss of that independence of mind which a manager's reader of plays nominally represented, especially if he happened to be an author himself.[17]

Although the easiest (and certainly cheapest) way for a manager to fill up his playbills was to stage adaptations of the latest novelties from Paris, it must not be supposed that all managers were uniformly hostile or indifferent to native drama. Some actively encouraged authors, even at the patent theatres. Robert Elliston tried (though unsuccessfully) to interest Scott, Thomas Moore, and others to write for the Drury Lane stage; George

Colman was a keen supporter of home-grown products at the Haymarket when he could afford it; and Ben Webster at the same theatre in the 1840s and early 1850s – perhaps because he was a playwright himself – enjoyed unusually friendly and productive relations with his authors such as Mark Lemon, Douglas Jerrold, and Dion Boucicault. In John Westland Marston's experience he never attempted 'to beat down the price of a piece by depreciation – by remarking, for instance, that it was risky, or that times were hard'.[18] Ironically, Webster's most dedicated attempt to stimulate new writing – the offer in 1843 of a £500 prize for the best comedy submitted – was a signal failure. Selected by committee, the winning entry, Mrs Catherine Gore's *Quid pro Quo; or, the Day of Dupes* (Hay 1844), was hooted off the stage on the first night. Like Webster, Macready had a keen eye for a good script both as actor and actor-manager. But he was a dutiful rather than enthusiastic reader of new plays: 'how much time', he wrote, 'I am forced to expend in this kind of unprofitable labour!'[19] However, his taste for legitimate drama fostered the dramatic aspirations of Browning, Mary Mitford, Barry Cornwall, and Sheridan Knowles. Moreover, Bulwer Lytton, perhaps his most important collaborator, would in all probability never have made it to the stage without Macready's constant reassurance, encouragement, and practical assistance.

Most of the vigour and the vividness of nineteenth-century drama was concentrated in the minor theatres. As the patent theatres dwindled, so the minors prospered. Some were blessed with exceptionally astute management and they acted as nurseries for aspiring playwrights. Able managers, quick enough to recognise (and, perhaps what is equally to the point, exploit) dramatic talent when they saw it, could produce spectacular results. Robert Elliston, though defeated by patent theatre management at Drury Lane, had special managerial talents which were put to good effect in the minors. On form (and sober) he had few equals. It was Elliston who brought Dibdin to the Surrey in 1810 and William Thomas Moncrieff as house dramatist to the Olympic in 1816. During his second term at the Surrey he persuaded Edward Fitzball to write for him and enticed

Douglas Jerrold as resident playwright there, describing him in 1829 as 'the most rising Dramatist that we have'.[20] Though Planché's longest partnership was with Madame Vestris (at the Olympic from 1831, then at Covent Garden and the Lyceum), his earliest debts were to the actor John Harley at Drury Lane and to managers Stephen Kemble and Elliston, who encouraged him 'to be a dramatist in earnest'.[21]

The de-regulation of the theatres in 1843, contrary to some expectations, produced no sudden explosion of formerly repressed dramatic talent. But while Covent Garden and Drury Lane virtually ceased to have any material role in the encouragement of new drama, fresh sources of dramatic skill did appear at the Haymarket, where Webster's successor John Baldwin Buckstone's continuity of management and ready enthusiasm for new writing assisted dramatists as diverse in quality and range as Tom Taylor and Charles Reade (with *Masks and Faces* in 1852), Leicester Buckingham, Westland Marston, and W. S. Gilbert. At Sadler's Wells, under the lengthy and benign management of Samuel Phelps, the author list included recently established writers like Tom Taylor and also more hazardous propositions, such as F. G. Tomlins, and John Abraham Heraud, the dramatic critic of the *Illustrated London News*.[22] Even John Hollingshead at the Gaiety in the late 1860s, though he never publicly pledged support for native British drama, was nonetheless proud of his achievement in 1869, when three out of his five plays for the season were original plays from native authors: Robertson, Gilbert, and H. J. Byron. At the Lyceum, Irving had a reputation for neglecting contemporary drama but he did try to encourage new playwrights and sustain more experienced ones, like W. G. Wills, Frank Marshall, Richard Voss, H. T. Johnson, Burnand, H. Guy Carleton and others. Possibly more than anyone else of the period, Wilson Barrett (Henry Arthur Jones's earliest mentor) proved most useful to the younger writers. As Clement Scott pointed out, '[m]any of our most successful dramatists owe their first start in [theatrical] life to him'.[23] Amongst the new actor-managers in the last quarter of the century, John Hare, the Kendals, Herbert Beerbohm Tree, and George Alexander were probably the most adventurous.

Always full of good intentions, Tree announced in 1890 that during established runs he proposed to reserve Monday nights at the Haymarket for new plays, preferably by native British authors. Equally if not more solicitous of new dramatic talent was Alexander, whose St James's Theatre was described as 'the nursery of the modern drama'.[24] It was a well-deserved reputation. In a managerial career spanning twenty-seven years he was responsible for a total of sixty-two full-length plays and nineteen one-acters, of which just eight were of foreign origin.

At the same time, however, the long run (usually reckoned to comprise more than 100 consecutive performances) – a feature which began to attract notice in the 1860s and took firm root in the 1870s – materially altered the theatrical climate for the worse by tending to squeeze new aspirants to the stage out of the market. Such long-running successes as *Our American Cousin*, *The Ticket-of-Leave Man*, *The Colleen Bawn*, *The Streets of London*, *The Octoroon*, and *Our Boys* effectively meant that whole theatrical seasons and longer (sometimes much longer, as with the last-named) could be sustained on perhaps a single play. It was Dion Boucicault's view, as he informed the 1866 Committee, that there simply were not enough theatres to go round. And, while readily agreeing that for the past fourteen months he had been one of the prime culprits by monopolising both the Princess's and 'to a great extent' the Adelphi, Boucicault declared that consideration for his fellow authors had prompted him to retire 'about seven months ago for the purpose of leaving the space free for a year'. In consequence, though it was a purely voluntary decision, he had been 'deprived of the market that I am entitled to, and would have, if there were more theatres in London, and if there were plenty of room for all'.[25]

However, the problem was not so much the number of theatres, though after 1866 this did begin to increase quite substantially, but the inherent conservatism of theatre managements. Sydney Grundy in 1879, as representative of the new generation of late Victorian playwrights, accused the leading London managers of being party to what was in effect a conspiracy to deny proper opportunities to new writers, resulting in 'the almost absolute extinction of English dramatic authorship'. It had been murdered out of existence, he argued, by the over-cautious and self-interested behaviour of the managers, who operated (albeit not consciously) a dramatic ring. New and original drama was ignored on a simple but disastrous principle of collective managerial cowardice which favoured only what was tried and tested.[26] Indeed, to a somewhat tongue-in-cheek John Hollingshead, the dramatic world had effectively narrowed to 'about three dramatic authors' and 'two recognised English adapters' from the French. In the competitive London theatre, managers were said to be at the mercy of the few reliable playwrights, who demanded careful and respectful treatment 'like a duchess at a Civil Service store'.[27]

But as Grundy well knew from his own experience, the only kind of play from a young and inexperienced author which stood any remote chance of acceptance was farce, in which he achieved considerable early success with *The Snowball* (Str 1879). He yearned to be a serious writer but, as he wrote to William Archer, 'I can, however, place nothing but farcical pieces.' 'If you want to make way as a playwright, at once give over writing or adapting good plays, like "The Supports of Society" [his translation of Ibsen's *Pillars of Society*]. There is no market for them. You must write rot before you will be allowed to write sense.' More than a year later he was reporting to Archer that 'I have hawked about what I consider good work, from theatre to theatre, till I am wearied out. Hitherto, I have kept clear of absolute inanity and drivel, but they *will* have it.'[28]

Managers, it is true, were not generally well disposed to accept serious new drama because of the commercial risks. But the introduction of matinée performances did help the untried playwright by offering him a chance of stage exposure. Hollingshead claimed to have introduced such 'trial trips of actors, actresses, authors, and pieces' at the Gaiety as early as 1871;[29] but while matinées became reasonably common during the 1880s as a source of extra managerial revenue by extending the number of performances possible in a week, it was not until the 1890s, under managers like Beerbohm Tree and George Alexander, that they really performed the function intended, that is, as alternatives to, rather than duplications of, the regular evening bill. In 1891 Tree listed Outram Tristram, Walter Besant, and Clotilde Graves as examples of new authors who had all benefited in this way.[30] For managers the advantage was that new talent could be given a trial without committing the theatre's resources – in other words the evenings could still be devoted to money-making plays – but, as Archer later pointed out, for any author new or established 'the one really decisive test [is] that of a regular evening performance'.[31] To a new playwright looking for an opening on the London stage, Shaw advised that his chances of acceptance were as good or better if he submitted his script to one of the leading performers of the day (in the hope of his being attracted by a good part) rather than to over-cautious and over-burdened managers. As for himself, the disincentives attached to being a radical and adventurous author were still as real as ever. As he wrote in 1896, '[n]owadays, no manager will produce one of my plays as long as there is one by Grundy available – or Jones, or Pinero, or Carton &c.'[32]

Important though the manager was in the decision-making process for a new play, the role of the actor or, more precisely, the acting company was if anything even more crucial. And what is more to the point, nothing was more crucial for the author in the actual writing process, since the play was in a very real sense determined by the available actors. Until late in the century when the practice of seeking out actors for specific roles in West End plays began to be accepted practice, few managers would be disposed to buy a new piece unless it could be cast from his pre-existing company, which contained actors who specialised in certain 'lines of business'. At a minimum this certainly required suitably prestigious parts for his leading players and probably also for those such as his 'low comedian' and 'eccentric comedian', his most individual players and amongst his most valuable assets in box-office terms. Indeed, in some cases, the relationship between play and acting company was so close that the MS might be written out initially with the names of the actors rather than the names of the characters.[33]

For well over half a century plays tended to be bespoke for a particular company so that a new play was always judged on its appositeness to resources rather than its intrinsic merits. At the 1832 Committee, Douglas Jerrold stated that his most recent play had been refused at the Haymarket because Morris 'said he did not think it would suit his company';[34] but it was later mounted at the Strand. The necessary congruity between play and acting company or at least the available leading actors lies at the heart of playwriting for much of the nineteenth century. There is a direct ratio between the success of early dramatists like Morton and Reynolds and the brilliance of the acting companies they wrote for. R. B. Peake attributed the success of his best play to date – *Before Breakfast* (EOH 1826) – as purely dependent on the presence in the company of Charles Mathews (for whom he had written it) and implied that Mathews's absence from the company since then had reduced his chances of further success.[35] Some later playwrights became reliant not on a company but on one specific actor: Knowles and Bulwer Lytton depended upon Macready, just as W. G. Wills at the Lyceum wrote only with Irving in mind. Although such close liaisons between actor and author could often be fruitful and highly successful, it is also true that they tended to cramp the range of dramatic writing and in no small degree reinforced the belief that the Victorian period was, in essence and in practice, an actor's rather than a dramatist's theatre. Henry Arthur Jones still complained about the practice of writing plays to order for a leading performer in 1891 and considered it responsible 'for the literary degradation of the modern drama and for the just contempt with which it has been viewed by the intellect of the nation during the last twenty-five years'.[36] Nevertheless, both Jones and Pinero did help to bring about an important change of practice, as the critical task of casting was shifted to a point after completion of the play rather than before starting to write it.

Beyond the manager lay the green-room, a crucially important hurdle in the progression of a new play to production. The primary function of this room, so called, it is said, from the colour of its traditional decoration and furnishings, was to serve as a common-room where actors and actresses would congregate during performances while not required on stage and where behind-the-scenes visitors might be received. At Covent Garden

during the Vestris–Mathews era the first green-room, handsomely fitted out with chandeliers and mirrors, was 'a most
agreeable lounging-place . . . where one could pass a pleasant
hour in the society of charming women and men of gentlemanly
manners, and from which was banished every word or allusion
that would not be tolerated in a drawing-room'.[37] But the
generally relaxed club-like atmosphere of green-rooms,
especially at the patent theatres, belied the inevitable frictions
that existed between some performers. For the dramatic author
it was alien and often intimidating territory because it was here
that his newly accepted play was first introduced and read in its
entirety to the acting company. In acquainting the actors with
the general character and development of a new piece, green-
room readings served an essential function in an age which, until
late in the century, perpetuated a practice, stretching back to
Elizabethan times, whereby individual actors were at no time in
possession of the full dramatic text, but merely of their own parts
and associated cues. Here before the tribunal of the green-room
an author's play could be made or broken.

The conceit of actors and singers was almost proverbial.
Generally until about 1860 the power and status of leading
actors in the nineteenth-century theatre reduced the dramatic
author to the role of a tradesman obsequiously offering his wares
to clients who had powers to reject them entirely or, at the very
least, to require substantial alterations to adapt the text to their
own notions of what constituted an appropriately strong and
theatrical part. Leading members of companies, jealously
guarding their positions by insisting on equality of status and
length of part with their fellows, were notoriously difficult to
please. Green-room readings were seized upon by the actors at
all levels and turned into occasions for status-seeking, to the
extent that 'star' performers were able to refuse parts if it was
discovered that superior roles were allotted to others.

Most leading players were permitted, under the terms of their
engagements, complete freedom in choice of part in all new
pieces. In George Colman's *John Bull* (CG 1803), Munden
refused his part (Sir Simon Rochdale) because his rival Fawcett
had a better role (as Job Thornberry). At the reading of

Planché's *The Knights of the Round Table* (Hay 1854) George Vandenhoff, much to the surprise of the manager and the disappointment of the author, selected the villain of the piece (a swindler and gambler) instead of the hero, the part intended for him by Planché. Ostensibly, he wished to avoid having to make love to the leading lady (whom he judged immoral), but he confessed that 'I thought I saw, besides, that Captain Cozens might be made the strong character of the drama: the result justified my judgment.'[38]

On the whole, dramatists would have found that the behaviour of their listeners ranged between attentive courtesy and silent indifference. George Colman junior apparently kept his green-room audiences rapt by the accuracy of his rendering of character.[39] But unknown authors could expect a grisly ordeal and even more experienced writers sometimes suffered. Frederick Reynolds had a chilly reception from the Covent Garden company at the end of his reading of *The Dramatist* (1789), when 'even my hero, Lewis, disliked his part'. And Tom Dibdin, though respected by the company as author and actor, reported that he was forced to write twenty different musical subjects before he could overcome the resistance of his leading actor-singers (Incledon, Braham, and Mme Storace) in his production of *The Cabinet* (CG 1802). On one particularly frustrating morning he nearly walked out of the theatre, carrying his MS with him.[40]

Gruelling though the exerience could be, the author normally read his play in person, but the task might be farmed out to an actor, stage manager, or prompter. Macready, as actor-manager, tended to do it himself in the case of important plays, especially when the author did not have the voice for it. Bulwer Lytton, for instance, was notorious for his unease as a public speaker (in spite of his parliamentary experience) and Macready read all of his plays for him. Dickens, on the other hand (whom Macready described as reading 'as well as an experienced actor would – he is a surprising man') read his own farce, *The Lamplighter*. But when Macready had the elderly prompter John Wilmott read Browning's *A Blot in the 'Scutcheon* (DL 1843), it was reported that the actors had 'laughed at it'.[41]

Those authors with some acting experience tended to fare better at this important task than others. Sheridan Knowles, with a long history of acting behind him (though none of it especially distinguished), was nothing if not distinctive. His reading of *Old Maids* (CG 1841) was performed 'in a loud, rollicking style, with marked emphasis, a theatrical effect, and strong dashes of the [Irish] brogue'; but he was described also as having the much-prized Victorian virtues of 'earnest intensity' and 'natural pathos'.[42] Certainly in the hands of a skilful author-actor this initial reading served as a useful starting-point for actors' interpretations of their parts. Later in the century the Bancrofts considered Boucicault, Robertson, Gilbert and Pinero especially useful in this respect. Each possessed the ability to hold their green-room audiences with expressive, animated readings, as did Francis Burnand, even though his acting experience was limited to the amateur stage. But H. J. Byron, despite his later modest success as an actor, was represented as 'devoid of the power'.[43]

From the green-room plays eventually found their way into rehearsal. Once again authors were normally expected to be present at least some of the time. At the patent theatres at the turn of the century rehearsal time for a new play varied considerably. Covent Garden gave Elizabeth Inchbald a week for *Lovers' Vows* (1798) and nearly three weeks for *Wives As They Were* (1797), though in actual time this might have amounted to no more than Richard Cumberland's nine hours for *The Wheel of Fortune* and fifteen hours for *The Jew*, both at Drury Lane in 1794.[44] Theatrical exigencies sometimes reduced this period even further: Robert Elliston did not even finish casting Byron's *Marino Faliero* (DL 1821) until a week before production date. At the minor theatres, where the helter-skelter of production was second nature, rehearsals would in general have been considerably shorter, sometimes in the case of *pièces de circonstance* as little as a day; in other words about as long as it took the author to write it.

New authors were habitually treated with scant respect. Reynolds relates how at the rehearsal for his tragedy *Werter* (Bath 1785), the actors 'took not the slightest notice' of his instructions and the actresses treated him with such 'cool contempt' that he was deposed by the managers, who installed themselves as 'viceroys over me'.[45] On the whole, Edward Fitzball's experience at Covent Garden was pleasant enough – rehearsals there in the late 1820s he described as 'agreeable and intellectual' – but his tragedy *Walter Tyrrel* (1837), though 'greatly approved in the green room', ran into difficulties when, in the midst of rehearsals, his leading actor John Vandenhoff quarrelled with the manager and peremptorily decamped for the USA.[46] No less inconveniently, William Farren, as Shekel the money-lender in Douglas Jerrold's *The Bride of Ludgate* (DL 1831), withdrew from the play on the day before its first performance. Such unsettling experiences were common for authors throughout the period. Their frequency led Reynolds to comment on the exception: his rehearsal of *Notoriety* (CG 1791), at which the actors were so keen on their parts and 'the stage business proceeded with such unusual concord, and with such expressions of satisfaction from all parties, that for once in my life, I found a rehearsal, an agreeable morning lounge'.[47]

Reynolds's description aptly sums up the character of rehearsals in the early part of the century. Their purpose was to allow actors to run through standard moves with no attempt made to work at character or expression, since that was considered exclusively the province of the actor involved, who interpreted or elaborated upon his text as he pleased. For this reason the author's role at rehearsal was in general fairly minimal, pushed into the background not just by actors but by all the paraphernalia of stage machinery and specialist contrivances for the creation of special effects, like waterfalls, cliff rescues, and conflagrations, in which the nineteenth-century theatre delighted. James Boaden discloses that as author he was forced into private tutoring of Palmer for his performance as Schedoni in *The Italian Monk* (Hay 1797). Most of the time it seems that the author was simply present to witness the mutilation of his text either to suit an actor who thought he could improve it or a stage manager who took a fancy to recasting his whole play. For Catherine Crowe, the affronted author of *The Cruel Kindness* (Hay 1853) – her only play – there was no defence against the incongruity of John Baldwin Buckstone's having 'greatly changed and broadened' his comic role in her serious drama because he called the tune as both actor and manager.[48]

The indiscipline of actors, which so evidently irritated Shakespeare, was just as common in the nineteenth century. An inability to stick to the authorised text afflicted even major performers. Dowton was notorious for his 'treacherous memory' and Planché recalled his saying to an author 'D[am]n your dialogue! give me the situations.'[49] In his dual role as author and stage manager Tom Dibdin – in response to the introduction of anachronisms and the conversion of his Chinese characters in *The Chinese Sorcerer* (DL 1823) to broad Cockneys – resorted at one stage to pinning up a notice in the green-room to the effect that the actors should speak no more than was writ down for them. Such an unprecedented and autocratic assertion of authorial control provoked the actors into taking Dibdin's caution literally, so that, as James Winston records,

the piece [went] off very dully – their jokes being the only ones in the piece. They sent an answer to Dibdin nearly as follows – Mr Elliston gave the performers a *carte blanche* to say what they please as they could say nothing worse than what [he] had given them. They would do that [which] would prevent the author ever sending them such another piece, it being beneath their talents, etc., etc.[50]

Dibdin maintained that it was only when he had his own theatre that 'this improper practice' was eliminated. In other circumstances it was possible only where the acting or stage manager was sufficiently authoritative to discharge habitual miscreants who, as he put it, set 'at naught the interests, experience, and feelings of an author'.[51]

The terms 'acting' and 'stage' managers in the first half of the nineteenth century are to some extent interchangeable. Broadly speaking, however, the former (as in the case of Winston at Drury Lane during the Elliston regime between 1819 and 1827) was in charge of the actors and all the ancillary staff of the theatre, their contracts of employment, their pay, and in many respects acted as a kind of deputy manager of the theatre. The stage manager, as his name implies, had charge of the stage: the scene-painters, the carpenters, the wardrobe; and was generally more closely involved with authors. He functioned as intermediary when necessary in the sometimes awkward triangular relationship between author, manager, and actor. In addition he was responsible for despatching a copy of the MS to the Examiner of Plays for licensing at the Lord Chamberlain's Office, blocking the play, arranging the business (reproducing any such business attached by convention to an old play with all the accuracy he could muster), and supervising the actual performance from back-stage. He was also sometimes responsible for casting the play (though in the first half of the century at Covent Garden, for example, this was normally done by the proprietors or manager) and for cutting it to a length suitable for the performing slot into which it had to fit – but again actor-managers like John Philip and Charles Kemble, and especially Macready, often appropriated this function themselves.

Stage or acting managers were expected to be in constant, more or less daily, attendance at rehearsal, though not all did so. Alfred Bunn, for instance, was notorious for his absenteeism from Drury Lane while he was stage manager there in the 1820s. His duties were more or less equivalent to those of the prompter, another essential cog in the early nineteenth-century theatrical machine. But as Tom Dibdin (who had experience in both capacities) recorded, the latter, though 'as important . . . in his place as the main-spring of a watch', yet 'has all the arduous tasks of stage management to perform without being entitled to the credit or profits of any of them'. Fitzball commented in 1859 that the old whip-cracking sort of stage manager had disappeared and that in general 'these things are now, I rejoice to say, *much* improved'.[52]

William Charles Macready is generally credited with having introduced a form of rehearsal which approximates more closely to that of the present day than anything previously. As an actor he incurred much mockery and some resentment within the profession for his addiction to rehearsal. During periods as manager of the patent theatres his insistence upon careful and often lengthy rehearsal of individual scenes and with individual actors was in direct contrast to the perfunctoriness and sometimes downright carelessness of most earlier practices. Leading actors of the early nineteenth century, as a matter of principle, almost never rehearsed their roles in old plays which formed part of their habitual repertoire, but they were sometimes equally negligent about new ones. George Colman junior claimed that *The Iron Chest* (DL 1796) failed purely on account of J. P. Kemble's gross inattention to rehearsal and published a preface (later suppressed) which said so.[53] By contrast, it is clear from Macready's diaries that rehearsals for Bulwer Lytton's first play *The Duchess de la Vallière* (CG 1837) took a whole month, much of which was spent in a team effort between John Forster, the author, and himself to improve the text. Rehearsals for the same author's *Money* (Hay 1840) extended to more than six weeks of difficulty and frustration. Lytton's presence at some of them was counter-productive and after one particularly difficult occasion Macready noted that he 'became very nervous – quite ill-tempered, and spoke harshly to the actors – haughtily, I should say, certainly unphilosophically'.[54]

To some extent, the professionalism of Macready's rehearsals helped to break the power of the actors and stage manager over the staging of plays. In this shift of control the author began to move away from the periphery of the representational process into a more central position whereby he could assert his own power over movement, gesture and, perhaps above all, characterisation and expression.

When, according to custom, Charles Mathews began adapting the dialogue of Boucicault's *Old Heads and Young Hearts* (Hay 1844) to suit his own tastes, the author flatly refused to accept the changes. Mathews' later report of the altercation claims that Boucicault had stated: 'I want no one's opinion but my own as to the *consistency* of the characters I draw – your business is to utter what I create.' For his part Mathews refused to subscribe to 'this inflated view of the relative positions of actor and dramatist' and both he and Madame Vestris withdrew from the production.[55] But in an equally uncompromising display of the power of the playwright Charles Reade insisted that an author knew better than any actor 'the meaning of his own words' and that in consequence author-centred rehearsals were a vital condition of theatrical success. 'How ludicrous', he commented, 'is the amour-propre of English actors . . . A play of mine loses so enormously when not rehearsed by me, that I fear I shall always torment them for the sake of my own credit.' And in illustration of the point he compared the two productions of his play *The Ladies' Battle*, one at 'a second-rate theatre under my rehearsal, [the Haymarket in November 1851] and at a first-rate theatre under Leigh Murray's [the Olympic in May 1851]'.[56]

Reade's friend and sometime collaborator Tom Taylor held similarly radical views. At Sadler's Wells in the late 1850s he was fortunate to find in Samuel Phelps a sympathetic and enlightened manager who allowed him to put his ideas into practice. Of his play *The Fool's Revenge* (1859), which had a successful and considerable run, Taylor records that it was 'the only one of all my plays put on the stage absolutely as it was sent into the theatre, without alteration of a scene, a speech, or even a line, as far as I remember, at rehearsal'. Rehearsals with Phelps were the epitome of what he considered they should be: a 'continuous, well-considered, patient, shaping of the play for public performance, in which not merely the groupings and movements of the personages were attended to, but the delivery of every speech watched, nay, the emphasis and pronunciation of every word noted'. Taylor described some actors with whom he had to deal as 'absurdly dense'; but he knew what he wanted and was prepared to drill his cast until he got it. In the case of *The Fool's Revenge* this amounted to three weeks of 'patient and laborious rehearsal'.[57]

The 1860s were described by Marie Bancroft as 'the era of much stage slovenliness'.[58] But the Bancrofts' management of the Prince of Wales was exceptional for their attention to detail in the careful dressing of their sets and their recognition of the importance of rehearsal as a process of fine-tuning. At rehearsal with irascible characters like Dion Boucicault they had to tread warily. As they recalled, Boucicault, though kind, was also extremely autocratic, so much so that they scarcely dared to interfere directly. Their occasional suggestions were cloaked under the pretence that such and such business was the author's own idea but 'discarded too hastily at a previous rehearsal'.[59] With Tom Robertson there was no such awkwardness. His notions of how his play should be acted and staged accorded perfectly with their own. Of rehearsals for *Society* (1865) Marie Bancroft observed that 'my views of acting so entirely agreed with Mr Robertson's that we encountered no difficulties what-soever, and everything went smoothly and merrily'. Rehearsals for *Caste* (1867), she notes, were for Robertson 'a labour of love'.[60]

To be sure, Robertson was no sentimental dreamer. On the contrary, he was a tough, practical man of the theatre schooled in just about every aspect of it, from stagehand upwards. His meticulous stage directions in his printed texts (including comments on dress and sometimes even accent) are, among other things, expressive of his desire to retain a measure of control over their staging after the plays' release into the public domain. W. S. Gilbert, who was allowed unlimited access to Robertson's rehearsals, was fully aware of his debt to his slightly elder colleague for teaching him so much about the mechanics of stagecraft. Indeed, as far as Gilbert was concerned, Robertson 'invented modern stage-management'.[61]

The reversal of the traditional stances of actor and playwright and elimination of managerial interference was at the heart of Boucicault's strategy in acquiring full control over the products of his pen. Gilbert, Arthur Pinero, Henry Arthur Jones and Bernard Shaw looked to achieve similar objectives. In this respect the author's superintendence of rehearsals and the authority that he acquired as a result was vital for the development of the playwright's professional integrity and independence. While to a large extent Boucicault fought and won his own corner, Gilbert was keen to pass on advice to new authors and encourage them to demand what he had begun to obtain by sheer determination and, in some cases, even the threat of litigation. Any author who was not his own stage manager was, in Gilbert's view, 'certainly at a serious disadvantage'.[62]

As autocratic as Boucicault, utterly unyielding on the absolute authority of his text, and determined that all authors should be guaranteed proper and adequate rehearsal as of right, Gilbert knew from experience just how cavalierly authors could be treated. His own comedy *On Guard* (Crt 1871) he describes as having been 'pitch-forked on to the stage in ten days'.[63] There was perhaps nothing particularly unusual about the shortness of the rehearsal period – for instance, when Boucicault staged *The Colleen Bawn* in New York it was written, rehearsed and produced all in the space of nine days – but Gilbert was insistent that the success of a play was directly proportionate to the amount of time spent in rehearsals. Almost all of Gilbert's successes up to 1872 had a minimum of between three and four weeks' rehearsal. In a letter to James Albery, he announced that he intended to call together 'all the leading dramatic authors' in an attempt to persuade them to stand up for their rights – 'the claims of dramatic authors to such full and satisfactory preparation of their pieces as is always accorded to them on the French stage'.[64] Following Gilbert's lead, Albery made it a rule always to supervise his own rehearsals.

Gilbert's forthright role in the advancement of the professional status of the playwright was impressive in execution and lasting in effect. For Gilbert, the author had absolute authority over every aspect of the play and its production, including a voice in casting and on costume. His mission was to wrest control of his plays not just from the actors but from managerial meddling as well. To Buckstone in 1872 he insisted that his pieces should not be performed in public 'until three days after a rehearsal in which all the "cast" are letter perfect'; whilst to John Hare in 1875 he observed that his opinions on casting 'should go – not only for *something*, but for a *very great deal*'.[65] In effect, at an early stage Gilbert usurped the stage manager's function. Though most productions carried a nominal stage manager he was hardly deserving of the title. It may be assumed that Edward Righton's experience of being 'entirely guided by the wishes of the author' – he was one of the principal actors as well as 'stage manager' in Gilbert's cheeky political burlesque *The Happy Land* (Crt 1873) – was very much the norm.[66] Gilbert's development of a model stage for blocking purposes, in which the actors were represented by small pieces of wood, completed his revolution in the art of authorial stage management. Its efficiency was such that he boasted to Archer that he 'sometimes had a piece perfect, so far as stage-management was concerned, in four rehearsals'.[67] Many of Gilbert's practices gradually found wide acceptance. 'If nothing else has been accomplished for the drama's sake nowadays', wrote Robert Reece in 1879, 'the confidence of managers in the intelligence of dramatists is, at least, established.' The argument that authors could not be trusted as directors of their own works was now 'a fast fading fallacy'; an author's place was in the theatre, supervising rehearsals.[68]

But while it is evident that Gilbert had much influence in establishing the authority of the author, it would be misleading to suppose that all playwrights shared his aspirations or, indeed, that they were capable of effective production control. W. G. Wills, for example, rarely attended rehearsals and was generally so little interested in the details of performance that his plays contained almost nothing in the way of stage directions. In rehearsal he was irritated at requests from actors or managers to make alterations in his text. But while preferring to leave interpretation 'to the imagination of the actors', he was also, as Ellen Terry records, sometimes willing to speak privately to them and in her case to 'tell me things which were most illuminating'.[69] His indifference to the minutiae of performance and interpretation was shared by his contemporary H. J. Byron. Unlike the former he was willing to write during rehearsals (which he abhorred) anything that was wanted, as and when required, but he was just as uninterested as Wills in the way that his text was represented on stage: he delegated 'the task of putting everything together to the actors, the stage manager, the musical director, and the manager'.[70] Late to arrive and early to leave, Byron by all accounts tended to prefer a seat in a nearby bar-room or club to the author's place in the stalls.

There was no such disdain for his appointed role in the case of Arthur Pinero. By the mid-1880s he had made further inroads into territory which traditionally had lain outside the author's direct control. Not only was he positively in charge of his own productions on the London stage, but his influence extended in varying degrees to specifications for performances in the USA and Australia. Set and costume designs from the first run were sold to foreign managers as an integral part of the deal. Pinero exercised firmest authority in America through establishing close links with R. M. Field in Boston and Augustin Daly in New York. During negotiations with the latter for *The Magistrate* in 1885 Pinero insisted that the American production should realise fully the original intentions of the author, as reflected in its London performance, which he stressed had been 'produced here under my sole direction and is animated with the life and character I have instilled into it'. A year later Pinero prepared to sail to New York to supervise personally the production of *The Hobby Horse* in order 'to give it the exact tone'.[71]

The St James's under George Alexander's management, to which Pinero returned in 1893 after a long absence, was a highly disciplined theatre, where rehearsals began promptly at 11 o'clock and finished equally promptly at 2 o'clock. As author-director in charge of his own rehearsals he gained a reputation for dictatorial benevolence in his dealings with actors, though everyone recognised his skill at the job. Mrs Patrick Campbell well remembered 'the awful fatigue' of rehearsals for *The Second Mrs Tanqueray*, and Pinero's imposing on actors 'every piece of characterisation – every inflection'. Many of the readings and gestures, she claimed, which critics had praised in his interpreters were actually introduced at the prompting of the author. Cyril Maude (playing Cayley Drummle) confirms that Pinero instructed all his actors with 'extraordinary care and attention', and that Mrs Pat in particular was tutored every inch of the way in her part of Paula Tanqueray: '[h]e taught her every word and every look'.[72]

The playwright in the role of author-director was confined to a relatively small, but influential group of leading West End writers. His presence in a theatre which by this period was having to assimilate a new breed of actor-managers tended, however, to produce a sometimes uneasy, even explosive, mix. Actor-managers had their own mark to make in the theatre and their ascendancy had serious implications for the role of the dramatic author. Writing in 1886, William Archer had singled out W. S. Gilbert as perhaps the one playwright with sufficient force of personality, determination, and 'mastery of the stage' likely to resist the growing autocracy of the actor-manager.[73]

Certainly Gilbert, who had a reputation of ruling at the Savoy with iron-like discipline, was at the forefront of the struggle, but Pinero and Jones also emerged as combatants in the same field, as did, at a lesser level, Grundy and R. C. Carton. Jones believed passionately in the idea that the author ought to be 'actor, theatre manager and stage manager in one', arguing that this combination 'brings the whole play into connection with the mind and direction of the man who wrote it'. But at London's West End theatres the 1890s were dominated by a string of actor-managers – Irving, Alexander, Beerbohm Tree, Lewis Waller, Mrs John Wood, Terry, Wyndham, and J. L. Toole – who were at their period of greatest power. It was, as Jones observed, a system ideally suited to 'the glorification of the actor' and simultaneously to 'the discouragement of the author'.[74] Shaw put the issue even more forcefully: 'the effect of the actor-manager system is to impose on every dramatic author who wishes his work produced in first-rate style, the condition that there shall be a good part for the actor-manager in it . . . The strongest fascination at a theatre is the fascination of the actor or actress, not the author.'[75]

Dramatists had always written plays with the requirements of specific acting companies or individuals in mind, including earlier actor-managers like Vestris and Mathews or Macready. Few authors with pretensions to stage performance could afford to ignore that basic fact of theatrical life. Jones's solution to the problem was to have a leading dramatist as director and manager of a London theatre, a role in which he felt Pinero might be most beneficially cast.[76] What was different in the 1890s from previous decades (even from the 1880s) was the sheer numbers of actor-managers and the difficulty of having a play accepted in the West End anywhere other than at an actor-managed theatre.

The artistic integrity of the author was not of course actively threatened in every case, but the strengths and weaknesses of the actor-manager system in relation to dramatic authors are well illustrated by George Alexander, who had professional contact with many of the leading dramatists at the turn of the century. During the run of *Liberty Hall* (St J 1892), R. C. Carton wrote:

'No dramatic author was ever more fortunate in his company – and *his manager*!' More surprisingly, Jones, who had no love for actor-managers as a species, also appreciated his working methods: of preparations for *The Masqueraders* (1894), he commented that he had 'never had so pleasant an association with any theatre as I have lately had with yours'.[77] This was a high compliment because Jones was, as his daughter confirmed, 'like a great many authors, difficult at rehearsals'. Having, unlike his colleagues, no acting background, Jones made a point of learning the art of direction by personal involvement in the production of all his plays, an apprenticeship which began with *The Silver King* (P'cess 1882) and ended in 1894, when he had arrived at the point where he 'could take a play to a manager, printed and ready for rehearsal without the alteration of a single line'.[78] Rehearsals were not the occasion for experiment either for Jones or Pinero. Both dramatists used printed rehearsal copies deliberately to underscore the privileged status of the author's text over any conscious or unconscious re-writing either by actors or managers.

Despite the presence of an underlying respect for authorship at the St James's, not all of Alexander's dramatists would have been prepared to give him such glowing references as Jones and Carton did. Oscar Wilde was in more or less constant attendance at rehearsal and was often truculent and addicted to continual interruption. Preparations for his first success, *Lady Windermere's Fan* (St J 1892), were riven with conflict between two men of strong personality. After one particularly fractious rehearsal Wilde wrote to Alexander seeking an assurance that there would be 'no repetition of the painful scene of last night. I have always treated you with personal courtesy, and I expect to be treated with equal courtesy in return.'[79] To be fair, however, the frictions were not limited to Alexander: Beerbohm Tree always used to say that he directed Wilde's *A Woman of No Importance* (Hay 1893) with the interference rather than assistance of its author.

Pinero's initially friendly relationship with Alexander in *The Second Mrs Tanqueray* also broke under the strain. In theory, the regulated approach of the manager seemed to mesh nicely with an author-director who, from descriptions by those who served under him, conducted his rehearsals in the most organised and exacting manner of any late nineteenth-century dramatist, with the possible exception of Shaw. But rehearsals for *The Princess and the Butterfly* (St J 1897) seem to have opened up a vein of latent rancour on Pinero's side such that when Alexander invited him to furnish a new work for the opening of the autumn season in 1900 Pinero refused absolutely to play second fiddle to the manager. 'I also have won – or have chosen to usurp – ', Pinero reminded him, 'a similarly autocratic position in all that relates to my work . . . To put the case shortly, there is not room for two autocrats in one small kingdom; and in every detail, however slight, that pertains to my work – though I avail myself gratefully of any assistance that is afforded me – I take to myself the right of dictation and veto.'[80] In effect the letter was Pinero's combined assertion of his sense of status as author and a declaration of complete independence from any form of managerial control. He did not work with Alexander again for nearly ten years.

Although not averse to the introduction of new business and occasional improvements in the natural course of rehearsals, Wilde was stout in his defence of his text against meddlesome managers and had no doubt of the author's right to dictate to the actors every nuance and inflexion in the dialogue. But George Alexander could often be intensely persuasive and his influence on Wilde's productions was stronger than on any other major dramatist of the period with whom he came in contact. Though Wilde's inclination was always to resist interference, on two very material alterations in *Lady Windermere's Fan*, both suggested and warmly urged by Alexander, he eventually capitulated: the curtain line to Act II and, more important (though this occurred after the first night), to Alexander's view that the secret of Lady Windermere's birth – that she is, in fact, Mrs Erlynne's daughter – be divulged to the audience during the same act, rather than delayed to the third, as originally written. It refined the dynamics of the drama by making it dependent on its emotional power and ability to generate suspense rather than relying on its quality as a guessing-game. Relations with Alexander were clearly not irretrievable and after two productions with Tree, Wilde returned to the St James's for *The Importance of Being Earnest* (1895). Again, the actor-manager's special instinct for dramatic rhythm surfaced, but this time with even more radical results. During the rehearsal process Wilde was induced to drop a whole act of the play, making for a reduction to three acts and removing in the process a character (the solicitor Grigsby) and all of the plot-line centred on Algernon's near arrest for debt. Having accepted that the structural change made for a more tightly focussed play, Wilde continued to harass the life out of the actors and manager until Alexander, in apprehension that the play would never be ready in time, had to persuade the author voluntarily to absent himself from the final stages of rehearsal. As always Wilde had the last word. Congratulating him after the first performance, he said: 'My dear Aleck, it was charming, quite charming. And, do you know, from time to time I was reminded of a play I once wrote myself, called *The Importance of Being Earnest*.'[81]

Henry Arthur Jones's closest relationship was not with Alexander but with Charles Wyndham, for whom he wrote his only bespoke play, *The Bauble Shop*, produced at the Criterion in 1893. It was Wyndham whom he recognised as the one actor-manager who could be relied upon never to take 'the least liberty with the dialogue or business – he was a model for that'.[82] Yet even Wyndham was, in Jones's eyes, guilty of a single fall from grace in his behaviour over *The Case of Rebellious Susan* (Crit 1894). The play was, for Jones, more morally unconventional than anything he had written up to that point and Wyndham's unease began even before rehearsals started. He considered that it was cheap and unworthy of 'a practical long-experienced dramatic author' even to hint that his heroine was guilty of adultery in the face of severe provocation from a demonstrably unfaithful husband. Whereas Alexander's interference in Wilde's plays was shrewd and made artistic sense, Wyndham's stemmed merely from middle-class prudery. Jones wanted the hint to remain; Wyndham was firmly of the opinion that Susan should be innocent and went so far as to suggest that if certain lines (such as 'I should kill myself if anyone knew') were not excised 'my participation in the piece will not only be useless but positively dangerous'. Given his views on the autonomy of the artist and the integrity of his text (which had become stronger as time progressed), it is not surprising that Jones flatly refused. The only trouble was that, in the end, he had no control over what the actors would actually say on stage and in this case, as he pointed out later, 'the actor was a bit delicate with his audiences and refused to utter a few lines' that made it clear that Susan's infidelity was genuine.[83] Against that kind of resistance to authorial intention the printed text, with its attendant preface addressed to Mrs Grundy, was the only defence.

Bernard Shaw never allowed his relative lack of practical experience in the theatre to impede his function as author-director and it was he who most determinedly carried the banner of the playwright's authority into the twentieth century. His attempt to break into the commercial West End theatre with *You Never Can Tell*, much of which was written in a reserved deck-chair in Regent's Park, could on the face of it hardly have been a worse disaster. Cyril Maude, actor-manager of the Haymarket with Frederick Harrison, took on the role of the waiter but the principals were hopeless, especially Alan Aynesworth (who had earlier scored such a success as Algernon Moncrieff in *The Importance of Being Earnest*) in the lead role. He utterly failed to appreciate what manner of play he was taking part in and could do nothing that Shaw required. After a fortnight the rehearsals were abandoned and Shaw, by agreement with the management, withdrew the play from production in the spring of 1897. Though he had to wait three years more for its first public performance at the Strand, the act of withdrawal was the firmest expression yet of the playwright's final authority over his play. And whatever the disappointment of the experience, Shaw had had the satisfaction of performing a kind of sweet revenge on behalf of the rest of the dramatic profession for its treatment at the hands of managers and actors, neither of whom he had any time for. Maude (alias here Bernard Shaw) describes his behaviour at rehearsal as showing 'the perversity of his disposition and his utter want of practical knowledge of the stage' – indeed, he was 'a veritable Svengali'. Not imperiously like Pinero or modishly like Wilde but kitted out in a crumpled suit 'that any self-respecting carpenter would have discarded months ago',[84] the author-director had unmistakably arrived. As Shaw remarked darkly in a letter to Ellen Terry just after rehearsal started, though the actors 'think me a very harmless author so far', they would very soon find out differently: 'their sorrows have only begun, poor things'.[85]

CHAPTER 7

The new professionals

I

The attempt to bring dramatic authors into professional association with one another belongs to the early Victorian theatre. The Dramatic Authors' Society was the only organisation in the nineteenth century specifically devoted to the needs of dramatists. Unlike the Royal General Theatrical Fund for actors, it was never a charitable body nor was it, strictly speaking, a social club, though some members tried to make it into one. It was first and foremost a business enterprise devoted to the collection of performance fees on behalf of its members and to guarding their interests in their copyrights. Growing out of copyright reform in 1833, the society gradually developed into an association representing most of the better-known dramatists of the period. As an agency for fee collection, especially from provincial managers, it was indispensable. It was important, too, as a grouping together of influential dramatists; but despite its aspirations as a truly professional body the truth is that, though its three principal secretaries (Thomas J. Serle, Joseph Stirling Coyne, and John Palgrave Simpson) were all practising playwrights, it was never able to shake off its gentleman-amateur image. In the end, its inability to keep pace with the growth in economic development of the dramatist in the second half of the century was its downfall. Its eventual absorption in the early 1880s by its younger and much more powerful sister organisation the Society of Authors was inevitable.

James Planché asserts that the Dramatic Authors' Society was founded on or immediately after 10 June 1833, following the

Royal Assent to Bulwer Lytton's Dramatic Copyright Act.[1] It seems likely, however, to have had a less formal status at least a year or so previously – possibly as early as 1830 or 1831 – as a grouping of disaffected playwrights agitating through parliamentary means, in the reformist spirit of the age, for redress on the two key issues of the patent monopoly and dramatic copyright.[2] But its essential purpose was fee collection and Stirling Coyne argued that the Dramatic Authors' Society came about as a consequence of pressure from managers rather than dramatists, on the grounds that under the new legislation 'they had so much trouble in applying for permission to play each piece that they would prefer to pay a fixed sum for all the list'.[3]

The Dramatic Authors' Society embraced never more than a small proportion of the huge number of dramatists who wrote for the Victorian theatre – in that sense it catered for a coterie – but it was a very significant proportion. By about 1836 the membership list was more catholic than it was ever to be in its later history, when clubbiness began to predominate over business and it became more choosey about whom it would accept. Embracing minor theatre dramatists as well as patent authors and even a few from the East End theatres, it included S. J. Arnold, William Abbott, Capt. Henry Robert Addison, Morris Barnett, William Bayle Bernard, J. B. Buckstone, Charles Dance, Tom Dibdin, John Farrell, Edward Fitzball, Henry Holl, Douglas Jerrold, James Kenney, Sheridan Knowles, Barham Levius, Joseph Lunn, John Gideon Millingen, H. M. Milner, W. T. Moncrieff, Thomas Parry, Richard Brinsley Peake, Planché, George Dibdin Pitt, R. J. Raymond, Walter Leman Rede, G. H. Rodwell, Thomas J. Serle, Charles Selby, T. J. Thackerary, Cosia T. de Trueba, Ben Webster, and Thomas Wade. Among the honorary members were Edward Bulwer Lytton, Joseph Lythgoe, Caroline Boaden, Felicia Hemans, Lady Barbarina Dacre, Isabel Hill, Mary Mitford, Mrs Cornwall B. Wilson, and Mrs J. R. Planché.[4]

Its founder-members included Jerrold and Serle, who were respectively its first chairman and secretary. Although later incumbents of the latter post were empowered on behalf of the members 'to grant conditional permission as the agent of the author' to managers for the performance of any member's play on a scale determined by the general membership,[5] the day-to-day business of fee collection in the 1830s appears to have been delegated to John Miller, the theatrical bookseller and publisher, of Henrietta Street, Covent Garden, who also became the Dramatic Authors' Society's first publisher of members' plays.[6] The scale of fees which applied to the provinces took into account the genre and length of play, the size and status of the theatre in which it was to be produced, and, in special cases, the eminence of the author concerned. In the 1830s the three most popular of Sheridan Knowles's plays (*The Wife*, *The Hunchback*, and *William Tell*) were rated five times higher than anybody else's. This over-pricing was a deliberate device to discourage country theatres from performing the plays – to keep them back 'until he (with Miss Jarman or Miss Tree)' had 'visited the various towns on a star-ing tour'.[7]

The system was especially useful for managers of provincial theatres, where frequent changes of bill would have made unworkable payments on a play-by-play basis. In the early days there was acute reluctance on the part of some managers to pay anything at all, especially in the more remote regions of the provinces. With the larger and respectable travelling companies like 'Old Wild's' there was never any problem, but in the case of some of the smaller ones (described as being led by 'disreputable and dishonest men, who go about from theatre to theatre') the difficulties of making them pay for copyright pieces was apparent as late as 1866. Indeed in 1878 it was reported that some of the more obscure provincial theatres were still in the habit of changing the titles of their plays purely to deceive the society.[8] But it was normally possible for responsible managers to negotiate a composite fee for performing the plays of any dramatist on the Dramatic Authors' Society list, lasting up to a whole season at a time.

Initially in London the system seems to have operated on a more individual footing at least at the patent theatres, which at this period often took up plays first performed at minor houses. The Covent Garden accounts for 1836, for example, show payments direct to the society at the rate of £1 per night for performances of Charles Selby's *Robert Macaire* (originally Adel 1835) and *The Nervous Man* in October and November.[9] But there was always some room for departure from the standard procedures and Selby is an example of a dramatist who declined to subscribe to seasonal arrangements. In a letter to William Emden he firmly declared that his 'terms for the "Boots" [Str 1842] are 10s. a night' and that as a matter of principle he was prepared to entertain no other scheme.[10]

Owing to the notorious complexity and imprecision of the 1833 and 1842 Copyright Acts, the Dramatic Authors' Society as an institution suffered continually from the ease by which the unscrupulous could circumvent the law. Because of the difficulties of designing a system to foil the freebooters which could apply equally across the whole of Great Britain, London managers were treated differently from those in the country. The former generally paid on a tariff basis and were granted rights over an author's plays for an agreed period, often as much as three years, after which time copyright reverted to the author. But in the provinces, where the possibility of abuse was greater, copyright was almost always reserved by the author.[11]

The basic rules and working practices of the society were established in the 1830s and refined by experience. Provincial managers were encouraged to send up to London monthly files of playbills, but the original practice of having an agreed scale based on the number of acts was soon abandoned, proving contrary to the best interests of authors. Instead, between 1840 and 1846, the society issued annual prospectuses, in which certain plays were individually priced. This meant that it could respond quickly, on the author's behalf, to popular pieces by charging higher prices. Although the old scales were not totally dispensed with, outstandingly successful pieces were singled out for special rates in response to the altered requirements of many theatres in the 1840s, when 'the newest and most popular one-act pieces . . . have assumed an importance they never before possessed; frequently, indeed, forming the staple of the evening's entertainment'.[12]

Information on performances in country theatres was relayed

to the Dramatic Authors' Society by a variety of means, which gradually became more sophisticated. During the secretaryship of Joseph Stirling Coyne (1856–68) the society retained agents in all important towns and cities to report on the activities of the local theatres. On occasion it also relied on anonymous informers. More comprehensively, the *Era* weekly newspaper provided a convenient and on the whole reliable repository of information. But in the end it was really all a matter of trust. Responsible managers regularly submitted their playbills for inspection, and to these managers the society made the concession of allowing them to perform plays in advance of paying the fees. This more streamlined system meant that some large provincial theatres were given permission to play all the pieces on its list for a stipulated annual payment. Manchester's Theatre Royal fell into this category and its manager was required to send files of his playbills directly to London so that the composite fee paid to the society could then be 'distributed among the authors *pro ratâ* according to the number of pieces that each author may have had acted during the year at that theatre'.[13] The walls of its Covent Garden premises at 28 King Street while Palgrave Simpson was in office in the 1870s were said to have been plastered with playbills 'from every part of the United Kingdom'.[14]

Membership of the society grew steadily. By 1865 it included prominent dramatists such as E. L. Blanchard, Shirley Brooks, H. J. Byron, Robert and William Brough, Mark Lemon, Charles J. Mathews, J. Maddison Morton, Thomas Morton junior, John Oxenford, Charles Lamb Kenney, Tom Taylor, John Westland Marston, and Augustus Harris. At this period there were in all about 2,000 pieces under the protection of the society, though some were not credited to the original author but to the copyright-holder (in most cases a theatre manager). In times of hardship or for other reasons authors had often sold copyright to other parties, including, of course, publishers. This accounts for the existence of the great rival to the Dramatic Authors' Society list – T. H. Lacy's. Ironically it was Lacy who published the 1865 catalogue for the society, but no play could appear on both lists. Generally speaking the Dramatic Authors' Society cted merely as agent for the author, while Lacy took the fees himself. But, according to Burnand, the one advantage of the Lacy list as far as managers were concerned was that the rates were cheaper.[15] The society published no further lists after 1865.

When John Palgrave Simpson (elected secretary in October 868 on the death of Coyne) appeared as a witness before the parliamentary committee on copyright which reported in 1878, he insisted that the society was in a flourishing condition. Fee income from the provinces, he claimed, had risen substantially over the years from about £800 annually to between £4,000 and £5,000.[16] But surface appearances were deceptive and his optimism was misplaced. Important members were leaving or had already left and the society was beginning to lose its effectiveness. With remarkable swiftness, in little more than five years, the Dramatic Authors' Society had disappeared from the theatrical scene.

The roots of decline are to be found in the mid- to late 1860s, when the dramatist at the top of his profession began to discover that the society's pricing policy no longer reflected the reality of the dramatic market, where larger incomes than ever before were possible for the conscientious and talented playwright. Boucicault left its ranks early – probably in the early 1860s and certainly before 1865 – after a quarrel on this very issue. Similar dissatisfaction with the unrealistically low fees charged by the society to provincial managers determined Francis Burnand's initial refusal to place his money-making burlesque *Black-Eyed Susan* (Roy 1866) on the society's list. He delayed doing so until he had toured the provinces himself with his own company and pocketed the increased fees he was able to levy.[17] This unilateral action, as Burnand put it, 'fluttered the dove-cot' of the society and soon both he and W. S. Gilbert followed Boucicault into a more remunerative exile. Others, such as Andrew Halliday, did the same. Thus deprived of its former monopoly on the best dramatic talent of the day, the society's standing as a professional association was irreparably damaged.

During the 1870s, in a vain attempt to recover its position, the rules were revised to permit members to keep new high-earning pieces out of the list for a certain period. Arthur à Beckett maintained that as a result of this revision some disaffected playwrights rejoined, but at this point the rules were inexplicably changed again to allow dramatists the freedom to do as they pleased. Almost immediately most of them, including all the high-flyers, elected to withdraw their plays from the list altogether, thus delivering what amounted to a final death-blow to the society.

As a result of a resolution at a special general meeting held in January 1883, the Dramatic Authors' Society ceased to exist as an agency for the collection of authors' fees on 25 March following. Its surviving members were advised to transfer their business to one Douglas Fox, employed in the service of the society for the last fourteen years, who proposed to set up on his own account as a dramatic agent. In its report of the society's imminent demise, *The Theatre* ventured to hope that it would carry on and take up the cudgels on the still unresolved issue of copyright law reform.[18] But the society was not about to do in weakness what it had had no success at in strength. Quite simply with the loss of its fee-collecting function, it had no rationale for continuing.

During its fifty-year history, the Dramatic Authors' Society had varying fortunes. Yet it undoubtedly contributed to the dramatist's early sense of professionalism, not merely as a collection body for fees, but by taking on for a time during the 1830s and early 1840s the mantle of publisher as well. In this way it helped to secure members against exploitation by ensuring that fees were retained by the author and did not go to the publisher. There was a proposal that it should re-enter the publishing market in 1870 but, according to Edward Blanchard, this was vetoed by the committee.[19] Whatever the reason for this failure of courage or lack of foresight, it was a pointer to the eventual inability of the society to fulfil a truly professional function in a rapidly changing world. Although it began out of agitation for copyright reform and though it spoke with a collective voice at important parliamentary committees in 1866 and 1878, it was not – except at the very beginning – a propagandist or proselytising association. Too old-fashioned to move with the times, its collapse was for reasons quite independent of the emergence of a rival organisation in the shape of the Society of Authors. The Dramatic Authors' Society just faded away and though it was said to have been merged with the latter in 1884, there is no trace of any such an amalgamation in its records.[20]

The Society of Authors presented itself as a vigorous new organisation determined to speak not only for the whole literary profession, but for authors in science, history, and theology. Potentially much more powerful than the Dramatic Authors' Society, with a prestigious list of members such as Matthew Arnold, Thomas Huxley, Cardinal Manning, and J. A. Froude, and with Alfred Lord Tennyson as its first president, the new society set out with an avowed purpose 'to protect literary property, to consolidate & amend dramatic copyright, [and] to promote international copyright'.[21] The reform of dramatic copyright was allegedly a high priority and dramatic authors had their own representatives in the administration and policy-making sections of the society, the earliest of them being Charles Reade (who also had responsibility in fiction), Herman Meri-vale, and W. S. Gilbert. Yet, despite the emergence of a formal dramatic sub-committee as early as 1884 (comprising J. Comyns Carr, Merivale, and Walter Herries Pollock), it does not appear to have been very vigorous in presenting the playwrights' case in either of the two areas which most preoccupied them in the final two decades of the century: dramatic copyright and the official censorship conducted by the Lord Chamberlain's Office.

Important though copyright still was as an issue for drama-tists in the 1880s and 1890s, it was overtaken by censorship, which, since about 1885 – William Archer saw this date as the watershed – had tended to become ever more prominent in direct ratio to the growing adventurousness of writers anxious to tackle seriously social and moral questions. Whereas in earlier periods the principal targets of the censors had been political and biblical allusion and morally *risqué* adaptations from the French, at the end of the century playwrights were increasingly constrained by the resistance to serious moral discussion on the stage.[22] Official attitudes, which were constantly defended by reference to the supposedly conservative nature of public opinion, were well represented by the view of the Examiner of Plays (Edward F. S. Pigott) that Ibsen was morally deranged nevertheless *Ghosts* was staged in defiance of the Lord Chamberlain at a private performance arranged by Grein's Independent Theatre Society at the Royalty in 1891. This followed a trend towards private or club performance initiated by Sydney Grundy in 1882, when his drama *May and December* (a retitled version of *The Novel Reader*, banned in 1879) was staged at the Globe Theatre, and the Shelley Society's single matinée performance of *The Cenci* at the Grand Theatre, Islington in 1886. While Shaw (*Mrs Warren's Profession*) and Wilde (*Salomé*) never had much respect at the Lord Chamberlain's Office, certain other playwrights like Jones and, more especially, Pinero, who had built considerable reputations with theatre audiences tended to get away with more in the relative moral unconventionality of plays like *The Second Mrs Tanqueray* (St J 1893), *The Notorious Mrs Ebbsmith* (Gar 1895), and *The Gay Lord Quex* (Glo 1900). On the other hand, despite his standing as a novelist Robert Buchanan was refused a licence in 1895 for a copyright performance of *The New Don Quixote*. The play bore a strong thematic resemblance to *The Iron Master* (St J 1884); but, as the Examiner in justification of the ban privately pointed out to his superior, Buchanan was 'not Mr Pinero'. To the aggrieved author's protest that an objection on moral grounds to his play revealed an attitude more 'suggestive of the Dark Ages or the Star Chamber than of the nineteenth century', the newly appointed Examiner George Redford, declining to be drawn into controversy, stiffly reminded Buchanan that the censor 'has no official cognizance of Authors as such'. As far as the Lord Chamberlain's Office was concerned, it was evident that the status of the dramatist was no higher at the end of the century than at the beginning.

While there was much public discussion of censorship in the 1890s in the periodical press because opponents such as William Archer and Bernard Shaw and supporters like Clement Scott raised it into such a high-profile issue, the Society of Authors, which might have added its voice to the debate, chose not to do so at this stage in its history. Perhaps this was because dramatist

were a minority in its ranks; though some novelists like Thomas
Hardy and George Moore were prepared to speak out publicly
in support of the anti-censorship lobby, the general issue of
official stage censorship tended to have little direct concern for
novelists. In pressing the other issue of copyright protection,
however, playwrights in the main were able to travel on the
coat-tails of the larger membership. In this respect novelists and
playwrights united to continue the process of raising the commercial value of authorship.

   Not until 1897, when Henry Arthur Jones was made chairman of the dramatic sub-committee[23], did the society begin to
act more authoritatively on behalf of the dramatist and to
attract into membership by the end of the century nearly all
playwrights of any consequence. By 1899 Pinero, Sydney
Grundy, R. C. Carton, Haddon Chambers, Louis N. Parker,
and W. S. Gilbert (rejoining after a lapse) were all members.
Typically Shaw, who joined in 1897, was keen to turn the sub-
committee into a kind of trade union by asserting authors' rights:
to have 'a minimum price established for plays', and to put 'a
stop to . . . the silliness and ignorance of authors'.[24] Although it
never fulfilled Shaw's dreams for it, the society did nonetheless
act as a forum for grievances of the literary and dramatic
professions. There were obvious benefits to be derived from
dramatists making common cause with their colleagues in the
novel and journalism, though it is ironic that at the time when
dramatists were riding highest they were deprived of an independent professional organisation, for which sub-committee
status within the larger society proved no proper substitute. Not
until 1908, when playwrights, dissatisfied as a group over
progress on censorship and copyright, threatened to break away
and form a new society altogether, was a fully-fledged Dramatic
Section set up within the society, embracing 'nearly all active
British playwrights'.[25]

II

The theatre of 1900 was a very different place from that of fifty
years previously, and still more different from a century earlier.
It was on the whole a quieter place with a usually attentive

audience, quite unlike the formerly boisterous, orange-throwing patrons of pit and gallery. Amidst the general rowdiness, Lytton in 1839 had singled out the presence of babies in the shilling gallery of Covent Garden on first nights as (in protest to Macready) 'my most bitter persecutors'.[26] But theatre-going having been largely restored to middle-class respectability and rectitude, fashionable audiences were flocking to the St James's or Haymarket well before the end of the century. Broadly speaking, the old distinction between patent and minor theatres had been replaced by a line of demarcation between the middle-class commercial theatre of London's West End – the favoured circle centred on Charing Cross – and the rest. Attitudes were similarly polarised between the glittering front-of-house sophistication of the former and the tawdry vulgarity of the latter, especially where it shaded off into music hall and variety. In both cases, the number of theatres had increased in anticipation of the relaxation of the monopoly laws with a great burst of theatre building in the 1830s and smaller surges in the last three decades of the century, when theatre management (and hence theatre building) became an attractive commercial proposition. By then West End theatres were for the most part more comfortable in their provision for their newly demanding audiences. At Gilbert's new Garrick Theatre, splendidly fitted up in the best Italian Renaissance style, the use of marble, mosaic, and polished walnut created an atmosphere of opulence appropriate to the fashion for society drama and drawing-room comedy, though, as Pinero pointed out, in the case of really successful plays (such as his own) 'a "packer" is employed in the pit for the purpose of fitting elbows into ribs'.[27] From the 1850s onwards conditions for licensing of theatre buildings became ever tighter – in London, dependent upon the appointed licensing authority, either through annual inspection by the Lord Chamberlain's Office or the local County Council – so that theatres were safer in terms of fire protection, access, and ventilation. Gas-lighting, introduced early in the century, had been almost completely replaced by electricity, so reducing the risk of fire as well as providing a new dimension in lighting effects on the stage.

Many new plays were first staged in the provinces on a trial basis before being brought to London, while the spread of the railway system had allowed provincial touring after a London success to develop into a standard feature of the British theatre. Stock companies populated by actors dedicated to specific 'lines of business' had virtually disappeared and performers were chosen to suit the play rather than the other way round. The universally accepted measure of success in the West End was the long run, reliance on which changed the whole nature of the theatrical climate. Early in the century a nine nights' run was considered a success and twenty nights exceptional, but in the 1890s plays tended to be regarded as failures unless they managed to attain a minimum of a hundred nights. Indeed, the whole economic basis of the theatre was beginning to change radically as the formation of syndicates to finance productions became established. As Shaw observed in 1898, 'Capital, which used to back the manager, especially the actor-manager, now backs the play, and hires its manager and company for the occasion just as it hires its carpenters.'[28] In commercial as well as technical terms, the dramatist in 1900 wrote for a theatre no different in its essentials from that of the modern day.

Such large-scale changes in his professional environment were accompanied by smaller but significant changes in methods of work. Tom Dibdin and his contemporaries in 1800 wrote hurriedly at sometimes terrifyingly short notice, more often than not to order, with an eye fixed on the permanent acting company. Writing conditions were casual. In mid-century Edward Blanchard, knowing that each completed act of a new play was worth 10 shillings to him, would buy some paper and retire to a coffee house, 'where, over a roll and butter and a cup of coffee, he would pour out the most powerful dramas'. And even in the second half of the century, a journey-man playwright like James Albery would still write principally commissioned pieces to a strict schedule in the manner, as he put it himself, of 'a bootmaker working to his last'.[29] By contrast, Henry Arthur Jones, Arthur Pinero, and most of their contemporaries, at any rate in the West End theatre, lived in an age in which the

dramatic muse was subject to fewer external pressures, not least
that of time. With more leisure to write – in the study, in the
country, or at the seaside – they were able to pace their
productions to fit in with often lengthy time-scales dictated by
theatre managers who looked ahead in terms of months or even a
season rather than the day after tomorrow.

In the same way that the theatre gradually acquired a new
respectability, so the playwright tended to slough off his Bohemian image of earlier days. In the 1860s bohemianism was kept
alive by those like Tom Robertson (notorious for his untidy dress
– 'a Bohemian to the heart's core' the Bancrofts called him) –
and later by W. G. Wills, who wrote most of his plays in bed on
the backs of used envelopes or scraps of paper. Even at literary
gatherings he was never seen but with 'a pipe sticking out of one
pocket, and, a roll of manuscript from the other'.[30] In the new
professional age of Arthur Pinero and Henry Arthur Jones
things were different. The former limited his composition to
between three and four hours a day, was scrupulously tidy and,
like Jones, lived the life of a respectable middle-class gentleman
with all the trappings of conventional well-off, middle-class
Londoners: a fashionable address, servants and long summer
vacations perhaps on the Kent coast, Suffolk, or occasionally
abroad in the south of France. This was the usual kind of lifestyle
that novelists like Dickens and actors like Macready had long
enjoyed; but for the dramatist the experience was a relatively
new one. Towards the close of his professional career Dion
Boucicault retired to the USA, but he maintained addresses on
both sides of the Atlantic. For fourteen years from 1887 Jones
dwelt in some elegance at Townshend House, North Gate,
Regent's Park (the former home of Sir Lawrence Alma-Tadema,
RA), where he had a study with a splendidly painted ceiling.
After turning professional playwright, Pinero lived not far away
at various addresses in St John's Wood, latterly (from 1893 until
the end of the century) at 63 Hamilton Terrace, a turreted,
heavy red-brick mansion, redolent of high Victorian respectability and professional achievement. Sydney Grundy lived in West
Kensington but had a summer residence at Margate. Likewise,
Francis Burnand enjoyed the luxury of one home in the smart

terraces of the Boltons in Chelsea (a former address of W. S. Gilbert) and another at Ramsgate. Indeed, Gilbert was grandest of all. Having built a new house to his own specifications at 39 Harrington Gardens, South Kensington, in 1883, he moved out into the country in 1890 to a large, multi-gabled residence at Harrow Weald attached to a 100-acre estate to live a secondary life as a country squire, whilst still retaining two homes in London. In contrast Shaw, in the years before his marriage and as yet without a secure income from the drama, lived with his mother on the upper two floors of what he described as 'a most repulsive house' at 29 Fitzroy Square, where in an attic room he wrote his first seven plays.[31]

The dramatist in 1800 wrote with goose quills and unreliable inks and his plays were laboriously copied out by himself or others to provide parts for the actors. At the end of the century he could enjoy the practical advantages of the new technology of wireless telegraphy (Jones's telegraphic address was 'Playfully London') and, perhaps most important of all for the playwright, the typewriter. When Pinero acquired one in 1893 he reported to William Archer that he only occasionally operated the machine himself as his speed was 'about 10 words per minute'.[32] Shaw learnt shorthand yet left the typing of drafts to Charlotte Payne-Townshend (the future Mrs Shaw); but Jones and Pinero employed paid secretarial assistance to deal with the increasing correspondence they received as professionals in the theatre. In Jones's case there was the additional burden of numerous articles for journals and extensive lecturing commitments. Most of his contacts with Macmillan in the late 1890s over the publication of his plays were through his secretary George Day. And even the grubby business of negotiating and collecting fees could, if desired, be left to a professional like Mr English, of Garrick Street, whom Arthur W. à Beckett employed in the 1870s and described as 'the best of dramatic agents'.[33]

At Covent Garden at the beginning of the century copyists were generally paid £1 a week. To the same drudges might sometimes fall the burden of copying out a whole play to serve as the licensing copy for deposit at the Lord Chamberlain's Office, though in some cases the author's MS was used for this purpose.

In retrospect, this turned out to be a perfect method of ensuring survival of the MS, but it was an inadvertent consequence. A number of playwrights were surprisingly careless of their authorial copy and unappreciative of its value in professional terms. Licensing copies of two early plays of Dion Boucicault's (dating from 1845 and 1846) are in author's MS, and no fewer than twelve of Edward Stirling's (of various dates between 1842 and 1851). Even Planché, who might have been expected to value his originals more highly, allowed four holograph MSS to disappear into the archives of the authorities up to 1852.

Printed texts were used only very occasionally for licensing purposes in the first half of the century, but from about 1870 they become much more common. Frequently, they were printed privately and overlaid with the legend that the text is 'for private circulation only'. But the majority of play scripts in the Lord Chamberlain's collection at this period were still handwritten, mainly the work of copyists rather than holograph MSS: some in school exercise-books, others in folded sheets of foolscap, still others neatly bound in leather-cased notebooks. Authors were relatively slow in taking proper advantage of the new technology of the typewriter (and its ability to produce multiple carbon copies), invented in the USA and slowly becoming available on the British market in the late 1870s. The first novelist to use a typewriter to prepare his text for the publisher seems to have been Mark Twain (for *Tom Sawyer* in 1875) but not until the mid-1880s does it begin to have even a small impact on the form in which plays were submitted for licensing to the Lord Chamberlain's Office – and equally, it may be assumed, in the form in which they reached the theatre for rehearsals or publisher for printing. As late as 1884 there are no more than eight typescripts to be found amongst over 200 plays licensed during that year, three of which originate from George Conquest and Paul Merritt of the Surrey Theatre, where they were joint-lessees and collaborators in dramatic authorship.[34] By 1890 typescripts account for about half the texts submitted for licensing and within a couple of years, certainly by 1895, the hand-written MS had all but disappeared.

Slowly dramatists began to appreciate the advantages of

professional-looking typescripts and to avail themselves of the new commercial services provided by office agencies. One of the first of these was mentioned in *The Theatre* in 1885, which described the activities of the 'Ladies' Type-Writing Association' of Lonsdale Chambers, Chancery Lane, as providing a useful service for 'rendering, quickly and cheaply, illegible manuscript into the clearest of print, thus providing "copy" from which it is impossible for compositors to misprint'. It was clearly a pioneering venture at the time and in the journal's opinion deserved to succeed on the grounds that it gave honourable employment to young ladies. On the whole, dramatists like Pinero, Jones, and Grundy adhered to the more expensive practice of privately printing texts for rehearsal and licensing purposes, but the Lord Chamberlain's copy of Jones's *The Tempter* (1893) is unusually in typescript, produced by one of the typewriting agencies, in this case 'Miss Dickens's Type Writing Office' of 3 Tavistock Street, Strand, which began to receive business from playwrights anxious to give a professional finish to their texts.[35] This particular agency produced work to such exacting standards that even Shaw patronised it. At the end of the century Ethel Dickens was entrusted with producing the final typescript from drafts made by Charlotte 'with such unprofessional speed as her housekeeping & wifely cares allow'.[36]

The end of the nineteenth century was when the professional dramatist finally came of age. It wasn't just that dramatists were no longer the servants of actors or minions of theatre managers, but that the dramatic art itself had discovered a sharper and more critical edge. In *The Theatre*, founded as a folio weekly in January 1877 and re-launched in the following year as a monthly (with Clement Scott as editor for nine years from 1880), dramatists enjoyed almost as much exposure as actors. No longer confined to gossipy and anecdotal coverage in the ephemeral columns of the newspapers, they also had a voice in the weightier journals of the period: commentary on dramatic issues was a regular feature in, for example, the *Athenaeum* in the second half of the century and, by the 1890s in the *New Review* and *Westminster Review*, while most other journals of a similar nature included occasional articles on the drama and its relationship to literature, morality, censorship, and modern life. In part this new interest was owed to a lively new generation of dramatic critics led by William Archer, A. B. Walkley, and, despite his notorious conservatism, Clement Scott. But dramatists themselves contributed in a way that they had never done previously. They were keen to respond to the challenge of Ibsen and to uncover new subject-areas for the stage. No one was more evangelistic about the theatre and the art of dramatic authorship than Henry Arthur Jones, whose book *The Renascence of English Drama* (1895) collected together his contributions to periodical literature; and no one was more controversial or stimulating than George Bernard Shaw in the columns of the *Saturday Review*. Even Sydney Grundy, who was in general opposed to the more adventurous (or 'advanced') drama of the 1890s, contributed to the *New Review* an article entitled 'The Science of the Drama'.[37] In this participation of the dramatist in the intellectual life of the period his professional standing was enhanced and he firmly staked his claim to be listened to outside the theatre as well as within.

Playwrights who thought about the issue at all seem never to have been in doubt as to their status as professionals even in the first half of the century. The Dibdins (Charles, Charles Junior, and Thomas John), for example, all insisted on it in the titles to their respective memoirs; Edward Fitzball wrote of his hatred for 'everything that tends to turn the profession, and the drama itself into ridicule';[38] and when in 1872 Planché came to write his reflections on a long life in the theatre he sub-titled it 'A Professional Autobiography'. That sense of professional identity, however, was stronger at the close of the century because it had a greater reality in that the profession itself was so much more secure – or at least as secure as any involvement in the theatre could ever be. Reynolds argued in the early years of the century that the modern dramatist was forced to write for money, not reputation, and, quoting the Horatian maxim 'nonum prematur in annum', recommended writing only four classical pieces in thirty-six years.[39] At the end of the century

dramatists like Pinero and Jones could afford the occasional
experiment and still retain both reputation and a highly profitable income. When in 1894 Shaw announced to a friend
(prematurely as it happened) that he was abandoning journalism for the stage – 'now, if I cannot make something out of the
theatre', he wrote, 'I am a ruined man; for I have not £20 saved
. . . I am about to begin the world at last'[40] – he was taking a
calculated risk; but the prospects for life as a professional
dramatist were actually never better. The author's proprietorial
interests in his work were more securely protected than ever
before through successive copyright reforms; he was paid at rates
which reflected the commercial value of a successful play; he
could publish in more durable and respectable form than the old
cheap, flimsy acting editions; and, despite the predominance of
actor-managed theatres, he was successfully asserting his authority over the staging of his plays through his new role as author-
director. Early in the century George Colman junior is reported
to have spoken of the profession of dramatic authorship as 'a very
good walking stick, but very bad crutches'.[41] The difference was
that in 1900 those who chose to follow the profession of playwright, even if only modestly successful, could expect to stand
securely on their own two feet.

Dramatic biography: a summary of contemporary reference sources

Given the unprecedented number of dramatists writing in the nineteenth century, many of whom wrote perhaps only one play and had no other claim to fame, or worked in only provincial or itinerant theatre, it is safe to assert that the vast majority do not appear in any of the biographical dictionaries. And there is a whole host of very active minor theatre melodramatists, such as H. M. Milner and John Walker, who are biographical blanks. Nonetheless, despite playwrights having on the whole been less well served than actors of the period, the range of reference materials available is reasonably extensive. In the summary which follows I have included all general sources consulted for the biographical material in chapter 1 and for the birth and death dates of dramatic authors (where known) appearing in the index of plays and playwrights.

The period is remarkable for its wealth of reminiscence and autobiography and some of the more prominent playwrights – for example, Thomas Holcroft, Tom Dibdin, Reynolds, Planché, Stirling, Fitzball, G. R. Sims, and Burnand – wrote substantial accounts of their respective careers. Others (e.g. Knowles and Robertson) were the subjects of more or less immediate posthumous biographies. Most of them, together with many of the other important dramatists of the period (as well as some lesser-known dramatists who had an additional literary aspect to their career) are entered either in the original issue of *DNB*, ed. Leslie Stephen and Sidney Lee (63 vols., 1888–1900), or in the supplement (3 vols., 1901), while dramatists who died in the present century are to be found in the appropriate continuation volumes. The omission from *DNB* of such older hack writers as Moncrieff and George Dibdin Pitt should perhaps cause no surprise; but also absent are popular middle-of-the-road writers like Sydney Grundy and G. R. Sims. The fullest biography of the former is to be found in *Encyclopaedia Britannica* (11th edn, 1910–11); though he also appears with many other still-living dramatists, including Sims, in the listings in the annual volumes of *The Green Room Book*, ed. Bampton Hunt *et al.* (4 vols., 1906–9), forerunner of *Who's Who in the Theatre* (1912, etc.).

Indispensable for late nineteenth-century theatrical biography – and at least as useful as *DNB* – is Frederic Boase, *Modern English Biography* (6 vols., 1892–1921; reprinted Frank Cass, 1965). Though on a much smaller scale, this was a contemporary rival to Leslie Stephen's dictionary and was proud of its insistence on independent research. It contains more than 100 entries on dramatists who died in the second half of the nineteenth century and early decades of the twentieth. Of these about half have entries in both dictionaries. Boase repairs many of the more obvious omissions of *DNB* (e.g. Moncrieff, Pitt, Stirling, and C. H. Hazlewood) and includes a range of lesser figures, such as Henry Robert Addison, Joseph Ebsworth, H. B. Farnie, T. C. Grattan, Henry Holl, Paul Merritt, John Gideon Millingen, Henry Howard Paul (under his actress wife's name Isabella Paul), and Charles Stansfield James, most of whom appear in no other contemporary dictionary. There are also biographies for a number of women playwrights, such as Sarah Lane and Emma Robinson. That neither has an entry in *DNB*, even though the latter was also fairly well known as an historical novelist, helps confirm the general impression that women dramatists are under-represented in that work. Where discrepancies occur between the two dictionaries in matters of date, I have sometimes preferred Boase over *DNB*.

For the early part of the century David Erskine Baker, *Biographia Dramatica; or, A Companion to the Playhouse* (3 vols. in 4, 1812) is occasionally useful (e.g. for James Boaden), as is, to a greater degree, for the later period, Charles Eyre Pascoe, *The Dramatic List* (1879, 2nd enlarged edn 1880). The latter, though primarily a dictionary of actors and actresses, does include biographical sketches of many dramatists who were also performers. A few nineteenth-century dramatists appear exclusively in W. Davenport Adams, *A Dictionary of the Drama* (1904) (e.g. George Almar, C. Z. Barnett, Thomas Longdon Greenwood); but its usefulness is limited because in some instances biographies lack dates and only the first volume ever appeared, covering initial letters A to G.

Nearly all the dramatic periodicals of the century, the vast majority of which were very short-lived, confine their biographical interests to actors. However, the long-running *Era* theatrical newspaper (which began in 1838 and gradually increased in stature) is an exception in both respects. Published from the same offices, beginning in 1868, the annual volumes of the *Era Almanack* are a mine of information, especially the issues for 1868 and 1869, compiled by Edward Ledger, which contain short biographies of selected living dramatic authors, including some unnoticed in other works of reference (e.g. George Roberts and Nelson Lee). A number of dramatic portraits, mainly autobiographical, printed in the influential and authoritative monthly periodical *The Theatre* (begun in 1878) are referred to in the bibliography, below. Also worth consulting for additional information on some late Victorian authors is Victor G. Plarr, *Men and Women of the Time. A Dictionary of Contemporaries* (14th, 15th edns, 1895, 1899).

The most useful guide to references in the principal biographical dictionaries (contemporary and modern) is J. P. Wearing, *American and British Theatrical Biography. A Directory* (Scarecrow Press Inc: Metuchen, NJ and London, 1979). Though in other ways comprehensive and reliable, it omits to index entries in Boase, *Modern English Biography*.

Dramatic Authors' Society

The following information is taken from Leman Thomas Tertius Rede, *The Road to the Stage*. New edn, rev. & improved (London: J. Onwhyn, 1836), pp. 72–3.

SCALE OF CHARGES AT PROVINCIAL THEATRES (*c.* 1836)

The object of the society was said to be 'not to impede performers or managers, but to attain the objects contemplated by the [Dramatic Copyright] act in an amicable and reasonable manner'. For the purposes of pricing plays, the provincial theatres were divided into three classes, as follows:

First-class theatres

Dublin, Liverpool, Manchester, Bath, York, Hull, and Edinburgh

Second-class theatres

Brighton, Bristol, Portsmouth, Exeter, Norwich

Third-class theatres

Chelmsford, North and South Shields, Coventry etc.

In addition certain special arrangements applied. All plays originally performed at the English Opera House, Adelphi, Surrey, and Olympic, 'as first pieces, whatever the number of acts, will be charged as first pieces in the country. And all one act pieces brought out at the Olympic Theatre will be charged as after pieces of two acts.'

The following charges applied to plays brought out before the passing of the Act:

Country theatres of the first class

A full piece, of Five, or Three Acts (per night)	£0	10s	0d
of Two Acts		7s	0d
of One Act		5s	0d

Second class

A full piece, of Five or Three Acts	7s	0d
of Two Acts	5s	0d
of One Act	3s	0d

Third class

A full piece, of Five or Three Acts	5s	0d
of Two Acts	3s	0d
of One Act	2s	0d

But three of Sheridan Knowles's plays – *William Tell* (DL 1825), *The Hunchback* (CG 1832), and *The Wife* (CG 1833) – were charged at much inflated rates designed to discourage performance until Knowles had exhausted their provincial touring potential himself.

At first-class theatres, *The Wife* cost £5.00 per night; *The Hunchback* £3.00; and *William Tell* £2.00.
At second-class theatres: respectively £3.00, £2.00, and £1.00. At third-class theatres: respectively £2.00. £1.00, and 10 shillings.

The scale concludes with the following warning:

The society expect managers to transmit files of their bills to Mr [John] Miller [of Henrietta Street, Covent Garden]; on doing so the pieces liable to charges are marked according to the foregoing scale. Persons who do not choose to furnish this information play the pieces at their own peril, and in some cases the penalty (40s.) has been sued for and obtained.

Notes

1 THE SMELL OF LAMPS AND ORANGE PEEL

1 [William Broadley Megson (ed.)], *The Original, Complete, and Only Authentic Story of 'Old Wild's'* ([1888], reprinted London: Society for Theatre Research, 1989), p. 77.

2 Dibdin, II, pp. 195–6. Some of herd died before *The Laplanders* came to the stage and Morris, no longer having any use for the piece, refused to pay for it. Dibdin sued him for the money owing in the Court of Common Pleas (*ibid.*, pp. 325–6).

3 James Boaden, *Memoir of the Life of John Philip Kemble* (London, 1825), I, p. 438.

4 Planché, p. 17. His early experience of the professional theatre covered the transitional phase when oil-lamps were in the process of giving way to gas-lighting, first introduced at the Lyceum and Drury Lane in 1817. The sale of oranges in the auditorium for consumption (and sometimes for throwing at the actors) was traditional.

5 See membership list in 1836, below, p. 175.

6 For a general note on sources for dramatic biography in this chapter, see appendix 1, pp. 192–4.

7 Planché, pp. 3–4.

8 Edward Stirling, *Old Drury Lane. Fifty Years' Recollections of Author, Actor, and Manager* (London, 1881), I, p. 69.

9 See H. Chance Newton, *Cues and Curtain Calls* (London: John Lane, The Bodley Head Ltd, 1927), p. 124; Stirling, *Old Drury Lane*, I, p. 133.

10 Westland Marston, *Our Recent Actors: Being Recollections, Critical, and in Many Cases, Personal, of Late Distinguished Performers of Both Sexes* (London, 1890), pp. 268–9.

11 Joseph Knight, *Theatrical Notes* (London, 1893), p. 59.

12 Genest, VII, p. 605.

13 Allan Wade (ed.), *Henry James. The Scenic Art. Notes on Acting and the Drama 1872–1901* (London: Rupert Hart-Davis, 1949), pp. 119–20.

14 William Blanchard Jerrold, *The Life and Remains of Douglas Jerrold. By his Son*, 2nd edn (London, 1869), p. 173. The first public performance took place at the Princess's on the following day (22 Jan. 1853).

15 Macready, I, p. 446; George Rowell, *Queen Victoria Goes to the Theatre* (London: Paul Elek, 1978), p. 22.

16 Dibdin, I, p. 254. Similar clubs developed around other theatres, including Sadler's Wells in the 1850s. See Clement Scott, *The Drama of Yesterday and To-day* (London, 1899), I, pp. 308–11.

17 Alfred Bunn, *The Stage: Both Before and Behind the Curtain. From 'Observations Taken on the Spot'* (London, 1840), I, p. 92; Planché, p. 114.

18 Burnand, p. 288. Membership was by election and the committee was said to exercise 'very vigilant care' (John Timbs, *Clubs and Club Life in London* (London, [1872]), p. 219). Macready and Irving were among those black-balled on initial application.

19 George R. Sims, *My Life. Sixty Years' Recollections of Bohemian London* (London: Everleigh Nash Co. Ltd, 1917), p. 41.

20 Jean Webster-Brough, *Prompt Copy (The Brough Story)* (London: Hutchinson, 1952), p. 30.

21 John Hollingshead, *My Lifetime* (London, 1895), I, p. 191. He describes Planché, 'antiquarian, dramatic author, man of the world, and honoured officer of the Herald's College', as 'one of the sticklers for the club idea' (I, p. 192).

22 Palgrave Simpson's evidence, 1878 *Report*, q. 2,374.

23 Planché, p. 90.

24 Burnand, p. 246; Scott, *Drama of Yesterday*, I, p. 329. Other playwrights who were members included Tom Robertson, Alfred B. Richards, Nelson Lee, H. J. Byron, Leicester Buckingham, Stirling Coyne, Palgrave Simpson, Robert and William Brough, F. G. Tomlins, and (for a short while) W. S. Gilbert (I, pp. 330–4). See also A. W. à Beckett, *Green Room Reflections* (London, 1896), p. 55.

25 Burnand, pp. 248, 313.

26 Dated 27 Oct. 1880 (Add. MS 45291, f. 282).

27 'The Critic-Dramatists: Old Type and New', *The Theatre* (July–Dec. 1895), 188. The charge was rebutted by several writers, including W. Davenport Adams (256–69).

28 Michael Holroyd, *Bernard Shaw*, I (London: Chatto & Windus, 1988), p. 281. *Widowers' Houses* was performed under the auspices of the Independent Theatre Society, founded by J. T. Grein in the previous year for the staging of plays not acceptable to commercial managements or refused a licence by the Lord Chamberlain.

29 William Schwenck Gilbert, 'An Autobiography', *The Theatre*

(Jan.–June 1883), 217, 219.

30 Scott, *Drama of Yesterday*, II, p. 249.

31 Hollingshead, *My Lifetime*, I, p. 166.

32 Jones, p. 57.

33 Fitzball, II, p. 166.

34 *Ibid.*, II, p. 182.

35 See below, p. 124.

36 Boaden, *Life of Kemble*, II, p. 73.

37 Reynolds, II, p. 399.

38 James Winston, *Drury Lane Journal. Selections from James Winston's Diaries 1819–1827*, ed. Alfred L. Nelson and Gilbert B. Cross (London: Society for Theatre Research, 1974) (entries for 6, 10 Aug. 1823), p. 71. He resented the interference of 'the great and clever man, Reynolds, who knows everything and can [do] things *better than others [who are] about Elliston*' (p. 91).

39 *Ibid.* (16 July 1821), p. 34.

40 1832 *Report*, q. 860.

41 Richard Brinsley Knowles, *The Life of James Sheridan Knowles. By his Son* (London: privately printed, 1872), pp. 100–1.

42 1866 *Report*, q. 4,299.

43 Scott, *Drama of Yesterday*, I, pp. 474–5.

44 Hollingshead, *My Lifetime*, I , p. 208.

45 1866 *Report*, q. 5,321.

46 Burnand, p. 446; 'Our Symposium' on 'The Dearth of Dramatists', *The Theatre* (Jan.–June 1880), 10.

47 Wyndham Albery (ed.), *The Dramatic Works of James Albery* (London: Peter Davies, 1939), I, pp. cix-cx.

48 Sims, *My Life*, p. 126.

49 à Beckett, *Reflections*, pp. 53–4.

50 Burnand, p. 313.

2 'A DEVIL OF A TRADE'

1 Reynolds, II, pp. 201, 421.

2 Richard Brinsley Peake, *Memoirs of the Colman Family; including their Correspondence with the Most Distinguished Personages of their Time* (London, [1841]), II, p. 128.

3 Kemble Memorandum (Add. MS 31972, f. 224).

4 Reynolds, II, pp. 182–3; 282. There was also £150 for the copyright of *Laugh When You Can*.

5 1832 *Report*, q. 2,692. Playbills for Fox Cooper's benefits at the Victoria and New Strand theatres in 1833 and 1836 are reproduced in F. Renard Cooper, *Nothing Extenuate. The Life of Frederick Fox*

Cooper (London: Barrie & Rockcliff, 1964), facing pp. 48, 58.

6　Receipts were £168 13s (Charles Beecher Hogan (ed.), *The London Stage 1660–1800. Part 5: 1776–1800* (Carbondale: Southern Illinois University Press. 1968), III, p. 2,168). House charges at this period stood at about £140.

7　James Boaden, *Memoirs of Mrs Inchbald: Including her Familiar Correspondence with the Most Distinguished Persons of her Time* (London 1833), II, pp. 50; 24–6.

8　1832 *Report*, q. 2,551.

9　Boaden, *Memoirs of Mrs Inchbald*, II, p. 76.

10　Reynolds, II, p. 282.

11　Peake, *Memoirs of the Colman Family*, II, p. 413. The theatre was said to have cleared in excess of £16,000 profit (David Morris's evidence, 1832 *Report*, q. 2,696). Morris suggests that Colman also had a fee 'something very near that' for *The Africans* (Hay 1808) (*ibid.*).

12　Peake, *Memoirs of the Colman Family*, II, p. 414; Reynolds, II, p. 341.

13　Reynolds, II, pp. 365, 377–8.

14　Dibdin, I, pp. 395–6.

15　*Letters of Charles and Mary Anne Lamb*, ed. Edwin W. Marrs, Jr (Ithaca and London: Cornell University Press, 1975–8), I, p. 179.

16　*Collected Letters of Samuel Taylor Coleridge*, ed. Earl Leslie Griggs (Oxford: Clarendon Press, 1956–71), III, p. 437.

17　Reynolds, II, pp. 263, 341–2, 404.

18　The seasonal receipts of Covent Garden from 1809–10 to 1831–2 are printed in 1832 *Report*, appendix 13, p. 249. Capt. Forbes's figure for average receipts during the period was higher at £86,000 (*ibid*, q. 1,847).

19　*Ibid.*, qq. 3,706–8.

20　*Ibid.*, qq. 1,825, 1,831.

21　Planché, p. 88. Elliston paid £10,200 per annum for Drury Lane from 1819 (Christopher Murray, *Robert William Elliston: Manager* (London: Society for Theatre Research, 1975), p. 84).

22　Winston, *Journal* (30 June 1827), p. 151.

23　Boaden, *Life of Kemble*, II, p. 74.

24　1832 *Report*, q. 2,686. Morris's evidence for this rather dubious statement referred to payments given formerly to popular authors like O'Keeffe (*ibid.*, q. 2,687), but he seems to have had in mind mostly plays first performed fifty years previously, like *The Son-in-Law* (Hay 1779), for which the author received only 40 guineas (q. 2,688).

25　*Ibid.*, qq. 2,307, 3,464. Beazley claimed to have received £840 in one year [1819–20] for three plays at Covent Garden (q. 2,315). In the period from 1824 to 1827 Peake's usual income was about £100 per play; his least profitable piece was *The Ramsbottoms at Rheims* at £40 (ledger entries 19 Apr. 1827 and 24 Feb. 1827, Add. MS 23167, f. 117).

26 1832 *Report* qq. 1,954–7; 1,961–2.
27 *Ibid.*, qq. 1,949–51.
28 Add. MS 23167, ff. 118, 136, 117. Most of these payments by instalments can also be traced in Add. MS 29641.
29 Add. MS 23167, f. 99; 1832 *Report*, q. 2,559.
30 1832 *Report*, q. 1,969.
31 Gabriel Harrison, *Life and Writings of John Howard Payne* (New York, 1875), p. 103.
32 The accounts (17 July 1824) record: 'in addition, after run of 20 nights £100' (Add. MS 23167, f. 117).
33 Add. MS 23167, f. 99.
34 Add. MS 23167, ff. 107, 81, 111. Weber had the exceptional sum of £500 for his music (1832 *Report*, q. 1,959).
35 The instalments for *The Woman Never Vext* were paid on 12, 26 Jan. and 24 Feb. 1825 (Add. MS 29641, ff. 120, 124, 129); and those for *Charles X* on 30 Apr. and 18 June 1825 (Add. MS 29641, ff. 136, 140); Add. MS 23167 ff. 111, 82.
36 *Macready's Reminiscences, and Selections from his Diaries and Letters*, ed. Sir Frederick Pollock (London, 1875), I, p. 209. Alan Downer, *The Eminent Tragedian: William Charles Macready* (Cambridge, Mass: Harvard University Press, 1966), p. 64, maintains that Knowles had '£100 better than was customary'; but £400 was not exceptional for a full-length play. The real benefit in the contract was the extension of the run, since the timing of the production would normally have precluded Knowles's collecting more than £300. Even so, he had to wait for his money: the final £100 was not paid to him until more than eighteen months later on 11 Jan. 1823 (Add. MS 29641, f. 50).
37 Winston, *Journal* (18 Nov. 1823), p. 76. Elliston also bought the copyright through Macready for £100 (*ibid.*).
38 Harrison, *Life of Payne*, pp. 72–4.
39 Letter dated 19 Nov. 1823 (Add. MS 29643, ff. 23v–24).
40 Payment for *Julian* was made in two instalments in May and Oct. 1823 (Add. MS 29641, ff. 65, 74): the first in cash and the second 'by an accepted Bill due 12 Oct. 1823' (Letter Book of Henry Robertson, 20 May 1823, Add. MS 29643, f. 10v).
41 Quoted from her *Journal*, in Eleanor Ransome, *The Terrific Kemble. A Victorian Self-Portrait from the Writings of Fanny Kemble* (London: Hamish Hamilton, 1978), p. 20.

42 Letter to Dr George Mitford dated 30 Oct. 1826; to Miss Mitford, 14 Dec. 1826 (Add. MS 29643, ff. 58, 59v). The half fee of £200 is entered in the accounts under Dr Mitford's name, 29 Dec. 1826 (Add. MS 23167, f. 114).

43 Letter dated 12 Nov. 1829 (Add. MS 29634, f. 70). The play was performed 5 Dec. 1828 and Morton had been paid his £100 on 11 Feb. 1829 (Add. MS 23167, f. 99).

44 Add. MS 29641, ff. 47, 54, 63, 76.

45 Egerton MS 2319 ff. 56, 65.

46 Letter to Poole dated 16 Oct. 1826; to Farley, 29 June 1827 (Add. MS 29643, ff. 58, 62).

47 Letter dated 30 June 1827 (Add. MS 29643, f. 62v).

48 1832 *Report*, qq. 1,971; 2,034.

49 *Ibid.*, qq. 4,095–6, 4,142; 4,093; 4,073–80. Nicoll mistakenly ascribes this opera to Covent Garden.

50 James Kenney, *The Pledge: or, Castilian Honour* (London, 1831), preface, p. vii. (The play was adapted from Victor Hugo's *Hernani*.)

51 Dibdin, II, pp. 211–12. Cf. Planché, pp. 87–8; *The Professional & Literary Memoirs of Charles Dibdin the Younger, Dramatist and Upward of Thirty Years Manager of Minor Theatres*, ed. George Speaight (London: Society for Theatre Research, 1956), pp. 119–20.

52 Nicoll, IV, p. 53, quoting *The Dramatic Magazine*, 1829.

53 1832 *Report*, qq. 1,228–9, 1,246; 1,230, 1,232; 1,655.

54 'Biographical Memoranda of Living Dramatic Authors', in Edward Ledger, (comp.), *The Era Almanack, 1868* (London, [1869]), p. 17; Jerrold, *Life and Remains of Douglas Jerrold*, p. 49.

55 1832 *Report*, qq. 2,792, 2,797. Jerrold commented: 'For that piece I received altogether as much as Mr T. P. Cooke has informed the Committee he received for six nights' acting at Covent Garden Theatre' (q. 2,791). Cf. also Stirling, *Old Drury Lane*, I, p. 193, who maintains that Cooke made £10,000 with the play.

56 1832 *Report*, qq. 1,168–9; 2,810–12.

57 Entry dated 21 Oct. 1835 (Add. MS 29642, f.21v).

58 1832 *Report*, qq. 3,145–7. At least six other adaptations of the same novel appeared over the next few years.

59 Preface to *Tom and Jerry; or, Life in London*, in *Selections from the Dramatic Works of William T. Moncrieff* (London, 1851), III, p. [v].

60 1832 *Report*, q. 3,026; cf. also evidence of William Dunn (Treasurer and Secretary to the Drury Lane Committee), qq. 1,141, 1,165.

61 *Ibid.*, qq. 3,335–36. Cf. Thomas Morton, q. 2,562, who, speaking of standard rates of remuneration, agreed that 'if there be a general rule', that was it.

62 Bunn, *The Stage*, I, pp. 71, 116. This was two months after

Knowles's *The Wife: a Tale of Mantua* came out at Covent Garden.
The offer of special terms was repeated on 23 Sept. 1833 (I, p. 118).

63 Dated 24 Sept. 1835, Bunn, *The Stage*, I, p. 294.

64 See Macready, I, p. 283; Bunn, *The Stage*, II, pp. 171–2.

65 The accounts (29 Oct. 1836) record: '[Paid] Mr Bulwer on account
of new Play' (Add. MS 29642, f. 21v).

66 Bunn, *The Stage*, II, p. 175. Macready, I, p. 372, describes Osbaldiston's behaviour as 'shabby' and Lytton's as 'high-minded and
proper'.

67 Macready, I, p. 383.

68 The accounts (5 June 1837) record: '[Paid] Mr Browning authorship of Strafford' (Add. MS 29642, f. 22). It seems there was an
intention to risk a fifth night but this was cancelled after Vandenhoff deserted the company. Its last performance was on 30 May
1837, when Edward Fitzball took it as a benefit.

69 Charles H. Shattuck (ed.), *Bulwer and Macready: A Chronicle of the
Early Victorian Theatre* (Urbana, Illinois: University of Illinois
Press, 1958), p. 76.

70 *Ibid.* pp. 122, 139–40, 166.

71 Dated May 1843, *ibid.*, p. 219. Ironically, this was the year when
Macready could still write of Lytton's being 'my hope among
authors' (Macready, II, p. 191).

72 1832 *Report*, q. 2,805; J. A. Sutherland, *Victorian Novelists and
Publishers* (London: University of London, Athlone Press, 1976),
p. 54.

73 There is a brief discussion of this topic in Michael Booth (ed.),
Revels History of Drama Vol. VI 1750–1880 (London: Methuen & Co.
Ltd, 1975), pp. 8–10.

74 See Knowles, *Life of Sheridan Knowles*, p. 132.

75 Dionysius Lardner Boucicault, 'The Decline of the Drama', *North
American Review*, 125 (Sept. 1877), 243.

76 Arthur à Beckett, 'The Earnings of Playwrights and Players', *The
Theatre* (July–Dec. 1895), 209. He notes that £300 was 'quite a
handsome sum for a three-act comedy'.

77 Malcolm Elwin, *Charles Reade. A Biography* (London: Jonathan
Cape, 1931, reprinted 1934), p. 101. Reade later estimated that the
play would have been worth £5,000 under the French system.

78 Clement Scott and Cecil Howard, *The Life and Reminiscences of E. L.
Blanchard* (London, 1891), I, p. 87, quoting from Blanchard's diary.
His total literary income (mostly from journalism) for 1851
amounted to £139 14s (I, p. 89).

79 These figures are derived from private papers belonging to Barry
Duncan, quoted in a review for *Theatre Notebook*, 21 (1966–7), 142.

In addition to this Pitt would have had his house author/acting manager salary, but on 26 Dec. 1845 this was reduced from 50 shillings a week to 30 shillings as house author and 5 shillings as acting manager.

80 [Megson (ed.).], '*Old Wild's*', p. 77. The Somerset pieces were *Home, Sweet Home, or the Labourer and his Dog*; *The Lion of the Desert*; and *The Slave, or, the Blessings of Liberty* – all of which Wild 'had the sole right of performing' (*ibid.*).

81 Stirling, *Old Drury Lane*, i, p. 191.

3 THE PROFIT-SHARING REVOLUTION

1 1866 *Report*, qq. 6,734–5.

2 Freeman Wills, *W. G. Wills. Dramatist and Painter* (London, 1898), p. 56; *The Letters of Robert Louis Stevenson*, ed. Sidney Colvin, 5th edn (London: Methuen & Co., 1901), i, pp. 304, 266; Robert Gittings, *Young Thomas Hardy* (London: Heinemann, 1975), p. 157. Other comparative figures are drawn from Victor Bonham-Carter, *Authors by Profession Volume I* (London: Society of Authors, 1978); Sutherland, *Victorian Novelists and Publishers*; and *DNB*. Cf. also A. S. Collins, *The Profession of Letters. A Study of the Relation of Author to Patron, Publisher and Public, 1780–1832* (London: George Routledge & Sons, 1928).

3 John Hollingshead, *Gaiety Chronicles* (London, 1898), p. 134; Elwin, *Charles Reade*, p. 201.

4 1866 *Report*, qq. 4,588–9, 5,374.

5 Richard Fawkes, *Dion Boucicault* (London: Quartet Books, 1979), p. 121.

6 *Ibid.*, pp. 123–4. This was probably the first example of a West End production on tour. Other plays went out on similar terms, e.g. *The Octoroon*, with a company headed by Dan Leeson (p. 147); but as is clear from the way in which Boucicault valued the respective copyrights at his bankruptcy in 1863, it never made as much money as *The Colleen Bawn*. See below, p. 213n.

7 1866 *Report*. qq. 4,171, 4,172.

8 Dated 13 Mar. [*c.* 1864], in Townsend Walsh, *The Career of Dion Boucicault* (1915; reprinted New York: Benjamin Blom, 1967), p. 95. 'I can spin out these rough-and-tumble dramas', he wrote, 'as a hen lays eggs. It's a degrading occupation, but more money has been made out of guano than out of poetry' (p. 96).

9 Fawkes, *Boucicault*, p. 148.

10 1866 *Report*, q. 5,370.

11 Squire and Marie Bancroft, *Mr & Mrs Bancroft On and Off the Stage. Written by Themselves*, 6th edn (London, 1889), pp. 117–18.

12 1866 *Report*, qq. 4,618, 4,614.

13 à Beckett, *Reflections*, p. 254.

14 Tom Taylor, 'Impressions of John Baldwin Buckstone', *The Theatre* (Aug.–Dec. 1879), 265.

15 1866 *Report*, qq. 4,613; 6,732, 6,734.

16 On this basis, his individual totals for these plays on their first runs would have been £165, £300, and £468, respectively (Booth, ed., *Revels History of Drama VI*, p. 51).

17 Dated 7 Dec. 1870, quoted in Bancroft, *Mr & Mrs Bancroft*, p. 148.

18 Burnand, p. 315; T. Edgar Pemberton, *The Life and Writings of T. W. Robertson* (London, 1893), p. 221.

19 Fawkes, *Boucicault*, p. 178.

20 Dated 2 Jan. 1871, quoted in Pemberton, *Life of Robertson*, p. 283.

21 Burnand, pp. 237, 239. In all Burnand made nearly £80.

22 *Ibid.*, pp. 291–8. From Burnand's share 5 per cent was deducted to pay the theatre owner Tom Mowbray 'for his trouble' as intermediary; and Miss Oliver took a further cut of £7 nightly from gross receipts for her own pocket.

23 F. C. Burnand, 'An Autobiography', *The Theatre* (Jan.–June 1883), 107.

24 Hollingshead, *Gaiety Chronicles*, p. 143. If necessary, Reade was also prepared to back any play of his with capital.

25 William Schwenck Gilbert, 'An Autobiography', *The Theatre* (Jan.–June 1883), 219. He took to heart the advice of W. S. Emden, the stage manager, 'never [to] sell so good a piece as this for £30 again'.

26 See Hesketh Pearson, *Gilbert: His Life and Strife* (London: Methuen & Co. Ltd, 1957), pp. 38–41. The piece had first run of about 150 nights in London, which suggests a fee income of around 500 guineas.

27 Quoted from Gilbert's 'Actors, Authors, and Audiences', in *Foggerty's Fairy and Other Tales* (1890), in George Rowell (ed.), *Plays by W. S. Gilbert* (Cambridge: Cambridge University Press, 1982), p. 5.

28 Dated 5 June 1870, Albery, *Works*, II, p. 766. The scheme used by Boucicault and Robertson was, in Knight's opinion, the only way in which a playwright was likely to make any money.

29 *Ibid.*, I, p. xxviii. See also H. J. Montague to Albery, letter dated 21 Nov. 1870, enclosing £18 'brain work' (i.e. a week's royalties) on *Two Roses* (II, p. 769).

30 Account from Wallack's Theatre, New York, dated 10 Jan. 1871 (*ibid.*, II, p. 770) (performances in New York gave Albery £5 a

night but less in other American cities); Capt. Roebuck to Albery, 19 Oct. 1879 (II, p. 828).

31 Mary Moore, *Charles Wyndham and Mary Moore* (Edinburgh: privately printed, 1925), p. 37. This is confirmed by the Lyceum account books for Irving's sixth season (1881–2).

32 Dated 2 June 1874, Albery, *Works*, II, p. 803; H. G. Hibbert, *A Playgoer's Memories* (London: Grant Richards, 1920), p. 20.

33 George R. Sims, 'An Autobiography', *The Theatre* (July–Dec. 1884), 16.

34 Sims, *My Life*, p. 126.

35 *Ibid.*, p. 128. The agreement, drawn up by Barrett's business manager Henry Herman, is dated 20 June 1881. Sims also records that 'within a fortnight a thousand pounds had been paid down on account of American rights'. The play ran for years in the USA, the receipts being, as he put it, 'then a record' (p. 131).

36 Hibbert, *Memories*, p. 133; 'The Finance of the Drama', *Era* (26 Mar. 1892).

37 H. Chance Newton, *The Old Vic*, quoted in Booth (ed.) *Revels History of Drama VI*, p. 52.

38 Marjorie Thompson, 'Henry Arthur Jones and Wilson Barrett: Some Correspondence 1879–1904', *Theatre Notebook*, 11 (1956–7), 43; Jones, p. 58.

39 Laurence Irving, *Henry Irving. The Actor and his World* (London: Faber & Faber, 1951), p. 461. Wills made only £12,000 during a dramatic career lasting from the late 1860s to the early 1890s (Wills, *W. G. Wills*, p. 145).

40 Henry Arthur Jones, *The Shadow of Henry Irving* (London: Richards Press Ltd, 1931), p. 110. Total production costs for this free version of *Faust* have been calculated by Alan Hughes, 'Henry Irving's Finances: The Lyceum Accounts, 1878–1899', *Nineteenth Century Theatre Research*, 1 (1973), 82. Only *Henry VIII* at £16,543 cost more.

41 These figures stand in the production account but without identifying the recipients. Hughes, 'Henry Irving's Finances', 81, speculates that they represent payments made to Wills and J. Comyns Carr. He calculates that over all Irving spent on *King Arthur* a total of £9,613 17s 2d.

42 Lyceum Accounts; Bram Stoker, *Personal Reminiscences of Henry Irving* (London: William Heinemann, 1906), II, pp. 134, 137. The list of aborted plays he provides totals nineteen.

43 *Ibid.*, II, p. 304.

44 See Ellen Terry, *The Story of My Life* (London: Hutchinson & Co., 1908), p. 242.

45 Holograph letter to Hallam Tennyson dated 16 Dec. 1879 (Tennyson Research Centre, Lincoln). His estimate of likely box-office receipts was fairly conservative. They varied between £150 and £200 at this period (Irving, *Henry Irving*, p. 323); but the absolute capacity of the Lyceum, until the remodelling of 1881, was actually £228 a night (though sometimes 'when every inch of standing room was occupied, we got in a little more') (Stoker, *Irving*, II, p. 311).

46 *The Falcon* produced a total royalty income of £42 (June Steffensen Hagen, *Tennyson and his Publishers* (London: Macmillan Press, 1979), p. 137); Mrs Bateman's embarrassed letter after the failure of *Queen Mary*, enclosing a cheque for £230, is quoted in Irving, *Henry Irving*, p. 274.

47 For 111 performances and not the recorded 112 – the one before the Queen at Windsor naturally didn't count for royalty purposes. The accounts show six more performances in the same year, eleven in 1894, and two in 1895 – all at the same fee. Provincial and American tours generated additional royalties, but, since the entry for authors' fees is composite, it is impossible to distinguish the share accruing from *Becket*.

48 Dated 13 Aug. 1892, quoted in Irving, *Henry Irving*, p. 565. The rights were bought up by E. S. Willard for the Comedy Theatre.

49 Shaw, I, pp. 620, 761. This signalled the end of negotiations, begun more than a year earlier.

50 Irving, *Henry Irving*, p. 590.

51 There is a receipt for this amount dated 12 May 1899, signed by the dramatic agent Elisabeth Marbury (1856–1933), who protected Sardou's interests outside France, in file no. 2,485 (Lyceum Theatre Archive, Theatre Museum, London). The Irving–Sardou contract is dated 17 Sept. 1897. On her business heading Miss Marbury is described as 'Representing Dramatists, And Sole Representative in Great Britain and her Colonies and in the United States of America and Canada. General Agents of the "Société des Auteurs et Compositeurs Dramatiques" of France.' She also acted for Wilde and Shaw (see below, p. 81).

52 Jones, p. 123.

53 Pinero, p. 169.

54 Jones, p. 178. He argued that the returns were 'considerably higher than the corresponding [ones] for *The Middleman* [Shaft 1889], which proved an enormous financial success in England and America' (pp. 177–8). See pp. 77, 208n, below.

55 Dated 22 Dec. 1897 (Add. MS 45291, f. 336).

56 A. E. W. Mason, *Sir George Alexander and the St James' Theatre*

(London: Macmillan & Co. Ltd, 1935), p. 43. Alexander's ne
profit on the play was £6,498 9s 3d (p. 84). Including matinées, i
ran for 201 performances into 1893, sandwiched between Alex
ander's two other great successes *Lady Windermere's Fan* and *Th
Second Mrs Tanqueray.*

57 Wendy Trewin *All on Stage. Charles Wyndham and the Albery*
(London: Harrap & Co. Ltd, 1980), p. 145. As the play ran fo
fifteen weeks, this suggests a total royalty income of well ove
£2,000, perhaps as much as £2,400.

58 Shaw, I, p. 631.

59 See Henry James, *Letters*, ed. Leon Edel, III (London: Macmillar
London Ltd, 1981), pp. 422–5.

60 Leon Edel, *Henry James, The Treacherous Years 1895–1901* (London
Rupert Hart-Davis, 1969), p. 81. Towards the end of the rur
receipts averaged an uneconomic £90 or less per night and
Alexander lost £1,873 7s 2d on the production (Mason, *Georg
Alexander*, pp. 72, 98).

61 Jones, p. 130. But he was careless with money and at his death
according to his daughter, he left only £15,000. This, about on pa
with Burnand (who left an estate worth £18,176), compare:
unfavourably with the sums left by Grundy (£37,957), Pinerc
(£63,310), and Gilbert (£111,971). See John Parker, comp. & ed.
The Dramatic List. Who's Who in the Theatre, 10th edn (London: Si
Isaac Pitman and Sons Ltd, 1947), pp. 1,934–57.

62 Wilbur Dwight Dunkel, *Sir Arthur Pinero. A Critical Biography wit
Letters* (Chicago: Chicago University Press, 1941), p. 19; Newton
Cues and Curtain Calls, p. 55.

63 Jones, pp. 76, 58.

64 Booth (ed.), *Revels History of Drama VI*, p. 53n., suggests that these
figures may include royalties from publication as well. Undoubtedly *Mrs Tanqueray* was a great money-spinner, earning gros
receipts of £36,688 13s on its first run of 227 nights (Mason, *George
Alexander*, p. 63).

65 Pinero, p. 67; Jones, p. 58. On profits from *The Middleman*, se
letters 26, 30 Oct. 1889 (Harvard Theatre Collection), in Russel
Jackson (ed.), *Victorian Theatre* (London: A. & C. Black, 1989), p
334.

66 Dated 15 Mar. 1896, *Collected Letters of Thomas Hardy*, ed. Richard
Little Purdy *et al.*, II (Oxford: Clarendon Press, 1980), pp. 113
114n.

67 Richard Ellman, *Oscar Wilde* (London: Hamish Hamilton, 1987)
p. 315 (quoting newspaper interview with Alexander in 1913)

This is the equivalent of £200 a week. The play ran for 197 performances: five months from Feb. to July 1892 and, following a break in the London run for a provincial tour, a further month in November.

68 Dated 13 Oct. 1892 ('Copy of original stamped agreement'), *More Letters of Oscar Wilde*, ed. Rupert Hart-Davis (Oxford: Oxford University Press, 1987), p. 118. Tree produced the play in Apr. 1893.

69 Dated [*c.* 12 Nov. 1900], *The Letters of Oscar Wilde*, ed. Rupert Hart-Davis (London: Rupert Hart-Davis, 1962), p. 841. This implies an income during the run of over £3,000, though it is just possible that Wilde was exaggerating for the benefit of his argument with Harris on the total absence of royalties over *Mr & Mrs Daventry*, the scenario for which Wilde wrote, and in which he claimed a share.

70 Dated 3 Oct. 1899, Christopher St John (ed.), *Ellen Terry and Bernard Shaw: a Correspondence*, 2nd edn (London: Constable & Co. Ltd, 1931), p. 361. Shaw said he obtained this information from Wilde's bankruptcy proceedings.

71 Dated 12 Apr. 1897, Wilde, *More Letters*, p. 138. Wilde's plays in the USA were also taken off (Ellman, *Oscar Wilde*, p. 430).

72 Sims, 'An Autobiography', 17.

73 Pinero, pp. 71–2, 80, 82, 84, 88.

74 See Jones's correspondence with the American impresario Albert Marshman Palmer in 1888–9 (Harvard Theatre Collection), in Jackson (ed.), *Victorian Theatre*, pp. 333–6. Palmer was one of the first American managers to pay royalties to foreign dramatists.

75 Wilde, *Letters*, pp. 376, 369.

76 Wilde, *More Letters*, pp. 104–6.

77 Letter dated 22 Feb. 1895 to Richard Mansfield (who had suggested Miss Marbury), Shaw, 1, p. 485. Her London office was under the charge of Miss A. Wooldridge at 36 St Martin's Lane.

78 St John Ervine, *Bernard Shaw. His Life, Work, and Friends* (London: Constable & Co. Ltd, 1956), p. 266.

79 Shaw, 1, p. 430. A draft contract incorporating strict stipulations on the sanctity of the author's text – what Shaw called a 'Shylockian bond' – indicating his choice of the latter course is located in the Berg Collection, New York Public Library (quoted 1, p. 441); 1, pp. 447, 621.

80 Dated 3 Oct. 1899, in St John (ed.), *Ellen Terry and Bernard Shaw*, p. 362.

81 Burnand, p. 313.

4 PIRACY AND THE DEFENCE OF DRAMATIC PROPERTY

1 T. J. Thackeray, *On Theatrical Emancipation, and the Rights of Dramatic Authors* (London, 1832), p. 20.

2 1832 *Report*, qq. 1,234; 2,496–7.

3 *Ibid.*, qq. 3,131–2, 3,139. Elliston seems to have behaved in equally high-handed fashion to the threat of an injunction from the publisher, John Lowndes. See Winston, *Journal* (7 June 1820), p. 11.

4 Tate Wilkinson, *Memoirs of his Own Life* (York, 1790), II, p. 240.

5 See Thomas Holcroft, *The Life of Thomas Holcroft. Written by Himself*, ed. Elbridge Colby (London: Constable & Co. Ltd, 1925) I, pp. 272–3. Genest, VI, p. 358, asserts that the whole project from translation to production took 'little more than a month'.

6 1832 *Report*, q. 3,045. Robertson was a victim of this form of piracy as late as 1867 (see below, p. 105). Cf. Thomas Morton, who intimated that the preferred method at this period was by 'feeing [i.e. bribing] the copyist' (qq. 2,536).

7 *Ibid.*, q. 2,567. It had been pirated in the provinces but Morton concluded that it was not worth legal action (qq. 2,568, 2,570).

8 *Ibid.*, qq. 2,688, 2,691, 2,730. In *Morris* v. *Kelly* (1820) over the case of *The Young Quaker* (Hay 1783), judgement was obtained against the actress Maria Kelly (who intended the play for her benefit night) and Samuel Arnold, manager of the English Opera House. See Sir Frederick Pollock (ed.), *The Revised Reports, Being a Republication of Such Cases in the English Courts of Common Law and Equity, From the Year 1785, As Are Still of Practical Utility*, 152 vols. (London: Sweet & Maxwell Ltd, 1891–1920), XXI (1819–20), pp. 216–17.

9 1832 *Report*, q. 1,659.

10 Genest, VIII, p. 478.

11 1832 *Report*, q. 3,048. At the Queen's Theatre Morris Barnett's *The Bold Dragoons* was pirated under the title *The Dragoons of Normandy* (q. 3,045).

12 Winston, *Journal* (8 Feb. 1821), p. 26. Elliston won an injunction prohibiting the Coburg performance; but it was revoked on discovery that the play was not Payne's, merely taken from the same French source (p. 156 n. 2).

13 Dibdin, II, pp. 301–4.

14 See *Murray* v. *Elliston* in Pollock (ed.), *Revised Reports*, XXIV (1821–4), pp. 519–22. Cf. also Murray, *Robert William Elliston*, pp. 95–6

15 1832 *Report*, qq. 2,799–801, 3,149.

16 *Ibid.*, qq. 2,797, 2,802. Agents like William Kenneth, who found their activities in piracy necessarily curtailed by the 1833 Act, also had a more legitimate side to their business. Kenneth sold published theatrical texts and helped to negotiate acting terms for actors (see Macready, 1, pp. 160, 309). In the 1835–6 season Covent Garden happily employed his services 'for Theatrical Agency'. There is an entry for £20 under this heading dated 11 Dec. 1835 (Add. MS 29642, f. 21v).

17 Planché, p. 102. The case was also referred to in Planché's evidence to the 1832 Committee; but there the sum involved is said to have been 5 guineas (about what Planché estimated he would have had to pay for a black-market copy) and he makes the additional point that Murray went on to make more money out of the piece by playing it as an after-piece at the end of its run at 'first price' (1832 *Report*, q. 3,864).

18 1832 *Report*, p. 5.

19 *Hansard's Parliamentary Debates*, 1833, XVI, 560–1.

20 On its activities in publishing, see below pp. 128–9. There is an outline history of the Dramatic Authors' Society below, pp. 174–81. See also Appendix 2 below, pp. 195–6.

21 1832 *Report*, qq. 3,767, 3,766, 3,775.

22 Planché, p. 139.

23 *Ibid.*, pp. 106–7. This followed the sale of the complete opera to D'Almaine and Co. by G. H. Rodwell, composer of the music, who 'contemptuously disregarded' Planché's protests.

24 *Ibid.*, pp. 194–5. Planché considered himself morally obliged to bring the case to protect not only his own interests but those of the Covent Garden management, who 'had paid me very liberally for my labour'. The case is reported in Pollock (ed.), *Revised Reports*, XLIV (1836–8), pp. 642–4. Cf. also Harry R. Beard, 'Some Notes on John Braham (1774?–1856) at the St James's Theatre', *Theatre Notebook*, 10 (1955–6), 87.

25 Fitzball, 1, pp. 271–2.

26 See *Letters of the Wordsworth Family From 1787 to 1855*, ed. William Knight (Boston and London, 1907), III, pp. 159–64. Cf. also Paul M. Zall, 'Wordsworth and the Copyright Act of 1842', *PMLA*, 76 (1961), 380–3.

27 As reported in *The Times* (1 July 1842).

28 See leading article *ibid.* (8 Apr. 1842) two days after the main debate in the Commons, which can be found in *Hansard's Parliamentary Debates*, LXI (Mar.–Apr. 1842), 1,348–1,403.

29 Some thirty-two amendments made by the Lords were accepted by

the Commons on 30 June (*Journals of the House of Commons*, xcvii 443). The Copyright Bill was given the Royal Assent on 1 July (445).

30 The details of the case may be found in Pollock (ed.), *Revised Reports*, civ (1854–6), pp. 745–56.

31 Planché, p. 32.

32 'Manifesto' quoted in T. Edgar Pemberton, *Dickens and the Stage* (London, 1888), pp. 143; 146–7.

33 See K. J. Fielding, 'Charles Reade and Dickens – A Fight Against Piracy', *Theatre Notebook*, 10 (1955–6), 106–9.

34 See *The Times* (19 Jan. 1861). *Reade* v. *Conquest* is fully documented in Pollock (ed.), *Revised Reports*, cxxvii (1860–2), pp. 869–75.

35 *Ibid.*, cxxviii (1860–2), pp. 508–11; cxxxii (1860–3), pp. 627–35. Reade's own record, however, was not totally unblemished in this regard. See Hollingshead, *My Lifetime*, ii, p. 48, on Reade's adaptation of Trollope's novel *Ralph the Heir* as *Shilly Shally*, for which Trollope claimed he had never given permission.

36 Pollock (ed.), *Revised Reports*, cxxxvi (1862–4), pp. 331–4. Tinsley won a perpetual injunction against Lacy.

37 In *All the Year Round* (27 Dec. 1862). The dramatic version written for Collins by William Bayle Bernard seems never to have been performed.

38 1878 *Report*, pp. 169, 177, 178.

39 See Pinero, pp. 58–66. Cf. his defence in *The Theatre* (Jan.–June 1883), 70–3.

40 The Copyright Amendment Act, prompted by recent agreement with France, supplemented two earlier enabling Acts on international copyright – 1 & 2 Vict. c. 59 (1838) and 7 Vict. c. 1 (1844) – which, in the absence of reciprocal agreements with major European countries, had yet to be put into effect.

41 1866 *Report*, q. 6,787.

42 F. C. Burnand, 'Authors and Managers', *The Theatre* (Feb.–July 1879), 17; Sydney Grundy, 'The Dearth of Originality', *ibid.* (Aug. 1878–Jan. 1879), 275. In defence of native drama, Grundy argued that there was about as much originality as could be expected in the circumstances, instancing playwrights like H. J. Byron, James Albery, Wills, Taylor, Burnand, and W. S. Gilbert as examples of original talent, adding that '[i]t is no detraction from their originality that the majority of these gentlemen have been adapters also' (277).

43 *Hansard's Parliamentary Debates*, 3rd ser., cxix (Feb.–Mar. 1852) 401–2.

44 1866 *Report*, q. 4,266.

45 Jones, pp. 54–5.

46 1878 *Report*, qq. 2,506, 2,587; Bancrofts, *Recollections*, p. 97.

47 *The Colleen Bawn* was valued at £2,500 and *The Octoroon* at £750 when, two years later in 1863, the bankrupted Boucicault was forced to sell eight copyrights in order to meet his debts (Fawkes, *Boucicault*, p. 146).

48 *Ibid.*, p. 134. Fawkes comments that Canada counted as a British performance in respect of copyrighting.

49 Dated 2 Aug. 1897, Hall Caine to George Redford (Theatre Museum, London).

50 For records of copyright performances, see the annual volumes of *Dramatic Notes*, ed. W. H. Rideing *et al.* (London, 1881–93) and, from 1886, monthly listings in *The Theatre*.

51 Shaw, I, p. 758. Copyrighting plays in the USA was a rather more expensive process. Wilde said it cost him a total of £20 a time, including Elisabeth Marbury's fee as agent (*Letters*, p. 688).

52 Pearson, *Gilbert*, p. 104, records eight versions in New York and six in Philadelphia alone.

53 Colin Prestige, 'D'Oyly Carte and the Pirates: The Original New York Productions of Gilbert and Sullivan', in James Helyar (ed.), *Gilbert and Sullivan. Papers Presented at the International Conference held at the University of Kansas in May 1970* (Lawrence, Kansas: University of Kansas Libraries, 1971), p. 126.

54 See playbill, reproduced in William Winter, *Life and Art of Richard Mansfield With Selections from his Letters* (New York: Moffat, Yard & Co., 1910), I, facing p. 46.

55 *The Theatre* (Jan.–June 1880), 108; W. H. Rideing (ed.), *Dramatic Notes: 1880* (London, 1883), p. 20. See also the *Times* leader (25 Mar. 1882).

56 Prestige, 'D'Oyly Carte and the Pirates', in Helyar (ed.), *Gilbert and Sullivan*, p. 128, who observes that this was a distinction 'unique in theatrical annals'.

57 See *ibid.*, pp. 130–5.

58 Holograph letter dated 22 Mar. 1892 (Tennyson Research Centre, Lincoln). Macmillan went on to suggest that no notice be taken of the *Daily News*, though if Hallam was really concerned he might 'take counsel's opinion as to the legality of what was done, but I see no advantage in doing so. It would cost you 10 guineas & you would be in no better position than you are.'

59 Michael Meyer, *Henrik Ibsen*, II (London: Rupert Hart-Davis, 1971), p. 306.

60 Dated 8 Dec. 1892, in Evan Charteris, *The Life and Letters of Sir Edmund Gosse* (London: William Heinemann, 1931), pp. 226–7.

The playbill is reproduced in Ann Thwaite, *Edmund Gosse: a Literary Landscape 1849–1928* (London: Secker & Warburg, 1984), p. 344. *The Master Builder* was published in Norway six days after the Haymarket performance; *Little Eyolf* appeared in print in Copenhagen, Christiania, London and Berlin on the same day as its London copyrighting performance at the Haymarket, 3 Dec. 1894.

61 Shaw, I, pp. 574, 595.

62 *Ibid.*, p. 758.

63 See St John (ed.), *Ellen Terry and Bernard Shaw*, p. 357.

64 Dated 8 Jan. 1899, Jones, p. 143.

65 Pinero, p. 121.

66 Pinero hoped that Augustin Daly in New York would not regard publication of *The Cabinet Minister* as a drawback to performance in the USA, emphasising that '[t]he piece is hardly one which the pirates will favour' (Pinero, p. 131). In Britain, pirates stood more risk of being caught. A pirate version of *Tess* (copyrighted by Hardy in London in 1897 at the same time as the New York production) was stopped in 1900 by injunction. See Michael Millgate, *Thomas Hardy: a Biography* (Oxford: Oxford University Press, 1982), p. 376.

5 BOOKSELLERS AND DRAMATIC PUBLISHING

1 Based on play lists in Nicoll, IV, V, these broad estimates take account only of plays known to have been published during the lifetimes of their respective authors.

2 Dibdin, II, p. 351; Burnand, 'Autobiography', p. 106; Burnand, p. 370. But Nicoll, V, records only about 20 per cent of Burnand's pieces as published, almost all of them by T. H. Lacy.

3 Dated 9 Mar. 1831, quoted in Eleanor Ransome, *The Terrific Kemble, A Victorian Self-Portrait from the Writings of Fanny Kemble* (London: Hamish Hamilton, 1978), p. 49. Murray's generosity was sometimes overdone: he paid 500 guineas for Milman's sacred tragedy *The Fall of Jerusalem*, never intended for the stage (Samuel Smiles, *A Publisher and his Friends. Memoir of the Late John Murray* (London, 1891), II, pp. 104, 106).

4 Genest, VIII, p. 533. The play ran to seven editions during the first year of publication.

5 See Sutherland, *Victorian Novelists and Publishers*, p. 12, who comments that it was 'the most stably priced and sized commodity in the whole nineteenth-century market place'.

6 See Macready, I, pp. 383, 390–1. The hazardous nature of the venture was compounded by the fact that *Strafford* was the first of Browning's works to come out at the publisher's expense.

7 W. Hall Griffin and Harry Christopher Minchin, *The Life of Robert Browning*, 3rd edn (London: Methuen & Co. Ltd, 1938), p. 125.

8 1832 *Report*, q. 2,832.

9 Dated 19 Oct. 1846 (in which Knowles also enquires about the terms for a novel), quoted in Harold G. Merriam, *Edward Moxon: Publisher of Poets* (New York: Columbia University Press, 1939), p. 127.

10 This agreement was probably negotiated on the author's behalf by John Forster, long since acting as business manager for Lytton's novelistic and dramatic interests, including collection of fees for performance. See James A. Davies, *John Forster: A Literary Life* (Leicester: Leicester University Press, 1983), pp. 53, 55. Chapman also published *Not So Bad As We Seem*, following its private performance in 1851 at Devonshire House, Piccadilly, with Dickens in the cast.

11 Sutherland, *Victorian Novelists and Publishers*, p. 34. This gave him a ten-year lease.

12 Boaden, *Memoirs of Mrs Inchbald*, II, pp. 87; 94, 130, 132–3.

13 For dating the various collections in this and (except where otherwise stated) in the following paragraphs I am indebted to R. Crompton Rhodes, 'The Early Nineteenth-Century Drama', *The Library*, 4th ser., 16 (1935–6), 91–112; 210–31.

14 Thomas Dolby, *Memoirs of Thomas Dolby, Formerly of Sawtry, In Huntingdonshire, late Printer and Publisher, of Catherine Street, Strand, London. Written by Himself* (London, 1827), p. 154; Rhodes, 'Early Nineteenth-Century Drama', 105.

15 Quoted in Rhodes, 'Early Nineteenth-Century Drama', 215, 216.

16 See publisher's notice dated 1 Mar. 1834 for his edition of *The Clerk of Clerkenwell* (SW 1834): 'For the gratification of the public, the patrons of *Cumberland's British and Minor Theatre*, and as a small acknowledgement of the kind support afforded by the profession, in universally adopting this Work for their prompt and part books, I do hereby give full permission to the Managers, for the space of six months from the day of the date hereof, to perform [the play] in any Theatre in the British Dominions – without fee or reward.'

17 See Planché, p. 141n.

18 E.g. the Coburg Theatre's *Bartholomew Fair* 'By the author of "Quentin Durward" / Printed for, and sold by G. Herbert, 88 Cheapside; and J. Limbird, 355, Strand. / —— / 1823. / [Price Threepence.]'.

19 *Richardson's New Minor Drama: With Remarks Biographical and Critical. by W. T. Moncrieff*, preface (dated 1 Dec. 1828), vol. 1. Most of the plays in this edition have separately dated prefaces.

20 Fitzball, 1, p. 159.

21 Rhodes, 'Early Nineteenth-Century Drama', 216. A quarter of the plays represented came from the Coburg/Victoria Theatre.

22 It is likely, but not certain, that this bookseller is the same as the one active earlier in the century, trading from 25 Bow Street (see above, p. 118) and other addresses who is referred to by Planché (p. 94) as having 'business communications with the United States'.

23 Rhodes, 'Early Nineteenth-Century Drama', does not notice this title, though he refers (101) to one of the plays within the series, namely, Planché's *High, Low, Jack, and the Game*, which was in fact published as no. 7.

24 See imprint for Thomas Egerton Wilks's *The Brothers*, first performed in 1832 (described as no. 31 in the series).

25 Rhodes, 'Early Nineteenth-Century Drama', 102.

26 See British Library copy of Fitzball's *Mary Melvyn; or the Marriage of Interest. A Melodrama in Three Acts* (London, 1843). Imprints on title-page and wrapper differ: the former has G. Berger of Holywell Street, Strand, while the latter has S. G. Fairbrother, 31 Bow Street, and Berger, Holywell Street. This edition as such is not noticed by Rhodes, 'Early Nineteenth-Century Drama'.

27 Burnand p. 233.

28 Wendy Trewin, *The Royal General Theatrical Fund. A History: 1838–1988* (London: Society for Theatre Research, 1989), pp. 48–9.

29 See advertisement seeking assistance from the dramatic profession in acquiring such texts, on wrapper of no. 394 (Albert Smith's adaptation of Dickens's *The Cricket on the Hearth*); and also the wrapper of no. 574 (*Jack in the Water*). Rhodes, 'Early Nineteenth-Century Drama', 230, claims that this advertisement first appeared on the wrapper of no. 614.

30 See William Archer, *The Old Drama and the New. An Essay in Re-Valuation* (London: William Heinemann, 1923), p. 252. Nearly all of Gilbert's pieces had been printed for private circulation, but Archer was referring to the two series, *Original Plays*, published by Chatto and Windus in 1876 and 1881.

31 Jones, p. 110.

32 Macmillan took over as publisher of all Tennyson's works in 1884, retaining the standard dark-green cloth boards with gilt lettering established by Tennyson's earliest publisher, Edward Moxon. Eventually all the plays were published in separate as well as collected editions with the poems except *The Falcon* (St J 1879) and

The Cup (Lyc 1881), which were published together in 1882 and the unsuccessful *The Promise of May* (Glo 1882), which was relegated to the back of the volume entitled *Locksley Hall Sixty Years After* (1884). Only the 1893 version of *Becket* ever had any pretension as an acting edition: it is described on the title page 'As Arranged for the Stage by Henry Irving and Presented at the Lyceum Theatre on 6th February 1893'. See also Hagen, *Tennyson and his Publishers*, pp. 136–7, 173–5, 182–4.

33 Holograph letter dated 9 Apr. 1891 (Add. MS 55013, ff. 1–2).

34 Dated 22 May 1896 (Add. MS 55013, ff. 10–11); 17 June 1896 (Add. MS 55013, f. 12).

35 Quoted in Jones, p. 176.

36 See Russell Jackson (ed.), *Plays by Henry Arthur Jones* (Cambridge: Cambridge University Press, 1982), pp. 34–5. Some of Pinero's private editions were also printed by the Chiswick Press.

37 Dated 9 Apr. 1891 (Add. MS 55013, f. 2).

38 Pinero, p. 131.

39 W. A. Lewis Bethany, 'Criticism and the Renascent Drama', *The Theatre* (Jan.–June 1892), 283.

40 *The Theatre* (July–Dec. 1891), 195; 271.

41 Shaw, I, pp. 423–4.

42 See letters written on Jones's behalf in 1896 by his secretary (Add. MS 55013, ff. 10–15).

43 Holograph letter dated 28 Sept. 1925 (Add. MS 55013, f. 44).

44 Pinero, pp. 131–2.

45 Shaw, I, p. 595; Holroyd, *Bernard Shaw*, I, p. 399. In 1900 Shaw learnt from Wentworth Hogg, managing director of Samuel French, that French's sold twenty times as many copies of Pinero as Heinemann, who supplied the firm at 'half price net'. They sold 'in batches like hot cakes' principally for amateur performance (Shaw, II, p. 202).

46 Sarah Bernhardt was to have played the title role. On the private reaction of Edward Pigott, the Examiner of Plays, to the French text as 'a miracle of impudence', see John Russell Stephens, *The Censorship of English Drama* (Cambridge: Cambridge University Press, 1980), pp. 112–13. Other examples of publication in defiance of official veto – e.g. Martin Archer Shee's *Alasco* (1824) and Emma Robinson's *Richelieu in Love* (1844) – are discussed pp. 39–41, 48–50.

47 See Wilde, *Letters*, pp. 341n, 344n.

48 Wilde, *More Letters*, p. 124.

49 According to Bernard Shaw, *Our Theatres in the Nineties* (London: Constable, 1932), I, p. 23, the former had a print run of 500 copies,

making it an enterprise equivalent in scale to Wilde's plays. (Lane habitually dealt in limited runs.)

50 Wilde, *More Letters*, pp. 159–60. At this time (Nov. 1897) the figure of £50 seems to have been agreed upon; but the agreement dated 27 Apr. 1899 whereby he surrendered to Smithers 'all his right and interest in the publication in book form' of the two plays confirms the lower figure (quoted p. 160n).

51 Wilde, *Letters*, p. 669.

52 Wilde, *More Letters*, pp. 173, 175, 178–9.

53 Shaw, *Our Theatres in the Nineties*, I, p. 24; Holroyd, *Bernard Shaw*, I, p. 401.

54 Shaw, I, p. 740; II, pp. 8, 63.

55 Holroyd, *Bernard Shaw*, I, p. 403.

56 Grant Richards, *Author Hunting By an Old Literary Sportsman* (London: Hamish Hamilton, 1934), p. 134.

57 Quoted in Jones, p. 146.

58 Dated 28 Sept. 1925 and postcard dated 6 Oct. 1925 (Add. MS 55013, ff. 44, 46).

6   FROM WINGS TO CENTRE STAGE

1 Dated 20 Feb. 1902, Jones, p. 211.

2 Rideing (ed.), *Dramatic Notes: 1880*, p. 29.

3 1832 *Report*, q. 2,575; Bancroft, *Recollections*, pp. 118–19. Mrs Inchbald was reported by Dibdin to have expressed surprise that he 'possess[ed] nerve sufficient to be present at the first representation' of his own farce *The Naval Pillar* (CG 1799) (Dibdin, I, p. 262).

4 Reynolds, II, p. 355.

5 Fitzball, I, p. 17; Wills, *W. G. Wills*, p. 119.

6 Ellman, *Oscar Wilde*, p. 346.

7 Fitzball, I, p. 252; letter from Gilbert dated 19 Jan. 1873, Albery, *Works*, II, p. 800.

8 Peter Quennell (ed.), *Byron: A Self-Portrait. Letters and Diaries 1798 to 1824* (London: John Murray, 1950), II, p. 633.

9 Dibdin, I, p. 92; see Hollingshead, *My Lifetime*, I, p. 191.

10 Boaden, *Life of Kemble*, II, p. 100.

11 Add. MS 29637, f. 127; 1832 *Report*, appendix 14 (dated 27 June 1832), pp. 249–50.

12 1832 *Report*, qq. 1,979, 1,986, 3,484.

13 Fitzball, II, p. 361. The play was *Auld Robin Gray* (Sur 1858).

14 1832 *Report*, qq. 2,074, 1,984.

15 Bunn, *The Stage*, III, pp. 157–62.

16 Planché, pp. 266–7.

17 Fitzball, II, pp. 268, 217; Tom Taylor, 'Mr Phelps and *The Fool's Revenge*', *The Theatre*, I (Aug. 1878–Jan. 1879), 340.

18 Westland Marston, *Our Recent Actors*, p. 155.

19 Macready, I, p. 227.

20 Murray, *Robert William Elliston*, p. 129.

21 Planché, p. 4.

22 Phelps had the additional merit of being a prompt reader of newly submitted MSS, which Tom Taylor described as 'gratifying as unusual' (Taylor, 'Mr Phelps and *The Fool's Revenge*', 339).

23 Scott, *Drama of Yesterday*, II, p. 384.

24 See *The Theatre* (July–Dec. 1890), 98; William Archer, *Theatrical 'World' of 1895* (London, 1896), p. 364.

25 1866 *Report*, q. 4,180.

26 See Sydney Grundy, 'The Dramatic Ring', *The Theatre* (Aug.–Dec. 1879), 273–7.

27 John Hollingshead, *Plain English* (London, 1880), pp. 13–14.

28 Dated 29 Mar. 1879, Add. MS 45291, ff. 276–7; dated 1 Oct. 1880, Add. MS 45291, f. 281. Archer's first Ibsen adaptation was eventually performed as *Quicksands; or, the Pillars of Society* (Gai 1880).

29 Hollingshead, *Gaiety Chronicles*, p. 180.

30 Letter dated 10 Oct. 1891, *The Theatre* (July–Dec. 1891), 244. This was in response to criticism in S. J. Adair Fitzgerald, 'The Matinée Question', *ibid.*, 157–60.

31 Archer, *Theatrical 'World' of 1895*, p. 49.

32 Shaw, I, p. 631.

33 Percy Fitzgerald, 'Playwrighting As It Is', *The Theatre* (Aug.–Dec. 1879), 75.

34 1832 *Report*, qq. 2,482, 2,780. The play in question was his comedy *The Golden Calf*.

35 1832 *Report*, q. 3,460. It played thirty nights during its first season.

36 Preface to *Saints and Sinners*, p. xii. Jones wrote a play to a manager's order only once: see below, p. 171.

37 George Vandenhoff, *Leaves from an Actor's Note-book: or, Anecdotes of the Green Room and Stage, at Home and Abroad* (London, 1860), pp. 47, 48. As at Drury Lane, there were two green-rooms, the second (of lower status) being usually reserved for the ballet company and chorus. Cf. also Planché, pp. 23–4.

38 Boaden, *Life of Kemble*, II, p. 342; Vandenhoff, *Leaves from an Actor's*

Note-book, pp. 259–60. Planché's piece ran for fifty-four nights.

39 Peake, *Memoirs of the Colman Family*, II, p. 302.

40 Reynolds, II, p. 32; Dibdin, I, p. 324.

41 Macready, I, pp. 488, 480–1; II, p. 194.

42 Vandenhoff, *Leaves from an Actor's Note-book*, pp. 53, 54.

43 Bancroft, *Recollections*, p. 187.

44 The rehearsal period for *Wives As They Were* lasted from 15 Feb. to 4 Mar. (Boaden, *Memoirs of Mrs Inchbald*, II, p. 9); Booth (ed.), *Revels History of Drama VI*, p. 112.

45 Reynolds, I, p. 304.

46 Fitzball, I, p. 177; II, pp. 100–1.

47 Prefatory 'Remarks' by [George Daniel] to Jerrold, *The Bride of Ludgate* (Cumberland/Davidson edition, n. d.). He comments that '[t]he playwright must propitiate, flatter, and succumb to —— *actors!*'; Reynolds, II, p. 124.

48 Boaden, *Life of Kemble*, II, pp. 201–2.

49 Planché, p. 23. Andrew Ducrow was similarly dismissive with his 'Cut out the *dialect* and come to the 'osses.'

50 James Winston, *Journal* (29 Apr. 1823), p. 66. Dibdin felt badly treated, regarding himself as being in status second only to George Colman, jr. Later Winston commented that 'Twenty years ago Dibdin was a great man at Covent Garden' (15 May 1823, p. 67).

51 Dibdin, II, p. 339.

52 *Ibid.*, pp. 10, 15; Fitzball, II, p. 225. There is a general discussion of the role of stage manager in 'carry[ing] through the discipline of the stage' in Boaden, *Life of Kemble*, II, pp. 369–71.

53 Peake, *Memoirs of the Colman Family*, II, p. 282. Cf. Boaden, *Life of Kemble*, II, pp. 156–9.

54 Macready, II, p. 96.

55 Letter from Mathews to Ben Webster, dated 5 Nov. 1844, quoted in Fawkes, *Dion Boucicault*, p. 57.

56 Notebook entry for June 1853, quoted in Elwin, *Charles Reade*, p. 75.

57 Taylor, 'Mr Phelps and *The Fool's Revenge*', 340, 342; Burnand, p. 398.

58 Bancroft, *Mr & Mrs Bancroft*, p. 97.

59 Bancroft, *Recollections*, p. 193.

60 Bancroft, *Mr & Mrs Bancroft*, pp. 96, 106.

61 William Archer, *Real Conversations* (London: William Heinemann, 1904), p. 114.

62 *Ibid.*, p. 130.

63 Preface to Gilbert, *Pygmalion and Galatea* (London: Judd & Co. privately printed 1872), p. [iii]. Marie Litton apparently threatened to sue but wisely thought better of it.

64 Dated 20 Feb. 1871, Albery, *Works*, ii, pp. 775–6.

65 Dated 3 Jan. 1872 and Dec. 1875, quoted in Pearson, *Gilbert*, pp. 41, 47.

66 Edward Righton, 'A Suppressed Burlesque – "The Happy Land"', *The Theatre* (Jan.–June 1896), 63. On the Lord Chamberlain's rather spectacular interference with this production, see Stephens, *Censorship of English Drama*, pp. 119–24.

67 Archer, *Real Conversations*, p. 130.

68 Robert Reece, 'Stage-Management', *The Theatre* (Aug.–Dec. 1879), 208, 209.

69 Wills, *W. G. Wills*, p. 124; Terry, *Story of My Life*, p. 141.

70 Hollingshead, *Gaiety Chronicles*, p. 259.

71 Pinero, pp. 80, 90.

72 Mrs Pat Campbell, *My Life and Some Letters* (Hutchinson & Co., n. d.), p. 69; Cyril Maude, *Behind the Scenes* (London; John Murray, 1927), p. 86.

73 William Archer, *About the Theatre. Essays and Studies* (London, 1886), p. 52.

74 Jones, *The Shadow of Irving*, p.109.

75 William Archer, *Theatrical 'World' for 1894* (London, 1895), introduction, p. xvi.

76 See Henry Arthur Jones, 'The Actor Manager', *Fortnightly Review*, n. s. 48 (July 1890), 14–15. On his own venture into management, see above, p. 74.

77 Mason, *George Alexander*, pp. 43; 94–5.

78 Jones, pp. 131. 437.

79 Wilde, *More Letters*, p. 112.

80 Mason, *George Alexander*, pp. 122–3. Alexander's amiable reply (quoted p. 124) implies that he was simply unaware that such competitiveness existed between them.

81 *Ibid.*, p. 79.

82 Jones, pp. 130–1.

83 See exchange of correspondence quoted *ibid*, pp. 162–7. Wyndham's secondary argument that the play would not be good box-office material was disproved by its 164 nights' run.

84 Cyril Maude, *The Haymarket Theatre. Some Records and Reminiscences* (London: Grant Richards, 1903), p. 212. (In a spirit of puckishness Shaw wrote the whole chapter on the vicissitudes of rehearsal himself.)

85 Shaw, i, p. 743. For a discussion of the development of Shaw's career as author-director, see William A. Armstrong, 'George Bernard Shaw: The Playwright as Producer', *Modern Drama*, 8 (1965–6), 347–61.

7 THE NEW PROFESSIONALS

1 Planché, p. [138].
2 On the early meetings of playwrights for reform, see Ernest Bradlee Watson, *Sheridan to Robertson: A Study of the Nineteenth-Century London Stage* (Cambridge, Mass: Harvard University Press, 1926), pp. 46–7. The patent monopoly is fully treated in Watson Nicholson, *The Struggle for a Free Stage in London* (1906, reprinted New York: Benjamin Blom, 1966).
3 1866 *Report*, q. 5,898.
4 Based on Leman Tertius Rede, *The Road to the Stage*, new edn (London, 1836), p. 71, which purports to be a complete membership list. (Errors in spelling and in the initials attached to some authors have been corrected.)
5 Planché, p. 139.
6 See above, pp. 128–9.
7 Rede, *Road to the Stage* pp. 72–3. See appendix 2, p. 195, for scales and the classification of provincial theatres.
8 1866 *Report*, q. 5,888; 1878 *Report*, p. [380].
9 Add. MS 29642, f. 21v.
10 Letter dated 4 Dec. 1857, quoted in Cecil Howard, 'Some Letters', *The Theatre* (Jan.–June 1891), 30.
11 1866 *Report*, q. 5,873.
12 This information comes from *Morton* v. *Copeland*, Pollock (ed.), *Revised Reports*, c (1853–5), pp. 825–7.
13 1866 *Report*, q. 5,876.
14 à Beckett, *Reflections*, p. 255.
15 Burnand, p. 236.
16 1878 *Report*, p. [378].
17 Burnand, p. 299.
18 Report in 'Our Omnibus Box', *The Theatre* (Jan.–June 1883), 195–6.
19 Diary entry for 10 March 1870, quoted in Scott and Howard, *Life of E. L. Blanchard*, II, p. 380.
20 See Carter, *Authors by Profession*, p. 99.
21 Add. MS 56868, f. 8.
22 For sources for this paragraph, see Stephens, *Censorship of English Drama*, pp. 138–150.
23 Add. MS 56868, f. 54.
24 Shaw, I, p. 812.
25 Add. MS 56869, f. 123.
26 Shattuck (ed.), *Bulwer and Macready*, p. 123.

27 Pinero, p. 172.
28 Shaw, *Our Theatres in the Nineties*, III, p. 340.
29 Scott and Howard, *Life of E. L. Blanchard*, I, p. 28; *Era* (28 June 1884), quoted in Albery, *Works*, II, p. 851.
30 Bancroft, *Mr & Mrs Bancroft*, p. 152; Wills, *W. G. Wills*, p. 56.
31 Holroyd, *Bernard Shaw*, I, p. 192.
32 Pinero, p. 148.
33 à Beckett, *Reflections*, pp. 266–7.
34 Licensing scripts for this year comprise twenty-two vols. (Add. MSS 55309–30).
35 Add. MS 53534. In the same volume Sydney Grundy's *Sowing the Wind* is a privately printed text.
36 Shaw, II, p. 92.
37 *New Review* (July 1891), 89–96. This is the conclusion to Henry Arthur Jones's article with the same title, pp. 83–9. Richard A. Cordell, *Henry Arthur Jones and the Modern Drama* (1932, reprinted Port Washington: Kennikat Press, 1968), p. 143, describes Jones as 'the only important spokesman of his profession for the new drama' before Shaw. He combined 'the straightforward simplicity of the great eighteenth century stylists with the vigor and bluntness of a Carlyle'. Cf. also William Archer, 'What does the Public Want?', *The Theatre* (Jan.–June 1885), 271, who saw it as a hopeful sign 'that some of our leading playwrights', such as Jones and Grundy, 'should take to theorizing. Their utterances claim all attention.'
38 Fitzball, II, p. 40.
39 Reynolds, II, p. 366.
40 Shaw, I, p. 448.
41 Peake, *Memoirs of the Colman Family*, II, p. 375.

Bibliography

MANUSCRIPT SOURCES

BRITISH LIBRARY, BLOOMSBURY, LONDON WC1

Accounts of daily receipts and payments at Covent Garden Theatre, Mar. 1822–Sept. 1826. Add. MS 29641

Accounts of payments at Covent Garden Theatre on account of rents and taxes, salaries, authors, licences, advertisements, wardrobe, etc., Sept. 1835–June 1837. Add. MS 29642

Diary of Covent Garden Theatre, containing the daily receipts and expenditure, the titles of the plays performed, etc., 11 Mar. 1822–16 May 1833. 7 vols. Add. MSS 23156–62

Ledger of Covent Garden Theatre, containing general expenditure, the titles of plays performed, etc., 11 Mar. 1822–30 June 1829. Add. MS 23167

Ledgers of Covent Garden Theatre, Apr. 1799–Mar. 1822. 21 vols. Egerton MSS 2298–2319

Ledgers of Covent Garden Theatre, Sept. 1808–July 1818 and Sept. 1820–June 1822. 10 vols. Add. MSS 29631–40

Letter Book of Henry Robertson, secretary to the committee of management of Covent Garden Theatre, 3 Feb. 1823–2 June 1849. Add. MS 29643

Letters of Henry Arthur Jones to Frederick Macmillan. Add. MS 55013

Letters of Sydney Grundy to William Archer. Add. MSS 45291–2

Papers of the Incorporated Society of Authors, Playwrights, and Composers: History of the Society (G. H. Thring). Add. MSS 56868–9

Plays submitted to the Lord Chamberlain (1824–51), Add. MSS 42865–43038

Plays submitted to the Lord Chamberlain (1851–99), Add. MSS 52929–53701

Professional Memoranda of John Philip Kemble. 4 vols. Add. MSS 31972–5

PUBLIC RECORD OFFICE, CHANCERY LANE, LONDON WC2

Papers of the Lord Chamberlain's Office (LC1: 325; LC1: 639; LC1: 357)

THEATRE MUSEUM, TAVISTOCK STREET, COVENT GARDEN, LONDON WC2

Account Books of the Lyceum Theatre, 1878–1901. 14 vols
Lyceum Theatre archive

TENNYSON RESEARCH CENTRE, CENTRAL LIBRARY, LINCOLN

Account for *Becket* (Bram Stoker)
Letters of Henry Irving and Frederick Macmillan
Programme for copyright performance of *The Foresters*

SELECTED PRINTED SOURCES

Albery, Wyndham (ed.). *The Dramatic Works of James Albery, Together with a Sketch of his Career, Correspondence Bearing Thereon, Press Notices, Casts, Etc.*, 2 vols. London: Peter Davies, 1939
Archer, William. *About the Theatre. Essays and Studies*. London, 1886
  English Dramatists of To-day. London, 1882
  The Old Drama and the New. An Essay in Re-Valuation. London: William Heinemann, 1923
  Real Conversations. London: William Heinemann, 1904
  The Theatrical 'World' for 1893–97. 5 vols. London, [1894]–98
  'What does the Public Want?', *The Theatre* (Jan.–June 1885), 269–75
Armstong, William. 'George Bernard Shaw: The Playwright as Producer', *Modern Drama*, 8 (1965–6), 347–61
  'The Nineteenth-Century Matinée', *Theatre Notebook*, 14 (1959–60), 56–9
Bancroft, Squire, and Marie. *The Bancrofts. Recollections of Sixty Years.* London: John Murray, 1909
  Mr and Mrs Bancroft On and Off the Stage. Written by Themselves. 6th edn. London, 1889
à Beckett, A[rthur] W. 'The Earnings of Playwrights and Players', *The Theatre* (July–Dec. 1895), 209–13

Green Room Reflections. London, 1896

'Benefits', *The Theatre* (Aug.–Dec. 1879), 67–9

'Biographical Sketch of Frederick Reynolds, Esq. (Accompanied with an Original Portrait)', *Monthly Mirror* (Dec. 1795), [67]–73

Boaden, James. *Memoir of the Life of John Philip Kemble, Esq. Including a History of the Stage, From the Time of Garrick to the Present Period*. 2 vols. London, 1825

   Memoirs of Mrs Inchbald: Including her Familiar Correspondence with the Most Distinguished Persons of her Time. 2 vols. London, 1833

Booth, Michael R. 'East End Melodrama', *Theatre Survey*, 17 (1976), 57–67

   (ed.). *The Revels History of Drama in English. Volume VI 1750–1880*. London: Methuen & Co Ltd, 1975

Boucicault, Dionysius Lardner. 'The Debut of a Dramatist', *North American Review*, 148 (Apr. 1889), 454–63

   'The Decline of the Drama', *North American Review*, 125 (Sept. 1877), 235–45

   'Early Days of a Dramatist', *North American Review*, 148 (May 1889), 584–93

   'Leaves from a Dramatist's Diary', *North American Review*, 149 (Aug. 1889), 228–36

Bright, Addison. 'George Alexander: Actor and Manager', *The Theatre* (Jan.–July 1892), 239–44

Browne, Alexander P. 'Sir Arthur Sullivan and Piracy', *North American Review*, 149 (1889), 750–60

Bunn, Alfred. *The Stage: Both Before and Behind the Curtain, From 'Observations Taken on the Spot'*. 3 vols. London, 1840

Burnand, Francis Cowley. 'An Autobiography', *The Theatre* (Jan.–June 1883), 105–8

   'Authors and Managers', *The Theatre* (Feb.–July 1879), 14–17

   Records and Reminiscences Personal and General. 4th edn rev. London: Methuen & Co, 1905

Calthrop, Christopher. 'Dion Boucicault and Benjamin Webster', *Theatre Notebook*, 32 (1978), 28–32

Carter, Victor Bonham-. *Authors By Profession. Volume I: From the Introduction of Printing until the Copyright Act 1911*. London: Society of Authors, 1978

Coleman, John. *Players and Playwrights I Have Known*. 2 vols. London, 1888

Collins, Jeremy F. Bagster-. *George Colman the Younger, 1762–1836*. Morningside Heights, New York: King's Crown Press, 1946

Cooper, F. Renard. *Nothing Extenuate. The Life of Frederick Fox Cooper*. London: Barrie & Rockcliff, 1964

Cordell, Richard A. *Henry Arthur Jones and the Modern Drama*. New York, 1932; reprinted Port Washington: Kennikat Press, 1968

Dark, Sydney, and Rowland Grey. *W. S. Gilbert: His Life and Letters*. London: Methuen & Co, 1923

Dibdin, Charles [junior]. *The Professional & Literary Memoirs of Charles Dibdin the Younger, Dramatist and Upward of Thirty Years Manager of Minor Theatres*, ed. George Speaight. London: Society for Theatre Research, 1956

Dibdin, Thomas. *The Reminiscences of Thomas Dibdin, of the Theatres Royal, Covent-Garden, Drury-Lane, Haymarket &c and author of the Cabinet, &c*. 2 vols. London, 1827

Dolby, Thomas. *Memoirs of Thomas Dolby, Formerly of Sawtry, in Huntingdonshire, late Printer and Publisher, of Catherine Street, Strand, London. Written by Himself*. London, 1827

Donaldson, Frances. *The Actor-Managers*. London: Weidenfeld & Nicolson, 1970

Donohue, Joseph. *Theatre in the Age of Kean*. Oxford: Basil Blackwell, 1975

'Dramatic Copyright', *Athenaeum*, 21 Nov. 1874

'Dramatic Copyright', *Era*, 30 Aug. 1884

['Dramatic Copyright'], *Era*, 10 Jan. 1891

Downer, Alan S. *The Eminent Tragedian: William Charles Macready*. Cambridge, Mass: Harvard University Press, 1966

Dunkel, Wilbur D[wight]. 'The Career of George W. Lovell', *Theatre Notebook*, 5 (1950–1), 52–9

 Sir Arthur Pinero. A Critical Biography with Letters. Chicago: Chicago University Press, 1941

Ellman, Richard. *Oscar Wilde*. London: Hamish Hamilton, 1987

Elwin, Malcolm. *Charles Reade. A Biography*. London: Jonathan Cape, 1931, reissued 1934

Ervine, St John. *Bernard Shaw. His Life, Work, and Friends*. London: Constable & Co. Ltd, 1956

Fawkes, Richard. *Dion Boucicault. A Biography*. London: Quartet Books, 1979

Fielding, K. J. 'Charles Reade and Dickens – A Fight Against Piracy', *Theatre Notebook*, 10 (1955–6), 106–111

'The Finance of the Drama', *Era*, 26 Mar. 1892

Fitzball, Edward. *Thirty-five Years of a Dramatic Author's Life*. 2 vols. London, 1859

Fitzgerald, Percy, 'Playwriting As It Is', *The Theatre* (Aug.–Dec. 1879), 74–6

 The World Behind the Scenes. London, 1881

Fitzgerald, S. J. Adair. 'The Matinée Question', *The Theatre* (July–

Dec. 1891), 157–60

[Genest, John]. *Some Account of the English Stage, from the Restoration in 1660 to 1830*. 10 vols. Bath, 1832

Gilbert, William Schwenck. 'An Autobiography', *The Theatre* (Jan.–June 1883), 217–24

Grundy, Sydney. 'The Dearth of Originality', *The Theatre* (Aug. 1878–Jan. 1879), 274–7

'The Dramatic Ring', *The Theatre* (Aug.–Dec. 1879), 273–7

'The Science of the Drama', *New Review*, 5 (July 1891), 89–96

Hagen, June Steffensen. *Tennyson and his Publishers*. London: Macmillan Press, 1979

Harrison, Gabriel. *The Life and Writings of John Howard Payne*. New York, 1875

Harrop, Josephine. *Victorian Portable Theatre*. London: Society for Theatre Research, 1989

Helyar, James (ed.). *Gilbert and Sullivan. Papers Presented at the International Conference held at the University of Kansas in May 1970*. Lawrence, Kansas: University of Kansas Libraries, 1971

Heraud, John Abraham. *The Present Position of the Dramatic Poet in England*. London, 1841

Hibbert, H[enry] G[eorge]. *A Playgoer's Memories*. London: Grant Richards Ltd, 1920

Hogan, Charles Beecher (ed.). *The London Stage 1660–1800. Part 5: 1776–1800*. 3 vols. Carbondale: Southern Illinois University Press, 1968

Hogan, Robert. *Dion Boucicault*. New York: Twayne Publishers Inc., 1969

Holcroft, Thomas. *The Life of Thomas Holcroft. Written by Himself, Continued to the Time of his Death From his Diary Notes & Other Papers by William Hazlitt*, ed., with introd. & notes, Elbridge Colby. 2 vols. London: Constable & Co Ltd, 1925

Hollingshead, John. *Gaiety Chronicles*. London, 1898

My Lifetime. 2 vols. London, 1895.

Plain English. London 1880.

Holroyd, Michael. *Bernard Shaw. Volume I 1856–1898: The Search for Love*. London: Chatto & Windus, 1988

Bernard Shaw. Volume II 1898–1918: The Search for Power. London: Chattos & Windus, 1989

Howard, Cecil. 'Some Letters', *The Theatre* (Jan.–July 1891), 28–31

Hughes, Alan. 'Henry Irving's Finances: The Lyceum Accounts, 1878–1899', *Nineteenth Century Theatre Research*, 1 (1973), 79–87

Hunt, Hugh (ed.). *The Revels History of Drama in English. Vol. VII 1880 to the Present Day*. London: Methuen & Co. Ltd, 1978

Irving, Laurence. *Henry Irving: The Actor and His World*. London: Faber & Faber, 1951

Jackson, Russell (ed.). *Plays by Henry Arthur Jones*. Cambridge: Cambridge University Press, 1982

  (ed.). *Victorian Theatre. A New Mermaid Background Book*. London: A. & C. Black, 1989

Jerrold, Douglas. 'Rights of Dramatists', *Monthly Magazine* (May 1832)

Jerrold, Walter. *Douglas Jerrold, Dramatist and Wit*. 2 vols. London: Hodder & Stoughton, [1914]

Jerrold, William Blanchard. *The Life and Remains of Douglas Jerrold. By his Son*. 2nd edn [London, 1869]

Johnson, Albert E. 'Real Sunlight in the Garden: Dion Boucicault as a Stage Director'. *Theatre Research*, 12 (1972), 119–25

Jones, Doris Arthur. *The Life and Letters of Henry Arthur Jones*. London: Victor Gollancz, 1930

Jones, Henry Arthur. 'The Actor Manager', *Fortnightly Review*, n. s. 48 (July 1890), 1–16

  'A Playwright's Grumble', *To-day*, Dec. 1884

  The Renascence of the English Drama. London, 1895

  'The Science of the Drama', *New Review*, 5 (July 1891), 83–9.

  The Shadow of Henry Irving. London: Richards Press Ltd, 1931

Jones, John Bush (ed.). *W. S. Gilbert: A Centenary of Scholarship and Commentary*. New York: New York University Press, 1970

Knight, Joseph. *Theatrical Notes*. London, 1893

Knowles, Richard Brinsley. *The Life of James Sheridan Knowles. By his Son*. London: privately printed, 1872

Macready, William Charles. *The Diaries of William Charles Macready, 1833–1851*, ed. William Toynbee. 2 vols. London: Chapman & Hall, 1912

  Macready's Reminiscences, and Selections from his Diaries and Letters, ed. Sir Frederick Pollock. 2 vols. London, 1875

Marston, Westland. *Our Recent Actors: Being Recollections, Critical, and in Many Cases, Personal, of Late Distinguished Performers of Both Sexes*. London, 1890

Mason, A. E. W. *Sir George Alexander and the St James' Theatre*. London: Macmillan & Co. Ltd, 1935

Maude, Cyril. *Behind the Scenes with Cyril Maude*. London: John Murray, 1927

  The Haymarket Theatre: Some Records and Reminiscences. London: Grant Richards, 1903

Meeks, L. H. *Sheridan Knowles and the Theatre of his Time*. Bloomington, Indiana: Principia Press, 1953

Megson, William Broadley (ed.)]. *The Original, Complete, and Only Authentic Story of 'Old Wild's' (The Yorkshire 'Richardson's', and the Pioneer of the Provincial Theatre): A Nursery of Strolling Players and*

the Celebrities Who Appeared There. Being the Reminiscences of its Chief
and Last Proprietor, 'Sam' Wild. Edited by 'Trim'. Reprinted from the
'Halifax Courier'. London, 1888; reprinted London: Society for
Theatre Research, 1989

Merivale, Herman C. 'New and Original', *The Theatre* (Aug.–Dec
1879), 10–14

Merriam, Harold G. *Edward Moxon: Publisher of Poets.* New York
Columbia University Press, 1939

Moore, Mary (Lady Wyndham). *Charles Wyndham and Mary Moore*
Edinburgh: printed for private circulation, 1925

'Mr George Alexander at Home', *Era*, 3 June 1893

Murray, Christopher. *Robert William Elliston: Manager.* London
Society for Theatre Research, 1975

Newton, H. Chance. *Crime and the Drama, or Dark Deeds Dramatized*
With an introduction by Sir John Martin-Harvey. London
Stanley Paul & Co. Ltd, 1927

  *Cues and Curtain Calls, Being the Theatrical Reminiscences of H. Chance
  Newton ('Carados' of the 'Referee').* With an introduction by Sir
  Johnston Forbes-Robertson. London: John Lane, The Bodley
  Head Ltd, 1927

Nicholson, Watson. *The Struggle for a Free Stage in London.* Boston, 1906
reprinted New York: Benjamin Blom, 1966

Nicoll, Allardyce. *A History of English Drama, 1660–1900.* rev. edn. 6
vols. Cambridge: Cambridge University Press, 1965–7

Northend, Marjorie. 'Henry Arthur Jones and the Development of
Modern English Drama', *Review of English Studies*, 18 (1942)
448–63

O'Keeffe, John. *Recollections of the Life of John O'Keeffe, Written by
Himself.* 2 vols. London, 1826

Peake, R[ichard] B[rinsley]. *Memoirs of the Colman Family; including their
Correspondence with the Most Distinguished Personages of their Time.* 2
vols. London, [1841]

Pearson, Hesketh. *Gilbert: His Life and Strife.* London: Methuen & Co
Ltd, 1957

Pemberton, T. Edgar. *The Life and Writings of T. W. Robertson.* London
1893

Pinero, Arthur Wing. *The Collected Letters of Sir Arthur Pinero*, ed. J. P
Wearing. Minneapolis: University of Minnesota Press, 1974

Planché, James Robinson. *Recollections and Reflections by James Robinson
Planché. Somerset Herald and Dramatic Author. A Professional Auto
biography.* New & rev. edn. London, [19]01

Pollock, Sir Frederick (ed.). *Macready's Reminiscences. See* Macready.
  *The Revised Reports, Being a Republication of Such Cases in the English
  Courts of Common Law and Equity, From the Year 1785, As Are Still of*

Practical Utility. 152 vols. London: Sweet & Maxwell Ltd, 1891–1920

Reade, Charles. *The Eighth Commandment.* London, 1860

Rede, Leman Thomas Tertius. *The Road to the Stage . . . To which is added . . . An Account of the Dramatic Authors' Society; the Members; Scale of prices; and a Copy of the Dramatic Copyright Act.* New & improved edn. London, 1836

Reece, Robert. 'A Bed of Roses', *The Theatre* (Aug.–Dec. 1879), 14–16

'Stage Management', *The Theatre* (Aug.–Dec. 1879), 207–10

Report from the Select Committee of the House of Lords and the House of Commons on the Stage Plays (Censorship), in *British Sessional Papers* (1909), VIII, 459–905

Report from the Select Committee on Dramatic Literature: With Minutes of Evidence, in *British Sessional Papers* (1831–2), VII, 1–252.

Report from the Select Committee on Theatrical Licenses and Regulations; together with the Proceedings of the Committee, Minutes of Evidence, and Appendix, in *British Sessional Papers* (1866), XVI, 1–420

Report of Commission on the Laws and Regulations relating to Home and Colonial Copyright, in *Reports from Commissioners, Inspectors, and Others* (1878), XXIV, 163–667

Reynolds, Frederick. *The Life and Times of Frederick Reynolds. Written by Himself.* 2nd edn. 2 vols. London, 1827

A Playwright's Adventures. London, [1831]

Rhodes, R. Crompton. 'The Early Nineteenth-Century Drama', *The Library,* 4th ser., 16 (1935–6), 91–112; and 210–31

'Some Aspects of Sheridan Bibliography'. *The Library,* 4th ser., 9 (1928–9), 233–61

Rowell, George. *Queen Victoria Goes to the Theatre.* London: Paul Elek, 1978

Theatre in the Age of Irving. Oxford: Basil Blackwell, 1981

The Victorian Theatre 1792–1914: A Survey. 2nd edn. Cambridge: Cambridge University Press, 1978

St John, Christopher (ed.). *Ellen Terry and Bernard Shaw; a Correspondence.* 2nd edn. London: Constable & Co Ltd, 1931

Scott, Clement. *The Drama of Yesterday and To-day.* 2 vols. London, 1899

Scott, Clement, and Cecil Howard. *The Life and Reminiscences of E. L. Blanchard.* 2 vols. London, 1891

Shattuck, Charles H. (ed.). *Bulwer and Macready: A Chronicle of the Early Victorian Theatre.* Urbana: University of Illinois Press, 1958

Shaw, George Bernard. *Bernard Shaw. Collected Letters 1874–1897,* ed. Dan H. Laurence. London: Max Reinhardt, 1965

Bernard Shaw. Collected Letters 1898–1910, ed. Dan H. Laurence. London: Max Reinhardt, 1972

Our Theatres in the Nineties. 3 vols. London: Constable, 1932

Sims, George R. 'An Autobiography', *The Theatre* (July–Dec. 1884), 14–17

   My Life. Sixty Years' Recollections of Bohemian London. London: Everleigh Nash Co. Ltd, 1917

Stedman, Jane. 'General Utility: Victorian Author-Actors from Knowles to Pinero', *Educational Theatre Journal*, 24 (1972), 289–301

Stephens, John Russell. *The Censorship of English Drama 1824–1901.* Cambridge: Cambridge University Press, 1980

Stirling, Edward. *Old Drury Lane. Fifty Years' Recollections of Author, Actor, and Manager.* 2 vols. London, 1881

Stoker, Bram. *Personal Reminiscences of Henry Irving.* 2 vols. London: William Heinemann, 1906

Sutherland, J. A. *Victorian Novelists and Publishers.* London: University of London, Athlone Press, 1976

Taylor, Tom. 'Impressions of John Baldwin Buckstone', *The Theatre* (Aug.–Dec. 1879), 261–7

   'Mr Phelps and *The Fool's Revenge*', *The Theatre* (Aug. 1878–Jan. 1879), 338–44

   'Some Personal Reminiscences of Alfred Wigan', *The Theatre* (Aug. 1878–Jan. 1879), 410–18

   The Theatre in England. Some of its Shortcomings and Possibilities. London, 1871

Terry, Ellen. *The Story of My Life.* London: Hutchinson & Co., 1908

Thackeray, T[homas] J[ames]. *On Theatrical Emancipation, and the Rights of Dramatic Authors.* London, 1832

Thompson, Marjorie. 'Henry Arthur Jones and Wilson Barrett: Some Correspondence, 1879–1904', *Theatre Notebook*, 11 (1956–7), 42–50

Tirebuck, William. 'Managers and Plays', *The Theatre* (Feb.–July 1879), 210–12

Tolles, Winton. *Tom Taylor and the Victorian Drama.* New York, Morningside Heights: Columbia University Press, 1940

Tomlins, F[rederick] G[uest]. *The Nature and State of the English Drama.* London, 1841

   The Past and Present State of Dramatic Art and Literature; Address to Authors, Actors, Managers, and the Admirers of the Old English Drama. London, 1839

   Remarks on the Present State of the English Drama. London, 1851

Trewin, J. C. *The Edwardian Theatre.* Oxford: Basil Blackwell, 1976

Trewin, Wendy. *All on Stage: Charles Wyndham and the Alberys.* London: George G. Harrap & Co. Ltd, 1980

Troubridge, St Vincent. *The Benefit System in the British Theatre.* London: Society for Theatre Research, 1967

'Fitzball and Elliston: or, How to Submit a Play in 1820', *Theatre Notebook*, 7 (1953), 64–5

Vandenhoff, George. *Leaves from an Actor's Note-book: or, Anecdotes of the Green Room and Stage, at Home and Abroad.* London, 1860

Walsh, Townsend. *The Career of Dion Boucicault.* New York, 1915; reprinted New York: Benjamin Blom, 1967

Watson, Ernest Bradlee. *Sheridan to Robertson: A Study of the Early Nineteenth-Century Stage.* Cambridge, Mass: Harvard University Press, 1926

Wilde, Oscar. *The Letters of Oscar Wilde,* ed. Rupert Hart-Davis. London: Rupert Hart-Davis, 1962

More Letters of Oscar Wilde, ed. Rupert Hart-Davis. Oxford: Oxford University Press, 1987

Wills, Freeman. *W. G. Wills. Dramatist and Painter.* London, 1898

Winston, James. *Drury Lane Journal. Selections from James Winston's Diaries 1819–1827,* ed. Alfred L. Nelson and Gilbert B. Cross. London: Society for Theatre Research, 1974

Index of plays and playwrights

This index includes (i) plays, operas, librettos – cross-referenced by author where known – play series, and play collections referred to in the text, notes, and appendixes; and (ii) playwrights, for whom birth and death dates are normally given. An * denotes those playwrights who also appear in the general index.

General index

Those entries marked by * are also entered in the index of plays and playwrights, above.